MUSIC, INFORMAL LEARNING AND THE SCHOOL:
A NEW CLASSROOM PEDAGOGY

In loving memory of my father, Ronald Sidney Green, 1924–2004

Music, Informal Learning and the School:
A New Classroom Pedagogy

LUCY GREEN

The Institute of Education, University of London, UK

ASHGATE

Published by
Ashgate Publishing Limited
Gower House
Croft Road
Aldershot
Hampshire GU11 3HR
England

Ashgate Publishing Company
Suite 420
101 Cherry Street
Burlington, VT 05401-4405
USA

Ashgate website: http://www.ashgate.com

British Library Cataloguing in Publication Data
Green, Lucy
Music, informal learning and the school: a new classroom
  pedagogy. – (Ashgate popular and folk music series)
  1. Music – Instruction and study 2. Non-formal education
  3. Education, Secondary
  I. Title
  780.7'12

Library of Congress Cataloging-in-Publication Data
Green, Lucy
  Music, informal learning and the school: a new classroom pedagogy / Lucy Green.
    p. cm. – (Ashgate popular and folk music series)
  Includes bibliographical references and index.
  ISBN 978-0-7546-6242-6 (alk. paper)
  1. School music–Instruction and study–United States. I. Title.

  MT3.U5G735 2007
  780.71–dc22

2007009799

ISBN 978-0-7546-6242-6 (Hbk); 978-0-7546-6522-9 (Pbk)

Printed and bound in Great Britain by MPG Books Ltd, Bodmin, Cornwall.

Contents

General Editor's preface

The upheaval that occurred in musicology during the last two decades of the twentieth century has created a new urgency for the study of popular music alongside the development of new critical and theoretical models. A relativistic outlook has replaced the universal perspective of modernism (the international ambitions of the 12-note style); the grand narrative of the evolution and dissolution of tonality has been challenged, and emphasis has shifted to cultural context, reception and subject position. Together, these have conspired to eat away at the status of canonical composers and categories of high and low in music. A need has arisen, also, to recognize and address the emergence of crossovers, mixed and new genres, to engage in debates concerning the vexed problem of what constitutes authenticity in music and to offer a critique of musical practice as the product of free, individual expression.

Popular musicology is now a vital and exciting area of scholarship, and the *Ashgate Popular and Folk Music Series* aims to present the best research in the field. Authors will be concerned with locating musical practices, values and meanings in cultural context, and may draw upon methodologies and theories developed in cultural studies, semiotics, poststructuralism, psychology and sociology. The series will focus on popular musics of the twentieth and twenty-first centuries. It is designed to embrace the world's popular musics from Acid Jazz to Zydeco, whether high tech or low tech, commercial or non-commercial, contemporary or traditional.

Professor Derek B. Scott
Chair of Music
University of Salford

Acknowledgements

The material on which this book is based was possible thanks to funding from the Paul Hamlyn Foundation's 'Musical Futures' project, the Esmée Fairbairn Foundation, and the UK Department for Education and Skills Innovation Unit. I would also like to thank Hertfordshire Music Service and the London University Institute of Education.

At my first meeting with Abigail D'Amore (née Walmsley), she demonstrated an instantaneous grasp of the aims and rationale of the project which forms the focus of this book. That led to many hours of work, talk, worry, exhaustion, celebration and laughter together as we travelled in her car between schools, shared cups of coffee and snacks in roadside cafés, and exchanged what must amount to hundreds if not thousands of emails. Abi, as she is known to her friends, has made a contribution to this study which it is hard to acknowledge sufficiently. Whilst I have attempted to indicate her particular input as the book goes along, there are undoubtedly issues in the final melting pot which must have originated in one of our many real or virtual conversations. She also made invaluable comments on a draft of the text, with her ever-ready eye for detail. Thank you Abi, for being nothing less than a fantastic colleague and friend.

John Witchell put his faith in the ideas behind this book at an early stage of their development, when he invited me to form a partnership with Hertfordshire Music Service. It has been a great privilege to have had that opportunity. I could not have hoped for a more enthusiastic and outgoing, let alone a better organized and active, Music Service team to work with. Moreover, the experience was at all stages enhanced by John's boundless wit, energy and long experience.

I was extremely fortunate that Dave Price and the Steering Group of the UK Paul Hamlyn Foundation 'Musical Futures' project saw potential in the initial stages of the work which is discussed between these pages. It has been a great honour to be a part of that major national venture. I have learnt and benefited from discussions with numerous music educators and others arising directly and indirectly from 'Musical Futures'. In addition, because of the vision, commitment and energy of Dave as well as Abi and many others on the team, the teaching materials and ideas that form the backdrop to this book have already received far wider dissemination than I could have imagined possible.

I would like to thank Hilary Hodgson at the Esmée Fairbairn Foundation, who took a step in the dark when she first agreed to look at a proposal for a pilot project. Without that, none of the rest could have happened. The Foundation also gave support towards study leave which was crucial for the final stages of the book.

I have been most fortunate that a number of people have read and commented on drafts of this book. They include, as well as Abi, my colleagues Keith Swanwick and Charles Plummeridge at the Institute of Education, and Sharon Davis in the United States. The refinement of many aspects of the text is thanks to their insight, knowledge and generosity. As Series Editor, Derek Scott has once again amazed me with his enthusiasm and efficiency.

I would like to thank Graham Welch for his unswerving support and patience; Chris Harrison for insightful feedback on the early stages of the project, and a number of other colleagues who sent me readings or contributed to discussions with me. Many music education students at the London University Institute of Education and other universities, as well as delegates at a number of conferences, have shared ideas and provided inspiring feedback. A special thanks to Evangelos Himonides for the exercise of extreme patience and skill in preparing sound files for the website.

This book attempts to explore and consider the views and actions of pupils and teachers in music classrooms as they try out and reflect on some new approaches to classroom music teaching and learning. My admiration of the way young teenagers are apt to describe and analyse their experiences when asked to do so, and the wonderful wealth of musicality and musical potential that they harbour, is deep indeed. I am grateful to all the young people who took part in the project. They will remain in my memory for years to come, and it is in large measure their words and their actions which form the backbone of what is here.

But if there is any value between these pages, it must ultimately stem from the integrity, commitment and judgement which were brought to the project by the teachers. My very deep thanks go to them – for turning around, downing tools and being willing to completely change their curricula in order to try out a new approach, about which they were offered no guarantee of success. I wish to make special mention of the five teachers who worked most closely with us for two full years and beyond in Hertfordshire: Anna Gower, Liz Grant, Jonathan Kemp, Cyd Waters and Birgitta Birchall. Not only did they play a full part in implementing the curriculum, attending meetings and contributing extensively to interviews and discussions, but they also became ambassadors for the project. This included contributing to a number of additional meetings, and especially in Anna's case, leading workshops and other events throughout the country. Their input soared way beyond the bounds of what had been expected or was ever asked of them. It is still continuing. In similar ways, I would like to thank the London teachers who took part initially for around half a year, and without whose enthusiasm and belief at the outset, I would never have had the courage to take the work any further. Many of them also continued to make inputs at induction meetings and in other ways long after their official involvement had ceased. They are: Louise Bowes-Cavanagh, Melinda Carr-Ruby, David Griffiths, Christine Chamberlain, Stuart Hughes and Paul Newbury.

I am also greatly indebted to the following teachers who put the project into practice during its research phase, developed ideas, attended meetings and contributed their experiences through a number of discussions and questionnaires. Many of them, too, are still making an input to further developments: Joanna Brignall, Neil Browne, Rodney Browne, Phill Bullas, Philippa Butcher, Matt Clarke, Sarah Cornell, Tish Ellis, Lyn Epps, Nadia Dyett, Elizabeth Hastings, Kirsta Johnston, Liz Lomas, Chloe Macdougall, Kevin McCalman, Joy Mendelssohn, Louisa Osmond, Caroline Ross, Colleen Sheridan, Elizabeth Sterling, Nigel Taken, Mark Taylor, Jonathan Walton, Adrian Warren, Sue Williams and Phil Wright.

Many more people, including peripatetic instrumental teachers, community musicians, student-teachers, administrators, animateurs, transcribers, film-makers, my own teenaged children and others, have contributed in different ways, either directly through their work or through conversations and the exchange of ideas and experiences. They cannot all be named here, but they include: Ruth Dalloway, Michael Davidson, Roger Drew, Jilly Dolphin, Danny Fisher, Sophie Ford, Marcus Ford, Oliver Gearing, Pippa Gearing, Tom Gearing, Mary Heyler, Gazelle Hill, David Hoskins, Ashka Komorowska-Jalal, Marion Long, Tania Rosato, Jeff Sayadian, René Steenvorden, David Stoll, Nick Sutton, Richard Thomson, Wendy Topping, Judith Webster and John Williams.

I would also like to thank Heidi May and the wonderful team at Ashgate for their efficiency, patience and professionalism.

This is the fourth book I have written, and the fourth time I have wanted to thank my husband, Charlie Ford. Acknowledgements to him always seem to come last nowadays – but that is because he has always been there at the end, just as he has always been there at the beginning. As usual, he read a draft and made his unerring criticisms; he continued to put up with endless discussions that seem to turn by default to the topic of music education, and he always challenged my ideas, including when I least wanted, and most needed, to be challenged.

Chapter 1

Introduction

The aims and rationale of this book

–Michael: Just play it once, just play it once.

–Ross: I'll go (plays guitar riff).

–Michael: You don't need to play that, so when I go (starts to play) if you be silent (guitar plays) and then you go silent for (bass plays).

–Ross: I know! So I'll just go (guitar plays).

–Billy: Are we going to have to do chords?

–Ross: Yeah, what we doing after that bit?

–Michael: Work out the first bit first. If we get the first bit done, so at least we can perform, and then (inaudible). 'Cause we're still not sure what Ross is doing.

　　　　　All start attempting to play/improvise on their instruments.

　　　　　CD comes on. They play along with the CD.

–Billy: It's too loud.

–Michael: So when I go (plays guitar) you be silent, 'cause it's quite hard.

–Ross: Come on, shall we just start again, shall we just listen to it?

–Billy: We're only doing the first one though aren't we?

　　　　　CD comes on again.

–Michael: Drums don't come in yet.

–Ross: You play five, you don't need to do that.

(Broadacres High School, concealed field recording)

The above extract is from a 'fly-on-the-wall' recording of a group of 13- to 14-year-old pupils working together in a school practice room. They were taking part in a research and development project which introduced and evaluated new pedagogical methods in the music classroom. The project's approach derived from a study of the informal learning practices of popular musicians (Green 2002a), and represented an attempt – which might at first seem an impossible task or a contradiction in terms – to bring informal music learning practices into the formal environment of the school classroom. The project became part of a major national music education programme in England called 'Musical Futures', and the resulting teaching strategies and curriculum resources are already available for teachers' use (Green with Walmsley 2006; <www.musicalfutures.org/PractionersResources.html>). But the aim of this book is to present a more detailed and theoretical analysis of what went on during the project, how things occurred, why, and what benefits and challenges the project seemed to offer to music education.

　　The book considers how pedagogy in the music classroom could draw upon the world of informal popular music learning practices outside the school, in order to recognize, foster and reward a range of musical skills and knowledge that have not previously been emphasized in music education. It investigates how far it is possible and desirable to incorporate informal music learning practices into formal music education; how the incorporation of such practices can affect young teenagers' skill and knowledge acquisition processes, and how such practices can change the ways pupils listen to, understand and appreciate music in and beyond the classroom. It raises questions about pupils' motivations towards music education, their autonomy as learners, and their capacity to work co-operatively together without instructional guidance from teachers.

In so doing, it considers how informal practices can affect teachers' approaches and perspectives in ways that we have, as music educators, often left unquestioned or taken for granted. Bringing informal learning practices into a school environment is challenging for teachers. It can appear to throw up conflicts with their existing views of professionalism, and may at times seem to run against official educational discourses, pedagogical methods and curricular requirements. But I hope to show that any conflict is more apparent than real. For informal learning practices can introduce fresh, constructive ways for music teachers to understand and approach their work, and worthwhile new perspectives on pupils' capacities and needs. Through examining such issues, the book touches on further current debates about pedagogy as well as curriculum, offering grounded examples and discussions of alternative approaches to classroom work and classroom relations, that may have relevance to a variety of curriculum subjects.

In the pupils' words quoted above, we can glimpse many of the themes that will be considered in greater depth as the book goes along. The task they were engaged in had not been broken down into a series of progressively demanding steps, but instead they were holistically approaching a piece of 'real-world', professionally produced music. They had no notation or other form of written instructions in front of them, but were using their ears to copy what they heard on a CD. Only one of them had any previous experience of instrumental tuition, yet they were all attempting to communicate instructions and ideas to each other through musical gestures and sounds; and were engaging in embryonic instrumental performance and improvisational skills. They had been given no instruction to analyse the music, yet they were beginning to listen structurally, observe entries and count repetitions. There was no teacher in the room, yet they were focused on the task. They had not been given separate or explicit roles, but were co-operating as a group, and trying to sort out what one of them should do as they worked towards a performance. Most importantly, perhaps, they had been given no guidance about how to approach the task, but they were engaging in self-directed, co-operative learning. Not only had they selected the content of the curriculum themselves – that is, the song that they were copying – but they were also responsible for organizing and structuring their own teaching and learning strategies.

Pupil motivation and take-up of music as a curriculum subject have never been high or widespread. Over the last forty years or so, music educators have made radical shifts towards raising motivation and widening participation. This has involved re-thinking the role of music as a minority subject that catered mainly for the success of children who took instrumental lessons, and that focused centrally on classical and folk music, singing and musical literacy. Music educators, along with teachers in many other subjects, have challenged the notion of education as a stable body of knowledge and skills which are unquestioningly possessed by teachers, and which should be imparted to pupils, regardless of whether such knowledge and skills are equally useful, relevant or valid for all pupils, or whether all pupils are equally capable of absorbing them. This challenge has included closing the gap between 'high' and 'low' musical cultures, and between 'Western' and 'non-Western' musics, and has involved recognizing and valuing pupils' 'own' musical cultures by bringing them into the curriculum.[1]

However, until recently one area within music education has remained relatively unaffected – that of pedagogy. For although the above changes brought in a huge range of music as new curriculum *content*, this new content was largely approached through traditional teaching *methods*. Thus a new gap opened up, particularly in the realm of popular, as well as jazz and 'world' musics. For whilst a huge range of such musics have entered the curriculum, the *processes* by which the relevant musical skills and knowledge are passed on and acquired in the world outside the school, have been left behind. These processes in most cases differ fundamentally from the processes by which skills and knowledge tend to be passed on and acquired in formal music education settings. In this sense, popular, jazz and world musics – and indeed other previous curriculum content including folk and traditional musics, and even in some ways classical music itself – have been present in the school more as a simulacrum of the real thing than the real thing itself.

Many young people who go on to become skilful and successful popular musicians report that the music education they received at school was unhelpful, or worse, detrimental. For some, instrumental lessons, even in popular music genres, also provided a negative and often short-lived experience (see, for example, Green 2002a, pp. 127–76). We can surmise that many children and young people who fail and drop out of formal music education, far from being either uninterested or unmusical, simply do not respond to the kind of instruction it offers. But until very recently, music educators have not recognized or rewarded the approaches involved in informal music learning, nor have they been particularly aware of, or interested in, the high levels of enthusiasm and commitment to music displayed by young popular or other vernacular musicians.

---

1   Scandinavian countries are probably among the first and most far-reaching in bringing popular music into the school curriculum. See, for example, Vakeva (2006), Stålhammar (2000, 2003), Faulkner (2003), Tagg (1998). For history, information, critical accounts and arguments concerning the entrance of popular music into the curriculum in the UK, see, for example, Swanwick (1968, 1992), Vulliamy (1977a and 1977b), Vulliamy and Lee (1976 and 1982), Green (1988, 2003); Shepherd and Vulliamy (1994), Gammon (1999), Byrne and Sheridan (2000), Lamont et al. (2003) and Odam (2004). For Australia, Malaysia, the USA, Hong Kong, Thailand and Japan respectively, see, for example, Wemyss (1999, 2004), Marsh (1995, 1999), Dunbar-Hall and Wemyss (2000), Dunbar-Hall (1996), Shah (2006), Ginocchio (2001), Humphreys (2004), Herbert and Campbell (2000), Newsom (1998), Ho (1999), Maryprasith (1999) and Koizumi (2002). For general discussions of popular music in education, see for example, Rodriguez (2004), Lines (2005a) or the special issues of the journals *Research Studies in Music Education* 13 (1999) and *International Journal of Music Education* no. 36 (2000).

In my previous book, *How Popular Musicians Learn*, I investigated popular musicians' informal learning practices, specifically with a view to what those practices could tell us as music educators. From my findings I hypothesized that such learning practices could possibly enhance motivation and increase a range of musical skills, in ways that were largely missing from pedagogy and from the school curriculum. I also considered that such practices could make music education more inclusive for pupils of all abilities and backgrounds, particularly those who have found it difficult or impossible to make their musicality shine in formal environments. In addition, I had observed that popular musicians seem to have a wide appreciation and respect for a range of musical styles going beyond the familiar, perhaps more so than other people of the same age who are not musicians. Therefore, I hypothesized that through informal ways of approaching music-learning, school pupils could also be brought to expand their appreciation of music, both in relation to what they already know and to what lies beyond it. Through this, the approaches could, I believed, help to demystify the world of music, including its commercial manifestations, making pupils more confident of their own musicality in relation to notions of musical value and musical ability, more discerning, or more 'musically critical'.

The final chapter of that book put forward a number of suggestions for adopting and adapting informal popular music learning practices within various formal music education settings, not as a substitute, but as a complement running side by side with existing approaches. The project on which the present book is based gave the opportunity to try out some of those suggestions in practice, within school classrooms.[2]

For the remainder of this introductory chapter I will first briefly discuss the main characteristics of informal popular music learning practices as these occur outside the school. Then I will explain in general terms how these characteristics were incorporated into the aims and strategies of the project, and will situate the project in relation to the historical context of music education in the present day. Finally I will outline the research methods used.

---

2   Increasing numbers of projects are, each in their different ways, currently bringing informal music learning practices into formal settings. For work in classrooms, see, for example: in Scotland, Byrne (2005) and Byrne and Sheridan (2000); in Holland, Evelein (2006); in the USA, Boespflug (2004), Emmons (2004), Jaffurs (2004), Seifried (2006) and Harwood (1998a, 1998b), and in Australia, Wemyss (1999). For work relating to instrumental music teaching in Scotland, see, for example, Cope (1998, 1999) and Cope and Smith (1997). For work in the 'non-formal' sector, also known as 'community music', see Renshaw (2005). For general discussions of informal learning within formal music education, see, for example, Folkestad (2005), O'Flynn (2006) and Westerlund (2006), and with reference to jazz at the HE level, Nielsen (2006). Information about such developments at a national level in the UK is available in Price (2005, 2006a and 2006b) and DfES (2006).

Background research: how popular musicians learn

The exact ways in which popular musicians go about acquiring their skills and knowledge vary between different sub-styles of popular music, different social and cultural contexts, and from one individual learner to another – the more so precisely because of the general lack of formal systematization involved in such learning. Increasing numbers of popular music learners nowadays are taking advantage of formal provision such as instrumental lessons on electric guitars, drums and other instruments that are almost wholly associated with popular music, and for which it would have been difficult to find a professional, formal teacher even a few decades ago. Some musicians nowadays also take national qualifications, from elementary exams right up to post-graduate degrees in popular music. There is in addition fast-growing provision through community music networks and many other organizations outside formal education, which is often referred to as 'non-formal' music education. However, such formal and non-formal provisions still mainly act as supplements or extensions to popular musicians' informal practices. These informal practices continue to form the essential core of most popular musicians' learning, and run alongside any additional formal or non-formal activities. Overall, in spite of differences between sub-styles of popular music, context, provision and individual musicians, informal popular music learning practices are undertaken, in one way or another, by nearly all popular musicians in nearly all sub-styles of popular music, in ways that can be characterized by a number of generalizable features.[3]

'Enculturation', or immersion in the music and musical practices of one's environment, is a fundamental factor that is common to all aspects of music learning, whether formal or informal. However, enculturation plays a more prominent part in some learning practices and with relation to some styles of music than others. In the traditional music of many countries, young children are drawn into group music-making activities on a daily basis, both within the home and beyond, almost from birth. Through being included in music-making by adults and older children around them, they pick up musical skills in ways that are similar to how they pick up linguistic skills.[4] These skills include all three of the main ways by which we engage with music: performing (whether playing or singing, even at a basic level), creating (whether composing or improvising) and listening (to ourselves and/or to others).

---

3   There is a growing literature on how popular musicians learn. One of the earliest and most thorough investigations was by H. Stith Bennett (1980). Also see Bayton (1997), Berkaak (1999), Björnberg (1993), Campbell (1995), Clawson (1999a, 199b), Cohen (1991), Davis (2005), Finnegan (1989), Green (2002a), Horn (1984), Kirshner (1998), Lilliestam (1996) and Negus (1999). For work in hip-hop, Jamaican dance culture and jazz respectively, which have many similarities as well as differences, see, for example, Dimitriadis (2001), Stolzoff (2000), Berliner (1994) and Monson (1996). The remainder of the current sub-section of this book is a rewritten version of Green (2004), and originates in Green (2002a).

4   For classic texts on enculturation and learning in traditional musical contexts, see Merriam (1964), Blacking (1976) and Nketia (1975). For discussions of the concept in relation to formal education, see, for example, Barrett (1996), Nettl (1983, pp. 323–5), Kwami (1989), Campbell (1998), McCarthy (1999) and Nwezi (1999).

Most folk and traditional musics of the world are learnt by enculturation and extended immersion in listening to, watching and imitating the music and the music-making practices of the surrounding community. In some folk and traditional musics, as well as in art musics of the world such as Indian classical music, and to a large extent in jazz, there are also systems of 'apprenticeship training' whereby young musicians are introduced, and explicitly trained or just generally helped by an individual adult or a 'community of expertise'.[5] In such environments, older musicians might provide specific guidance, as in a 'master–apprentice' or 'guru–shishya' relationship; or they may allow learners to 'sit in' with a band or join a group of older musicians, as in jazz or African drumming. Most importantly, the older musicians act as expert musical models whom learners can talk to, listen to, watch and imitate.

Popular musicians also tend to acquire musical skills and knowledge, first and foremost through being encultured in, and experimenting with, the music which they are familiar with, which they like, and which they hear around and about them. This involves early experimentation with an instrument or the voice, and discovering what different sounds they can make through trial and error, before stringing sounds together into embryonic musical phrases, rhythms or harmonies.

However, there are some crucial differences between how most folk and traditional musics are passed on, and how most Western popular musics are passed on – differences which it is tempting to overlook, but which are very significant for music education. They include, firstly, the fact that, unlike in most folk and traditional fields, most young popular musicians in Western or Westernized musical cultures are not regularly surrounded by an adult community of practising popular musicians who they can talk to, listen to, watch and imitate, or who initiate them into relevant skills and knowledge. Hence young popular musicians tend to engage in a significant amount of *solitary* learning. Secondly, in so far as a community of practice *is* available to young popular musicians, it tends to be a community of peers rather than 'master-musicians' or adults with greater skills. The significance of this is profound, as it affects the entire way in which skills and knowledge are transmitted in the popular music field, taking the onus of transmission away from an authority figure, expert or older member of the family or community, and putting it in large measure into the hands of groups of young learners themselves.

By far the overriding learning practice for most popular musicians, as is already well known and is also clear from existing studies, is to copy recordings by ear. It seems an extraordinary fact that this practice has developed in only the eighty or ninety years that have elapsed since the spread of recording technologies, across many countries of the world, through the activities of children and young people, basically in isolation from each other, outside of any networking or formal structures, and largely without adult guidance. I wish to distinguish between two extreme ways of conceiving of this practice, each situated at the opposite ends of a pole. At one extreme there is what I call 'purposive listening' (Green 2002a), that is, listening

---

5   See Lave and Wenger (1991) for elaboration of this concept. For discussions of apprenticeship learning in relation to music, see the references in note 4, and Nketia (1975), Merriam (1964, pp. 150–61) and Campbell (1991).

with the conscious purpose of adopting and adapting what is heard into one's own practices. At the opposite extreme there is 'distracted listening'. This occurs when music is heard in the background, but is not attended to in a focused way, so that it enters the mind almost entirely through unconscious enculturation. Not only purposive listening, but also distracted listening carry on beyond the early learning stages and into professional realms.

Copying recordings is almost always a solitary activity, but as already indicated, solitude is not a distinguishing mark of the popular music learner. On the contrary, group activities occurring in the absence of adult supervision or guidance are of great importance. They are characterized by two aspects. One is 'peer-directed learning'. This involves the conscious sharing of knowledge and skills, or even explicit peer teaching, through, for example, demonstration of a rhythm or chord by one group member for the benefit of another. The other aspect is 'group learning', where there is no *conscious* demonstration or teaching as such, but where learning takes place through watching and imitation during music-making, as well as talking about music during and outside of rehearsals.

Bands are formed at very early stages, even if the players have little control over their instruments and virtually no knowledge of any chord progressions, licks or songs; or even if they have no instruments to play. Often they start up a band or a series of bands within a few months of beginning to play their instrument, mostly in their mid- to later teenage years. Schools are a vital social institution to band formation, even though many bands start up without the aid of teachers. For the resources of the school, any instruments or practice spaces that it can provide, and more importantly, its ready-to-hand population of hundreds of pupils, are crucial. However, although early bands are nearly always formed with peers, age is less important than musical ability, or in other words, the fact that the band-members should all be at a roughly similar standard.

Most bands involve themselves in a range of practices including jamming and other forms of improvisation, playing covers they know and like, and making up their own music. As already indicated, conscious and unconscious peer-directed learning and group learning take place: different band members will demonstrate learnt or original musical ideas to each other, and players will engage in joint compositions that often involve every member of the band putting in their own ideas. Therefore performance, composition and improvisation abilities are acquired, not only individually, but crucially, as members of a group, through informal peer-directed learning and group learning, both conscious and unconscious. As indicated earlier, all this mainly occurs in the absence of an adult or other person who can provide leadership or bring greater musical experience to bear.

It is well known that notation plays hardly any part in the popular music world, although it is used in a few cases such as highly professional function or theatre bands, or in an occasional manner such as when a musician scribbles something down on a piece of paper (usually to be screwed up and binned as soon as the instruction is internalized). Session musicians are more likely to have constant work if they can read. But the main means of learning and passing on music is through recordings, either commercial ones or 'demos' passed between the musicians. Even when notation *is* used, it is never used on its own, but is always heavily mixed in with purposive listening and copying. It is reasonable to suppose that less than 40 per cent of pop musicians may know how to read notation – although I am not aware of any recent research on this – mostly having been introduced to it through some amount of formal music education. However, even given this adult guidance, when operating in the informal realm the musicians none the less tend to adapt any notational skills to their own use in highly idiosyncratic ways.

Aural copying of course pays attention to a number of factors which are not readily communicated through notation. These include idiosyncratic and non-standardized timbres, rhythmic flexibility, pitch inflection and many other aspects, not least those never-to-be-defined but always recognizable qualities, groove, 'feel' and swing. Here again, not only conscious, focused, purposive listening and copying, but also loose imitation related to continuous, unconscious enculturation and distracted listening, are relied upon as essential parts of the learning process, and continue to be the principal means through which music is transmitted and reproduced throughout a popular musician's career.

The concept of technique as a *conscious* aspect of controlling the instrument or voice comes late to most popular musicians, and is in many cases incorporated into their activities either immediately before or some time after becoming professional. However, having taught themselves to play their instruments or sing in their own ways, the adoption of standard techniques at a late stage comes with surprising ease.

As distinct from the executive psycho-motor *technique* involved in playing or singing, the musicians also acquire, to varying degrees, knowledge and understanding of musical *technicalities*, or 'theory'. Such knowledge and understanding usually come haphazardly, according to whatever music is being played and enjoyed at the time. To begin with, the musicians are able to use musical elements in stylistically appropriate ways, but usually without being able to apply names to them, or to discuss them in any but vague or metaphorical terms. As listening is the prime source of learning, working out the relationships between sounds follows on from that. Thus learning about theory tends to be led by excitement about the music. As time goes by, the pieces of the jigsaw puzzle fall into place, to differing degrees depending on the individual, and can of course lead to highly sophisticated levels of theoretical knowledge and understanding. Not surprisingly, all this emphasis on listening also leads to the development of perceptive and effective aural capacities.

Some musicians practise their instruments for five or six hours a day in the early stages of learning, others practise for considerably less time, and some hardly ever practise at all. They tend to approach practice according to their mood, other commitments in life, or motivation by external factors such as joining a new band or composing a new song. Their development is in many cases marked by some periods of relatively intensive practice, interspersed with other periods without any practice at all. Most importantly, practice is something they do only so long as they enjoy it.

Along with these learning practices go attitudes towards musical value and musical ability that tend to emphasize expressive qualities such as 'feel', 'sensitivity', 'spirit' or other similar attributes over and above complexity or technical ability. Popular musicians also place high value on friendship amongst themselves, tolerance, shared taste, and commitment. I am not suggesting that all young popular musicians are exceptionally well-balanced individuals who never have arguments;

but that co-operation, sensitivity to others, commitment and responsibility are explicitly highly *valued* by the musicians. Furthermore, this emphasis on friendship and commitment concerns not only the social relationships that surround the band practice or performance, but are necessary conditions of two further aspects. One is that, since the music being played is arrived at through choice and group negotiation, all the productive activities of the band are reliant on a consensus of taste, and/or the willingness to tolerate the potentially differing tastes of others, as well as the ability to co-operate and the responsibility of arriving at rehearsals and gigs at the correct place and time, bringing the correct equipment. Without such co-operation (especially in the absence of incentives such as fame and money, but even *with* such incentives), a band will eventually disintegrate. A second aspect is that friendship, co-operation and the ability to be sensitive to other people also affect the precise nature and 'feel' of the music being produced, in ways that relate to musical communication in performance, and particularly to group composition and improvisation.

Playing popular music in a band tends to raise the self-esteem and the perceived peer group status of the participants. The values surrounding their music and the musicians in their group are intimately tied up with deeply felt issues of personal identity. Finally, one thing that all popular musicians unfailingly report is the extremely high levels of enjoyment that accompany their music-making and music-learning activities. As I mentioned earlier, in the informal realm there is no imperative to practice unless they feel like practising, no teacher or parent telling them they must do it, no homework, no tests or exams, no coursework. Not only do popular musicians love what they are doing, but also from such a starting point many of them go on to develop a deep passion for music and a thirst for listening, often seeking out and becoming familiar with a wide range of different styles, including classical music.

The underlying principles of the project

With all the above in mind, I devised a pedagogical project which aimed to investigate whether it would be possible and beneficial to bring at least some aspects of informal popular music learning practices into the realms of the school classroom.[6] The first step was to locate some defining characteristics of informal popular music learning practices, and to consider how they differ from formal educational approaches. Drawing from the research described above, I formed these characteristics into five fundamental principles, which were placed at the heart of the project.

---

6   As indicated in the Acknowledgements, the early stages of the project were indebted to funding from the Esmée Fairbairn Foundation. Its further development was possible thanks to the Paul Hamlyn Foundation's 'Musical Futures' project, in which it formed a partnership with the Hertfordshire Music Service. We also had support from the UK Department for Education and Skills Innovation Unit. A large number of other institutions and individuals were involved in many different ways as the project proceeded, many of whom are named in the Acknowledgements. The teachers' resource that arose from the project is available in Green with Walmsley (2006), and can be downloaded from <www.musicalfutures.org/ PractionersResources.html>, Section 2. Information about the 'Musical Futures' project as a whole is available on <www.musicalfutures.org>.

Perhaps the prime factor is that informal learning always starts with music which the learners choose for themselves. Therefore, it tends to be music which they already know and understand, like, enjoy and identify with. This is distinct from most formal educational settings, in which the main idea is to introduce learners to music that they do *not* already know, and which is usually selected by the teacher.

Secondly, the main method of skill-acquisition in the informal realm involves copying recordings by ear. This is very different to learning through notation, or some other form of written or verbal instructions and exercises lying beyond the music itself. Although teachers in the music classroom employ a wide variety of approaches, aural copying from a recording has rarely, if ever, been amongst them, at least until very recently.

Thirdly, informal learning takes place alone as well as alongside friends, through self-directed learning, peer-directed learning and group learning. This involves the conscious and unconscious acquisition and exchange of skills and knowledge by listening, watching, imitating and talking. Unlike the pupil–teacher relationship in formal education, there is little or no adult supervision and guidance. Along with this, friendship and identification with a social group such as a particular sub-culture or other markers of social identity form an important part in the choice of music to be played. These factors are also central to negotiation over music-making and music-learning practices amongst the members of the band.

Fourthly, skills and knowledge in the informal realm, not surprisingly given the above, tend to be assimilated in haphazard, idiosyncratic and holistic ways, starting with 'whole', 'real-world' pieces of music. By contrast, in the formal realm learners tend to follow a planned progression from simple to complex, often involving specially composed music, exercises, a curriculum or a graded syllabus, under the direction of a teacher.

Finally, informal approaches usually involve a deep integration of listening, performing, improvising and composing throughout the learning process, with an emphasis on personal creativity. This is distinct from the greater differentiation of skills that tends to mark the formal realm, and its emphasis, very often, on reproduction more than on creativity.

At the same time as acknowledging differences between the informal and the formal realms in relation to learning strategies, it is important to recognize that there are also deep and remarkable similarities in many of the attitudes and values which are shared by popular musicians and formal educators alike. These include placing a high value on 'feel' over and above technique; demanding and valuing group co-operation in order for music-making to work; being aware of the huge amount of enjoyment that is to be had from music-making; believing that making music can raise self-esteem, and appreciating and respecting a wide range of music, often going into realms far removed from the familiar.

As will be explained in more detail in the next chapter, the project involved the development of classroom activities which drew as much as possible on the above fundamental characteristics of informal music learning.

The project in historical perspective

The music appreciation movement of the twentieth century

The music appreciation movement of the twentieth century is often associated with an image of school pupils seated in neat rows, passively listening to gramophone recordings of high-quality classical music.[7] In this sense, 'music appreciation' seems on the surface to have little in common with the approach of the project. For, as will be seen, the latter involves active music-making, and at least to begin with, allowing pupils to bring in their own choice of music rather than designating 'good' music for them to study. However, there are many respects in which the aims and outcomes of the music appreciation movement are shared by those of the project. These particularly include the notion that pupils' listening skills can and should be enhanced by education – although the means to this enhancement might be different – and that pupils should develop a critical appreciation and discernment in relation to a wide range of music. I will discuss this issue further, and attempt to substantiate these claims, in Chapter 4.

The creative music movement of the 1960s and 1970s

At first sight it could be assumed that the project strategies have a lot in common with what became known as the 'creative music movement' of the late 1960s and 1970s, which was itself a part of the broader notions of 'progressive education' and 'child-centred education' that were influential at that time.[8] The most obvious similarities include the fact that both the creative music approach and the project, as will be seen, involve pupils working together to create music in small groups. However digging a little deeper, there are significant differences.

One of the main differences concerns the notion of 'child-centredness'. Drawing from the wider educational context of the time, the creative music movement was explicitly child-centred, in that it placed the responsibility for learning in the hands of the child, with the possibility of open-ended learning outcomes, rather than making each step the responsibility of the teacher and geared towards pre-specified learning objectives. However, there was a crucial aspect in which it fell short of being child-centred. For rather than starting with music that pupils were familiar with and enjoyed, it introduced them, through compositional stimuli and

---

7   For discussions of the music appreciation movement, see, for example, Martin (1995, pp. 230ff.), Rainbow with Cox (1989/2006, pp. 276ff.), Scholes (1972, p. 48) and Simpson (1976). The project's relationship with the concept of 'music appreciation' is considered more fully in Chapter 4.

8   The adoption of creative music-making as a part of education dates back to before that time, as in the work of Carl Orff. It became influential through new channels during the 1960s in the work of, for example, Dennis (1970), Paynter and Aston (1970), Paynter (1982), Schafer (1967) and Self (1967). The notion of child-centred education can be traced as far back as Rousseau (1762), and has been much discussed within education studies generally. For a helpful recent overview of this concept and its historical role within educational theory and practice, see Moore (2000).

other means, to musical styles that they would be unlikely ever to come across in the world outside the school. This mainly focused not so much on the mainstream of classical music as on atonal or other modernist twentieth-century music of many varieties. The distance of this music from pupils' existing musical tastes, knowledge and skills made it difficult for pupils to connect their learning with their lives outside the school.

Another difference was that the creative music movement implicitly centred on a theoretical understanding of the nature of composition and pupil creativity, derived from the world of 'serious' or classical music. It did not, in the main, base its approaches on real-world composing practices, and did not involve pupils at the outset in copying an already-existing, familiar piece of music. Such copying may have been regarded then – and now – as 'slavish' and lacking in creativity. Also, in the creative music movement, teachers gave quite precise stimuli for pupils to build their compositions around, so that the compositional tasks were relatively structured. The project, however, does not give any compositional stimuli, but expects pupils to spontaneously carry over what they learn through copying tasks into compositional creativity as time goes by. The stimuli are therefore implicit, and once again, involve what is already familiar.

Overall, whilst there are both similarities and differences between the creative music movement and the project, the teachers in the project were in agreement that the differences overrode the similarities.

The popular music and 'world music' movements of the 1970s and on

The project also has many aspects in common with the early entrance of popular music into the curriculum in the UK and many other countries during the 1970s and 1980s. Popular music entered the curriculum partly in response to criticisms, such as those described above, that the creative music movement was not pupil-centred enough because it overlooked the very music that pupils already knew and were familiar with. In response to that criticism, a number of educationalists and teachers sought to reflect their pupils' musical tastes and identities by including popular music in their curricula (see notes 1 and 2).

However, it is pragmatically, economically and also ideologically very challenging for curriculum content, especially on a national level, to keep genuinely up-to-date with pupils' 'own' music. For one thing, pupils' ideas of what counts as 'popular' music change with alarming rapidity. Partly in response to this problem, and partly for reasons to do with the ways in which music is valued in the society at large, popular music in the curriculum, and particularly in national exam syllabi, has tended to centre mainly on 'classic' songs and bands. These include a range of music from early blues to bands such as The Beatles and Queen. Such music is perceived either to offer some authentic, rather than commercial, expression of its time and place; transcendent, universal qualities, and/or sufficient formal and harmonic complexity to warrant study. The inclusion of 'classic' popular music has in this way tended to reproduce traditional, accepted notions of musical value, and with those, of what counts as musical ability. But such music is often, from pupils' perspectives, as far removed from their lives and identities as mainstream classical music or twentieth-century atonal music.

The entrance of world music into education took place in a number of countries mainly during the 1990s.[9] That development has raised a huge number of important issues that are relevant to the project. These include the difficulties of incorporating music from one culture into another; the challenges of adopting, within formal education, music which is transmitted outside formal education; the lack of fit between the cultural assumptions that surround music and musical practices in different cultures; and many more. Unfortunately it is not possible to enter into such problems in this book, although many of the issues that I will be discussing can be directly or indirectly related to current debates in the literature on world music and cultural diversity in music education. But one issue that can be noted here, is that the introduction of world music in schools is also subject to the same tendencies as those identified in the paragraph above. Firstly, educators' particular choices of world music can reflect similar ideological values to their choices of popular music, that is, music which is considered to be an authentic, traditional, rather than commercial, expression of its time and place, and to have universal, transcendent qualities, and in some cases sufficient complexity. Secondly, by its very nature, world music in the curriculum tends to involve musical styles which are largely unfamiliar to most pupils.

Thus, although the newer music curriculum appears to challenge the previously more narrow selection of music from a mainly white, middle-class culture, the *values* which accompany it do not necessarily do so; and the musical identities of most pupils continue in many cases to be distanced. The social-class and cultural patterns of musical success and failure which are entailed therefore remain to a large extent unchallenged. (This position is argued more substantially in Green, 1988, 1999a, 1999b, 2003a and 2003b.)

Current trends and the aims of the project

In order to more thoroughly or accurately reflect pupils' musical identities, it seems appropriate to give pupils some autonomy to select curriculum content for themselves: that is, to choose the music they work on in class. An immediate objection to this is that it will 'pander', 'dumb down' and generally fail in the main educational endeavour, of leading learners beyond what they already know and can do into further, deeper and better realms. However, I hope to show that there are benefits to allowing such choice. One is that pupil-selection of curriculum content breaks down the reproductive effects of many previous music curricula, which by ignoring the musical identities and tastes of vast numbers of pupils prevented many of them from demonstrating or even discovering their musical abilities. Such pupils tended to be labelled, for *cultural* rather than musical reasons, as 'unmusical' or 'uninterested' in music (Green 1988, 1999a, 1999b, 2003a and 2003b). Another benefit is that starting from pupil-selected curriculum content can form the basis, not

---

9   See, for example, Campbell (1991), Campbell et al. (2006), Lundquist and Szego (1998), Volk (1998) and T. Wiggins (1996).

only for leading pupils out into unfamiliar territory, but also for making them more aware in relation to what they *do* already know and *can* already do. Just because they identify with and listen to certain music outside the school of course does not mean that they have a critical understanding of it. Rather than making that assumption, I will argue that we need to invoke a notion of 'critical musicality' as an educational aim, and address it to pupils' *own* music as much as to any other.[10]

More importantly, pupil-selection of curriculum content is only one side of bringing informal learning practices into the school. The more radical and far-reaching side concerns pupil autonomy in relation to learning *strategies*. Rather than approaching popular music through recognized, formal teaching or pedagogic strategies, in seeking to reflect the informal learning practices of popular musicians the project gave pupils autonomy to *direct their own learning*. Such autonomy presents a significant challenge to previous patterns, including fundamental issues such as how success and failure are constructed and measured. It will form a central issue to be addressed in many subsequent parts of this book.

Research methods

The empirical part of the project took place from 2002 to 2006, and involved altogether 21 secondary schools, 32 classroom teachers and over 1,500 pupils. General information about each school and its particular involvement is given in Appendix A.

We collected quantitative and qualitative data from all the project schools, but focused in detail on seven classes of 13- to 14-year-olds, one in each of seven schools, which I shall refer to as 'main-study' schools.[11] Three of the main-study schools were located in London, and four in Hertfordshire, a county just north of London. The

---

10   This notion is linked to those of 'critical literacy' and 'critical pedagogy', which run through the education, as well as music-education literature in a variety of guises. Within education these terms are principally associated with the work of Paulo Freire (1972, 1974). Recent helpful discussions are available in, for example, Bentley (1998), Buckingham (2005), Edwards and Kelly (1998), Goodson (1998), Hartley (2006), Kincheloe and Steinberg (1998), Kress (2006), McFarlane (2006), Moore (1999, 2000), Somekh (2006) and Young (2006). In music education, for sentiments and values that also resonate with these notions in various implicit or explicit ways, see, for example, Abrahams (2005a, 2005b), Allsup (2004), Bowman (2005), Boyce-Tillman (2000), Campbell (1998), Campbell et al. (2006), Elliott (1995), Glover (2001), Jorgensen (1997, 2003), Koopman (2005), Lines (2005b), Odam (1995), Regelski (2005), Ross (1998), Small (1977), Stålhammar (2006a and 2006b), Westerlund (2002), J. Wiggins (2001), T. Wiggins (2006), Wright (2007), Woodford (2005) and many more.

11   I have elsewhere referred to three of these as 'pilot schools' (for example, Green with Walmsley 2006, Green 2005a and 2005b). However, since they undertook exactly the same strategies as the other main-study schools for the first two stages of the project, and since the first stage forms the main focus of this book, it makes more sense to refer to them as main-study schools in the present context. The only sense in which they were pilots was that they were the first schools to try out the strategies, and they completed only two stages of the project. Another school, which I shall refer to as a 'pilot' school, was the very first to try out the strategies, but I did not conduct interviews with pupils there.

data-collection methods included the following: unstructured participant observation of pupils working together in small groups within class music lessons; observations of whole-class lessons or sessions within lessons; audio recordings of group work; audio and video recordings of performances and other whole-class activities; tape-recorded semi-structured interviews with pupils and teachers at regular intervals, and tape-recorded teacher team meetings. In addition, a number of conversations took place in corridors and over cups of coffee in busy staffrooms, which were in many cases recorded and transcribed or written up in field notes. The detailed findings from those seven classes, and the approximately 200 pupils and 11 teachers involved with them, form the main focus of this book.

A pilot school in London undertook the first one out of seven stages of the project, during the final term of the academic year 2001–2002. The three main-study London schools then undertook the first two stages only, during the academic year of 2003–2004. At that time, I was the sole researcher, observing one lesson per class per school per week of the project, and conducting all the interviews with pupils and teachers, the initial induction, and a final teacher team meeting. I was extremely fortunate to be joined by Abigail D'Amore (née Walmsley) and others when the project became part of the national Paul Hamlyn Foundation's 'Musical Futures' venture for the following two years. Abigail became the Research Officer and Project Manager, and during 2004–2005 she and I together or individually observed almost all the remaining lessons in the further four main-study schools that are discussed in detail in this book. These schools undertook all seven stages of the project, lasting almost one academic year.

During the following year Abigail oversaw and co-ordinated all the practical work in 17 schools. These included the four main-study schools from the previous year, which repeated the project, developing and incorporating it into their curricula in their own ways. It also included 13 schools new to the project, which I shall refer to as 'extension schools'.

Three of these were specialist institutions. One was for children with 'moderate learning difficulties', known in the UK as an MLD school, and the other two were for children with 'emotional and behavioural difficulties', known as EBD schools. The project had not been designed for such contexts, and I am unable to give them any special attention here, although I was thrilled that the teachers involved were not only interested in trying out the strategies, but stayed on board for the entire year and beyond. A dedicated study would be needed to evaluate the suitability of the project for such schools, and also the ways in which the teachers adapted it to the needs of their pupils. However, the findings from those three schools are included amongst those from all the others, and where appropriate, findings from the two EBD schools are identified separately. I have also included a brief note at the end of Chapter 6, concerning how the work was progressing, at the time of writing, in those and other schools for children with special educational needs. It should also be mentioned that there were a small number of pupils with special educational needs in most of the mainstream classes in which we worked.

In that year of the project we no longer conducted observations and interviews, but used the following data-collection methods instead. One was an anonymous quantitative questionnaire to teachers in all 15 schools which were still involved at the very end of the project. Two schools had stopped the project, since one Head of Music was on maternity leave and the other had moved away. We received responses from 17 teachers across all 15 of the remaining schools. This included one Head of Music from each school, plus an extra classroom teacher from two of the schools. We also used qualitative and quantitative anonymous pupil questionnaires, transcribed teacher meetings at the end of each term, and open-ended teacher feedback forms. Abigail visited the schools as often as possible, observed lessons on an informal basis, and kept in constant contact with the teachers by phone and email. The findings from the seven main-study schools have been cross-checked with the findings from these extension schools, and were presented, discussed and agreed in the extension school teacher meetings. As the book goes along I will occasionally refer to the findings from the extension schools and the results of the anonymous questionnaire, mainly in footnotes. At the time of writing, a number of schools in the UK have taken up the project strategies, but it remains to be seen to what extent their experiences will match those of the schools discussed here.[12]

There are many disadvantages to this kind of research. For one thing, there was bound to be a 'halo effect', especially in the four main-study Hertfordshire schools, where the teachers and pupils were particularly aware of participating in a nationally recognized project. In addition, the teachers were part of a small team working intensively together and having regular meetings. This in itself would be likely to make them feel more positive, involved and enthusiastic about their work than usual, regardless of what the project actually entailed. To some extent such problems were held in check by the findings from the extension schools. For although their teachers had an induction session and a meeting once a term, they worked at a greater distance from the researchers, had fewer meetings, and were generally more 'out on a limb'. In addition, the pupils in those schools were not so aware of participating in a national project, and had few, if any, visits from a researcher. Reference to other weaknesses and disadvantages, as well as strengths, of the qualitative approach is woven into the discussion below.

Interviews and meetings

In the seven main-study schools the pupils were interviewed in small groups, corresponding as much as possible with the groups they had been working in during class time. The teachers were interviewed individually, and also gave their views in group discussions during meetings. All the interviews, and some of the discussions, were audio-recorded and transcribed. Other formal and informal discussions were recorded in field notes. The interviews were semi-structured. Each one involved around five questions which were put in the same way to all respondents (or as nearly the same way as possible, according to the context of the preceding conversation). They were all open questions such as: 'Can you tell me what you enjoyed most, and what you enjoyed least about the project?'. We were careful to avoid putting

---

12   Although the main research phase of 'Musical Futures' project has come to an end, the Paul Hamlyn Foundation is monitoring its take-up and effects in schools nationally, and providing some support for teachers. Details are available on <www.musicalfutures.org>.

in our own suggestions or asking leading questions. Thus all substantive ideas and concepts came from the respondents themselves. In follow-up questions we tried to probe meanings, but again to avoid making suggestions.

There are obvious disadvantages to interviewing people as part of research, and particularly when the interviewers have previously been working alongside them as participant observers. Both pupils and teachers may have wanted to avoid saying negative things in case of upsetting the interviewers. They may also have felt pressure from peers and others to appear supportive rather than critical. The teachers were often quite anxious about the project at the start, and may not have articulated their anxieties quite as forcefully in an interview or a meeting as they may have done privately to each other or to their friends and family. In addition, some pupils in one of the London schools spoke very little English; others in many of the schools seemed unable to express themselves, for uncertain reasons perhaps including shyness, peer-pressure or lack of confidence; and even those who were willing to speak at length could not always put their views or feelings into words in the way an older person might.

One particularly helpful check on such problems, was to compare the interview responses with the anonymous, quantitative questionnaire results. Indeed, positive evaluations usually came over slightly more strongly in interviews and meetings than they did in the tick-box results. For example, whereas in a meeting the teachers explicitly declared themselves unanimous on a point, it may be that when they filled in their questionnaire tick-boxes at the end of the project, only 12 or 13 out of the 17 responses were unanimous on that point. In such cases I always make this clear in a footnote. Another check was that there were indeed occasions when teachers expressed doubts in meetings, and in which one or two pupils disagreed with others in the group, often entailing some discussion in which divergent or negative opinions were put forward openly. The areas that involved doubts or divergence particularly included teachers' concerns about standards and classroom management, and pupils' views about listening and classical music. This suggests that the high levels of consensus that tended to be reached around most other topics were at least in some ways relatively authentic. Besides, all human beings form their views and responses to things as a part of a group; there is no such thing as total individuality. Therefore if the group influenced views, then that was a significant influence and can be expected to happen if similar circumstances prevail elsewhere.

However, rather than being seen as a 'nuisance', some qualitative aspects of the research process became part of our recommendations. By taking time out to talk to pupils, or asking them to write down their views, we and their teachers were granted fascinating and often unexpected insights, not only into their opinions about teaching and learning strategies, but into how perceptive, analytical and constructive young teenagers can be if given the opportunity to show it. More importantly perhaps, there is evidence to suggest that pupils are more likely to perceive themselves as valued and valuable, and teachers are more likely to understand and respond to pupils' needs constructively, if such conversations are built into the educational environment as a matter of course.[13] The fact that teachers also may have benefited from discussing their work and meeting each other is, for similar reasons, integral rather than extraneous to the process of doing this kind of research. Overall, a tick in a box is hard to interpret meaningfully. The deeper explanations that teachers and pupils gave of their views during interviews and discussions provide far more valuable insights.

Observations

Our weekly observations of pupils working in small groups, and of whole-class sessions, were unstructured and participatory. We occasionally made notes during the observation, but on the whole this was done after the lesson. Observation of this kind naturally has many disadvantages, particularly since pupils are unlikely to behave in exactly the same way when we were in the room as they did when they were alone. One check on this, which has perhaps provided some of the best insights and may have been our most revealing research tool, was a digital MiniDisc recorder. We used only one MD-recorder per class (not per group), per lesson. Recordings from it were transcribed the same day or very soon afterwards. On some occasions, and sometimes for periods lasting up to an hour, pupils did not notice that the MD-recorder was in the room (although they later gave permission for the recording to be used in research). Those recordings are particularly illuminating. On most occasions pupils *did* know the recorder was there, but they seemed to become accustomed to its presence very quickly, and it is fair to suggest that its overall effect on their behaviour appears to have been fairly minimal. (There were occasions when the transcriber was almost deafened by a pupil picking up the microphone and shouting loudly into it at close range; not always involving the politest of language!)

During observations we attempted to retain the normal classroom environment as much as possible, although there were times when this cannot be said to have been achieved. One reason, in the four main-study Hertfordshire schools, was that across the year, a film crew was present during three or four lessons and some interviews for each class. However, I hope that the obvious disadvantages of this are counterbalanced by the value of the resulting film itself, which is available on the website.[14] It graphically illustrates some audio and visual aspects of the project that would not otherwise be captured, including footage of the pupils at work, audio examples of pupils' products, and clips of pupils and teachers talking about their experiences.

---

13 The literature on 'pupil voice' provides a rich support to this claim. See, for example, Fielding (2004) or the journal *Theory in Practice, Special Issue: Learning from Student Voices* (1995), vol. 34, no. 2, including articles by Dahl (1995), Johnston and Nicholls (1995), Lincoln (1995) and Oldfather (1995). In music education, see, for example, Jackson (2005) and Jorgensen (1997).

14 The film can be downloaded, with the other resources, from <www.musicalfutures. org/PractionersResources.html>, Section 2: Classroom Resources for Informal Learning. It was produced by MMT Openplay, filmed and edited by Nick Sutton.

Another difficulty in retaining normal conditions was that in the four main-study Hertfordshire schools, the Music Service had provided an instrumental teacher to help the classroom teacher. This related to the development of policies and practice concerning provision, whose effects cannot be considered here. The presence of one or two researchers, and occasionally other visitors in each classroom of course altered the normal situation as well. I have carefully compared the findings from the schools affected by this, with those in which no additional people, or only one additional person, was present, and can conclude that there appears to have been no significant effect on findings overall. Having said that, it is undeniable that additional adults in a classroom, making a film, helping, or observing, is obviously bound to have an effect, and there is no way of measuring the extent of this with precision.

More so than the interviews, the observations were not just a part of the research process, but had been put in place from the start, as a central building block of the project strategies, relating not only to the researchers', but the teachers' roles. This is an issue that I will address in the following chapter, and many other parts of the book.

Transcription

It must be mentioned how difficult it was to transcribe the tape-recordings of pupils working in groups, and also how chaotic everything sounds. It was impossible to hear every word that was said during group work, mainly because of the additional noise of instruments and music being played simultaneously within one group, let alone disturbance from neighbouring groups. Therefore the observation and group-work transcriptions are presented as sketches rather than blow-by-blow accounts. Missing passages can be ascertained by consulting the given timings, and some passages are presented as loose *des*criptions of what went on, rather than *trans*criptions. I have used square brackets for any insertions that were added after original field notes or transcriptions were made, but many of them also contain parentheses that were put in at the time for various reasons.

The interview transcriptions are complete, except for the usual convention of using ellipses to indicate missing text, but they do not include every 'um', 'er' or minor interjection of the interviewer, nor statements in which the interviewer simply repeated what an interviewee just said. I have inserted a dash at the end of a word to indicate when a speaker was interrupted, or simply stopped talking in mid-sentence, as people often do. The layout of transcriptions makes clear the difference between what was a conversation between a group of people, such as in a group interview, and what was a comment by an individual that has been isolated from its context. This is done by leaving a space between different interviews or comments. The pupils often used musical or quasi-musical terms in colloquial ways that might not be familiar to some adults. There is a discussion of their uses of musical vocabulary in Chapter 4, (pp. 68–71).

In most of the pupil interviews each speaker is named, but in transcriptions of group work or similar settings this was not always possible. Throughout the book (apart from the Acknowledgements), all names of schools and persons have been substituted with fictitious ones. In giving pseudonyms to the pupils and teachers I have attempted to retain cultural overtones as accurately as possible, for example by replacing names that are associated with a particular culture, nation or religion with another name that is also associated with those things.

Interpreting and reporting results

In qualitative research of this kind it is virtually impossible to give completely accurate descriptions of participants' actions and views. For one thing, during interviews and meetings pupils and teachers were engaged in discussion, and between such events they continued to be involved in further music-teaching and learning activities. They sometimes changed their minds, or unwittingly contradicted themselves in different parts of an interview or meeting, or between one interview and another; and they expressed themselves in complex ways. Therefore, in describing the findings I have often had to make generalizations such as 'a small minority of pupils suggested that ...', rather than giving actual numbers. Wherever possible, such statements are backed up and illustrated by representative examples of the actual words that were said. I have at all times tried to make it as clear as possible where statements illustrate general views, and where they were idiosyncratic. Again, the anonymous quantitative data provides a more objective, if less rich, alternative check on my interpretations, and this is given mainly in footnotes.

The quantity of data we collected was quite overwhelming, including not only over 800 pages of transcriptions and field notes, but over 100 audio recordings, most of which lasted more than an hour. Overall, because of the amount of data, as well as the variety of research tools used, rather than attempting to give any further blow-by-blow account of it all here, I have instead tried to make clear what was done and how it was done as I go along. I have of course attempted to be as systematic, thorough and objective in my analyses and presentation of all data as is humanly possible, but ultimately I am presenting here one person's qualitative analysis of a huge range of material, and the analysis is bound to be susceptible to some bias and error, for which I can only apologize in advance.

This was a practice-based research and development project, which took the views and assumptions of participants at face value. Its reliability and validity rest to a large extent, not only on the thoroughness of the researchers, but on the sincerity and perceptivity of the pupils, and the professional judgement of the teachers involved. They were all essential participant-researchers. The pupils' contribution was immeasurable, unpredictable and, to me at least, fascinating. But it is, in particular, the considered opinions of the teachers, based in most cases on extensive experience and previous knowledge of their pupils in that same environment, which provide the bedrock of any claims that I will make. Their incredible skill, dedication, enthusiasm and above all willingness to take a risk in trying out new ways of working lie at the heart of this book.

The beginning, and the ends, of the project

The first lesson of the project began with a class discussion, in which pupils were asked how they thought popular musicians go about the business of acquiring their musical skills and knowledge. While pupils suggested all sorts of ideas, many of which were accurate, we did not come across a single pupil in any of the 21 schools who showed awareness of, or who described, informal popular music learning practices with any precision. Answers included:

–They practise.

–They get lessons.

–They just play what they feel and stuff.

–I dunno. I think that some people, like Christina Aguilera, they do it 'cause, they, like, what happened in their life, and then afterwards they just start singing, 'cause, the way they think it is, yeah, to show how it, it's not, I dunno.

–Sometimes it comes naturally.

–They probably like have a talent and then they go to someone that can help them bring it out, like.

–Some of them teach them by themselves, like, you get, you know when you get the books, and you get all the notes in it, you, some people teach themselves …

–They get a guitar, and they go up to their bedroom.

I find it interesting and provocative that the pupils seemed to lack awareness of, or seemed unable to describe, popular musicians' informal approaches in more concrete ways, especially the idea of aural copying from a recording. At the same time they seemed unaware of the workings of the music industry in relation to the production of stars, either as highly trained performing commodities, sex-symbols or skilled musicians. As mentioned earlier, in jazz, folk and traditional musics, as well as in many non-Western popular and classical musics, it is often the case that older musicians induct younger ones into an adult 'community of expertise'. But young popular musicians in Western, mainstream styles, by comparison, have been very much left to their own devices. Therefore, large numbers of children in many countries and musical cultures have been unlikely ever to discover the simplicity and availability of informal music learning practices at all. The above findings, gleaned from over 1,500 pupils in 21 schools, would seem to confirm this. Whilst, as I will argue later, there is something almost natural about informal music learning practices, our society has for decades or even centuries, alienated us from them by removing them from the realm of everyday life, as well as from that of formal music education, so that we are now in a position of having to teach them back to ourselves!

The main benefit that I hope this study offers is an illustration of young people's responses to informal learning practices that have been adapted for the music classroom. Despite being fundamentally as old as the hills, these learning practices have been taken up in new ways, by only a minority of young people, outside schooling, following the invention of sound recording technology during the last century. They are learning practices, moreover, that young people can use in their own time, without the need for elaborate, expensive resources or specialist tuition. Most importantly, according to our findings, they are learning practices that can awaken many pupils' awareness of their own musicality, particularly those who might not otherwise be reached by music education, put the potential for musical development and participation into their own hands, open their ears, and enhance their appreciation and understanding of music, not only in relation to what they already know, but also taking them beyond the known as more critically aware and open-minded listeners.

Alongside that, I hope to offer an alternative pedagogy for music, not as a substitute for, but as a complement running alongside existing approaches. In the end, all 17 of the Hertfordshire teachers in the final questionnaire agreed that using informal approaches in the classroom had 'changed their approaches to teaching for the better'. If there is any strength in the approach, I think it must lie in the fact that the strategies were developed by learners, through learning, rather than by teachers through teaching. They derive, not from a theory of learning drawn from an experimental or formal educational situation, or from an analysis of a musical outcome, but from observation and analysis of real-life learning practices by musicians in the world outside formal education. In this book I wish to explore the pupils' skill and knowledge-acquisition, responses to and views of the project, setting them alongside the changing perspectives of teachers, in such a way as to foster ideas and discussion about ways in which we can take classroom music education forward. I do not know whether teachers in other subjects would find the approaches too musically specific to be of any interest; but there are indications of many possible echoes.

Chapter 2

The project's pedagogy and curriculum content

This chapter begins with a brief description of the project's pedagogy and curriculum content. The project was organized in seven stages, but in this chapter I will describe the first five stages only. The final two stages, which involved informal learning with classical music, are given separate consideration in Chapter 7. Appendix B contains a résumé of each stage. Having introduced the stages briefly below, I will discuss the teachers' initial responses to them. Then I will give an overview of the teachers' roles, and consider how their views of these developed as time went by.

For the remainder of the book, apart from Chapter 7, I will focus in detail almost entirely on the first stage of the project, referring only more briefly or generally to the others. Thus all quotations from teachers and pupils, and all field notes and transcripts, come from Stage 1 unless otherwise stated. The reason for this is partly that the quantity of data involved in the project is too great to consider as a whole. But it is mainly because the first stage is the one that most deeply reflects the nature of popular musicians' informal learning practices as these occur outside the school, and most fully represents the principles at the heart of the project. It was also the stage which presented the first and most radical challenge for the project teachers, and it was undertaken by all 21 of the schools, in many cases more than once.

Stages 1–7: overall pedagogy and content

As discussed in Chapter 1, the aims of the project were to adopt and adapt aspects of popular musicians' informal music learning practices for use within the formal arena of the school classroom, and to evaluate the extent to which this is possible and beneficial. Each of the project's seven stages placed at its centre two or more of the five characteristics of informal learning that were identified in Chapter 1 (page 10). These were: using music that pupils choose, like and identify with; learning by listening and copying recordings; learning with friends; engaging in personal, often haphazard learning without structured guidance, and integrating listening, performing, improvising and composing in all aspects of the learning process.

The stages were not conceived so much as 'modules' or 'units' within a 'scheme of work' or curriculum, but rather, as an *approach to teaching and learning* centred on these characteristics. Each stage usually lasted from four to six lessons of 50 to 90 minutes once a week during normal curriculum time, the exact duration depending on the particular school and teacher. (Music education in most UK classrooms takes the form of a general or liberal education which is provided for all pupils up to the age of 14, regardless of ability or choice. Pupils engage in listening, performance, composition and improvisation, covering music from a wide range of styles, times and places. In the majority of schools this happens once a week for a period of around an hour. In some schools music is rotated with other arts subjects, which was the case for one of our extension schools.[1]) There were of course many resource needs, mainly in the form of enough practice spaces for the classes to break into small groups, and enough instruments for pupils to make choices. However, this book is not the place to deal with such practicalities, which are instead discussed in the teaching materials.[2]

We recommend that teachers should introduce more formal lessons in between the project stages, since the project does not claim to address all possible musical skills or to be a complete curriculum. As already mentioned, it was designed to complement, not act as a substitute for more formal approaches. However, in the seven schools considered in detail in this book, the project took place almost entirely without additional lessons. As already mentioned, the three London schools undertook only Stages 1 and 2, whilst the four Hertfordshire schools ran the entire project (except that one school did not run Stage 7). They all followed the given order of the stages, as did most of the extension schools, but it is possible to change the order after Stage 1 if desired. Most of the extension schools did not approach Stages 6 and 7. (Appendix A contains information about which school did what.)

It is important to again emphasize that the central features of the project reside in Stage 1. That stage contains the core of the approach, since it is the one that most closely replicates informal music learning practices as they occur outside the school. It also acts as the blueprint for the role of the teacher, which runs through the whole project. Unless otherwise stated, I therefore devote the majority of the discussion to that stage and to the interviews and discussions that took place before, during and immediately following it throughout the book, with the exception of Chapter 7.

The role of the teacher in brief

The role of the teacher throughout the project was to establish ground rules for behaviour, set the task going at the start of each stage, then stand back and observe what pupils were doing. During this time teachers were asked to attempt to take on and empathize with pupils' perspectives and the goals that pupils set for themselves, then to begin to diagnose pupils' needs in relation to those goals. After, and only after, this period, they were to offer suggestions and act as 'musical models' through

---

1   The National Curriculum for Music in England is available online at <http://www. qca.org.uk/>. Wales and Northern Ireland have slightly different national curricula; Scotland does not have a national curriculum as such, but pupils there do have a similar entitlement to music education. For general discussions of the nature of contemporary music education in the UK, see, for example, Welch (2001), Mills (2005), and for historical perspectives, see Cox (2002), Pitts (2000) and Rainbow with Cox (1989/2006).

2   As mentioned earlier, these are contained in Green with Walmsley (2006), and can be downloaded from <www.musicalfutures.org/PractionersResources.html>, Section 2: Classroom Resources for Informal Learning. Documentary films of the different stages in action, and aural examples of the pupils' products can also be accessed on that site.

demonstration, so as to help pupils reach the goals that they had set for themselves. Teachers told their pupils that they would be available for help if required, but that they would not be instructing in the normal way. The role of the teacher was thus rather different from a normal, formal educational role, and was particularly challenging for all of the teachers involved. It will be considered in more detail later on in this chapter. For now, I will describe the bare bones of the teaching and learning strategies for each stage.

Stage 1: the heart of the project – dropping pupils into the deep end

Stage 1 involved 'dropping pupils into the deep end' by asking them to emulate as closely as possible the real-life learning practices of young, beginner popular musicians. The first four of the five fundamental principles of popular music informal learning practices, as put forward above, were emphasized: learning music that pupils chose for themselves; learning by listening and copying a recording; peer-directed learning without adult guidance, and learning in holistic, often haphazard ways with no planned structure of progression. The fifth principle, involving the integration of listening, performing, improvising and composing, was implicit, particularly with regards to listening and performing, and also to some extent improvising.

Pupils were asked in advance to bring their own music to the first lesson. In all cases they brought popular music drawn from recent chart hits or albums. As illustrated at the end of Chapter 1, there was then a brief whole-class discussion of the question: 'How do you think pop musicians learn to play their instruments, sing, improvise and compose music?' At the end of the discussion pupils were informed that pop musicians may indeed learn by taking lessons, practising, using computers and in other ways that pupils might have suggested; but that they also learn by informal means, that is, listening to their favourite music and copying it, alone and with friends. Pupils were then told they were going to learn in this way, as far as possible, by choosing their own music, copying it by ear using instruments of their choice, and directing their own learning in friendship groups of around three to five members. (Two groups had as many as eight; one pupil worked on her own.)

Teachers were able to relate the work to overall teaching and learning policies within their schools (see Green with Walmsley 2006). However, they did not set targets and objectives for every lesson. Rather, the generic aim of listening to a song and copying it was an ongoing objective that stretched over a number of lessons. Some lessons ended with class performances and discussions, which replicated informal learning practices in the sense that peer assessment, listening to and watching each other are central parts of such learning.

Stage 2: modelling aural learning with popular music

Having been given this relatively high level of autonomy in the first stage of the project, pupils were then offered a little more guidance and structure at the start of Stage 2. Thus the approach involved fewer of the five characteristics of informal learning identified earlier. Choice of music and allowing haphazard learning without structured guidance were dropped, since Stage 2 involved a pre-selected piece of music, pre-prepared curriculum materials, and some demonstration of how to use them by the teacher. But it retained informal qualities and pupil autonomy to the extent that, *once* the task had been set up, the pupils were again required, as in Stage 1, to aurally copy the music from a recording, select instruments and direct their own learning in friendship groups, whilst the role of the teacher continued to be one of standing back, observing, diagnosing, suggesting and modelling.

Pupils were given a CD with an instrumental and vocal version of the funk hit 'Word Up' by the band Cameo. I chose this song for two main reasons. One was that, although unlikely to be selected by pupils themselves, its style was broadly familiar to most of them, or in other words, they were encultured in this music. The second reason was that the song is built on a multitude of short riffs, one to four bars long, most of which are easy to remember and to play (depending on what instrument is being played). Rather than being as unstructured as Stage 1, the teaching CD also contains a broken-down version of the song in the form of 15 separate tracks, each of which contains a different, isolated, single riff, or in some cases two or three riffs in harmony, repeated for around two minutes. The tracks range progressively from relatively easy to relatively difficult. A worksheet gives note names, but not pitch contour or rhythm. The task was to listen to and copy the song in whatever way pupils wished, using the tracks of isolated riffs as a guide if desired, in order to make up their own version of it as a band.

Stage 3: the deep end revisited[3]

Stage 3 was simply a repetition of Stage 1. The aim was to give pupils a chance to build on the skills they had already acquired, and to observe to what extent this was realized. (This stage does not have to follow on from Stage 2, but could be placed at any point in the project. However, most of the project schools did place it at that point. Some repeated it again later.)

Stage 4: informal composing

Pupils then moved into their own composition. The aim was that they would build on what they had learned through listening and copying in Stages 1, 2 and 3. This structure replicates informal music learning practices, since popular musicians usually begin creating their own music by spontaneously basing ideas upon what they have learnt through listening and copying. Many pupils had already received guidance about composing in previous lessons, either as part of the national curriculum for music during the previous year at school or elsewhere. However, no further guidance was given at this stage of the project.

---

3   As explained, from Stage 3 to Stage 5 inclusive, only 4 of the 7 schools studied in detail, along with 12 of the 13 extension schools, took part. One extension school was unable to do so, due to a rotating timetable with another subject. Details of which school ran which stages are available in Appendix A. Many of those who did not run the latter stages of the project repeated earlier stages instead, or carried on the project by incorporating earlier stages into their existing curricula.

Stage 5: modelling composing

Next, pupils were offered a 'musical model' of song-writing taken from the 'real' world of popular music. This was organized by either inviting in a band (or duo) from outside the school, or organizing a peer demonstration by a band of same-age or nearly same-age pupils from within the school. The aim was to help pupils understand how a song can be put together 'from the inside', by engaging with live music and musicians' perspectives. It also allowed them to learn by watching more expert musicians play, including peers. Once the demonstration was over, the visiting musicians, whether older people or peers, took up similar roles to the teachers.

Stages 6 and 7: informal learning with classical music

As already mentioned, the final two stages used informal learning practices with classical music. Whilst in many ways the findings overlapped with those for earlier stages, the aims of the strategies and the focus of the research were somewhat different. Therefore, although I will occasionally mention findings from those stages in the following four chapters, I have left a description of their strategies and a detailed examination of their findings for later (Chapter 7).

Teachers' initial responses and the apparent conflict with official approaches

Everyone in the project team was in a wondering, and in some cases fairly anxious frame of mind before the project started. Musicians in the 'community music' realm are much more accustomed to informal ways of working with groups of teenagers than school teachers are. In theory at least, community musicians may not see anything unusual about the project strategies, and hopefully they will find echoes with many of their approaches in them. However, despite that, many such musicians do consciously or unconsciously tend towards formalizing their approaches to some extent when they are working within a formal educational environment. This is undoubtedly because that environment, and the very idea of 'teaching' or 'delivering' education, place complex demands upon practitioners. In addition, school teachers have a number of responsibilities which are not usually the same for community musicians in out-of-school settings, or even when such musicians come into the school as visitors. Not surprisingly, every school teacher in the project found the strategies new, and in many cases radical and challenging.[4]

The majority of school music teachers in the UK and most other countries have classical backgrounds.[5] It could be tempting to use this as an explanation for the

---

4   See Moore (2000) for some helpful discussions of how teachers deal, or could deal, with such conflicts, especially conflicts between government requirements and their own intuitive knowledge of the complexity of such matters in classrooms. It is probable that music teachers in England would have been less anxious about the strategies before the 1988 Education Act, when they had more autonomy from governmental directives.

5   York (2001) found that out of 750 Heads of Music in schools, 78 per cent had a degree based in classical music and 69 per cent performed in classical music, with only 8.5 per cent

project teachers' wariness about the project, since informal learning practices, especially aural copying from a recording, are likely to be unfamiliar to many of them; and also the value of such practices might not be immediately apparent. However, classical training cannot on its own explain the reasons for their hesitation. For one thing, a minority of classically trained teachers, especially younger ones, do increasingly double up as popular, jazz and traditional musicians, with one foot in formal education and one in informal learning. Secondly, every school music teacher is required to develop basic knowledge and versatility in relation to a number of styles, including popular music, as soon as they begin their teacher education, in order to fulfil the diverse requirements of contemporary music education, and all music teachers continue to gain experience in a range of styles once they are in post. Thirdly, although many teachers may not have much experience of aural learning in a popular style, or of group learning or playing in a pop, rock, jazz, folk or similar band, that does not mean they are at a complete loss when asked to undertake such activities. As part of our teacher induction for the extension schools, for example, and in many further workshops organized by Musical Futures around the UK, school teachers were asked to undertake the project's Stage 1 strategies, completing in one hour what pupils were required to do in four to six lessons. The task was greeted enthusiastically by the great majority of participants, and all groups produced worthy and fluent renditions of their given songs. So, I would suggest, rather than only the musical training backgrounds of teachers, the reasons for their nervousness about the project strategies lay in the implications that the pedagogy had for teachers' legal and professional roles and responsibilities.

Many countries have a national curriculum or other centralized set of requirements, such as official standards or textbooks, indicating the curriculum content and, either implicitly or explicitly, the pedagogic strategies that teachers are expected to use. In England, the National Curriculum for Music is mandatory unless special permission is obtained for innovatory work; however, such permission is very rarely sought and we did not seek it for the project. There are also a number of regularly revised government guidelines on what constitute good or desirable approaches to teaching. This is supported by regular inspections and other mechanisms for evaluating quality, including, at the time of the research, the potential presence of government inspectors as observers within classrooms. Whether mandatory or not, all guidelines are taken extremely seriously by teachers. Failure to 'deliver' the required curriculum, or being seen as a 'poor' teacher, officially or unofficially, can have disastrous consequences, both professionally and personally.

The main challenge for teachers at the start of the project was that 'we don't know what's going to happen', and many felt, as one Head of Music put it, that 'this is really going to be different'. Firstly, there were fears about the project's commensurability with the requirements of the National Curriculum. The project involved open-ended learning outcomes, a high degree of pupil autonomy, and a low level of teacher direction; whereas any national curriculum or other official educational directive, by its nature, is bound to give some specifications about what

---

performing in pop/rock. He also found that the teachers were unfamiliar with contemporary popular music.

pupils should have learnt by particular stages of development, as well as implicit or explicit indications about desired curriculum content and teaching strategies. In fact, as time went by it became apparent that much of the conflict with such directives was related to the means, rather than the ends of the educational endeavour. At the end of the project we were able to map out the activities quite precisely to show how they met almost all of the National Curriculum specifications for this country (Green with Walmsley 2006), and the results of the exercise were unanimously agreed by all the teachers present at the final project team meeting. However, at the start, although teachers did not think the project would conflict with the National Curriculum in a legal way, this mapping was not available. Furthermore, the mapping does not mean that the project *on its own* would meet all the requirements, as certain areas to do with theory, technical vocabulary and musical literacy are not necessarily covered by it. I will discuss some issues arising from this in the final chapter of the book.

Secondly, a variety of government guidelines in the UK at the time of the project, as well as to date, include the notion that lessons should be clearly structured in distinct parts, including an introduction with explicit aims, a variety of activities in the middle, and a closing activity. The project lessons were, however, relatively unstructured, and some of them, particularly in the hands of individual teachers who were willing to go to the furthest extreme, had no structure at all beyond the pupils coming into the music area, finding a space, making music, and going out again. As already mentioned, teachers in the UK, as in many countries, are inspected regularly by government representatives, and many felt that if they were observed undertaking the kinds of activities involved in the project they could face serious criticism. Again, however, in cases where project teachers were inspected, the results were highly favourable.[6]

Not only are there legal and professional responsibilities relating specifically to music teaching, but there are of course other general responsibilities that go along with the teaching of almost any subject in almost any country. In different ways, teachers and schools have to produce and meet targets; make formal assessments of pupil attainment and ability; write reports to parents, employers and others; give written and verbal feedback to pupils; tailor their educational programmes so as to benefit, as well as interest, all pupils; address themselves to learners who may come from a huge diversity of backgrounds and will exhibit a range of ability, usually all in one class at the same time, and meet many, many more demands. Most importantly, perhaps, teachers have to maintain worthwhile, educationally beneficial and trusting relationships with children, who attend their classes out of compulsion, not choice

---

6   One of the project schools was deemed by inspectors to have 'serious weaknesses' during the time of the project. However, this did not apply to the Performing Arts Department. Following an inspection of a project lesson, the report stated: 'Pupils' achievements in a number of special activities, such as Musical Futures, are very good or excellent. ... The project is designed to investigate how pupils can take control of their own learning, and addresses the low take-up of music nationally after Year 9. It demonstrated high motivation and very good progress in lessons.' Similar stories occurred in some of the extension schools. Musical Futures asked the Chief Inspectorate of Music to produce a report on all its activities at the end of the two-year period. At the time of going to press, the report, as well as a variety of guidelines, are available at <www.ofsted.gov.uk>.

– relationships that can last for years. Beyond such positive educational aims, and beyond the personal relationships of individual teachers and pupils in particular schools, is the vast complex of social, political and ideological educational effects that occur in the wider society, despite the intentions and outside the control of those people who participate in the educational endeavour.

In view of all these demands and complexities, it is no surprise that the project looked rather daunting from the perspective of a teacher. However, in the spirit which characterized their approach throughout, the teachers greeted it as a challenge rather than a threat:

–Denise: This is great, it's really exciting; it's going to be so interesting seeing what happens.

–Ken: It was actually quite exciting not knowing.

Where doubts were felt, they were expressed in terms such as:

–Richard: When I first heard about the project, I was a little sceptical. I think lots of music teachers now – I mean the Key Stage 3 Strategy [government guideline] has kicked in, the way we structure lessons, with starters and objectives and two-part pupil activities with a plenary at the end. And this is sort of quite divorced from that, in that it all goes out the window really, in terms of the style of the project, of informal learning. So yes I was sceptical. I was a little bit concerned also about abandoning my principles – what I thought were good lesson structures.

Overall, there was a feeling of anxiety, and words including 'panic', 'dread' and 'terror' were used. Even when group composition began in Stage 4, by which time teachers had become far more accustomed to the strategies, the idea of giving pupils freedom to compose music without any guidelines, stimuli or explicit objectives caused concern all over again:

–Debbie: I'm terrified about the lesson today; just letting the kids go off and jam. I'm actually scared of letting them do this. But I am interested to see what they'll come up with.

–Sandra: … in teaching composition we can normally direct it so much, that it's scary giving them free choice, and you just don't know what they'll be able to do.

During the rest of the book I will trace how these doubts and fears developed as the project went along.

The role of the teacher: an overview

The issue of the teacher's role also forms a strand that runs throughout the book, but here I wish to focus on it specifically, in relation to two main component parts: firstly, that of standing back and observing during the first few lessons of each stage, and secondly, that of diagnosing, suggesting and demonstrating during the latter lessons, at which point the teachers' roles became more developed.[7] I will focus on Stage 1, as that was the first time that the teachers had taken on this role, and it provides the blueprint for the later stages. Then I will briefly present how the teachers' views of this aspect developed as the project went on.

Stage 1: standing back and observing

Standing back occurred most radically during the first two or three lessons, depending on the school, length of lesson and so on. During the very first lesson, when pupils were choosing their music to copy, there was literally no pedagogic role for teachers to play. It was important that they should not intervene in order, for example, to help pupils choose songs that were more suitable or easier to play, since the free choice of the learners was one of the essential learning strategies that was drawn from the practices of popular musicians. Once the pupils had chosen their music (which usually occurred during the first or second lesson), teachers were asked to continue standing back as much as possible while pupils selected instruments and started trying to sing and play through aural copying.

All the teachers, myself included, found it hard to stand back and watch, particularly when, for example, a pupil might be holding a guitar upside down or across their knees. In extreme and obvious cases such as those there was indeed a tendency for many of us to suggest an alternative position, but ideally even that should wait for half an hour or more, rather than being jumped on immediately.

Some teachers found it harder to stand back than others. The teaching team could be divided into those who saw themselves as 'control freaks', and those who were more 'laid-back'. The 'control freaks' were tempted to structure the lesson, set explicit objectives, issue instructions about how to approach the task, and specify what outcomes they expected. Before starting, Richard wanted to know how long each phase of the lesson would take. He stressed to us: 'because this is a *school*'. At the end of Stage 1 the teachers reflected on this aspect:

–Richard: I'm a control freak, really. And I've hated standing back. I've found that very difficult. Mainly because I felt I haven't earned my money. Mainly because I like things to be at my fingertips and at my control. And I've had to learn to stand back and let the pupils in a sense, decide their own learning, informally. So that's a struggle I've had to come to terms with ...

–Debbie: I'm a total control freak! And I've found that really hard. I found that really hard at first and I didn't enjoy it at first. ... Knowing my kids, knowing what they're like in

---

7   For related discussions of the role of the teacher as standing back in some way, see, for example: Alderson (2003, 2004), Bentley (1998, pp. 156ff); Kincheloe and Steinberg (1998), Osler (2006), Watkins (2005) and Weimer (2002). Goodson (1998) suggests an approach to standing back very similar to that adopted in the project. Moore's (2000, pp. 149f.) concept of the 'reflexive teacher', who takes their own assumptions as problematic, is also similar to the project conception in many ways, although it does not explicitly include the notion of teaching as observing. Also see notes 2 and 10 in Chapter 1, and elsewhere in this volume for other commensurate views. In relation to music education, related concepts of the role of the teacher occur in, amongst others, Allsup (2004), Glover (2001) and Jorgensen (2003).

other areas, I had a bit of a panic attack, because from knowing for example from the Maths Department, you have no structure at the moment, it's like 'hard-hat country' down there at the moment, it's like, you go in and you brace yourself as you go in. And that is the way that the kids are. I didn't want the kids to see music as a 'Let's just go in and sit, chat and doss', 'cause I've worked hard to get away from that. … And it's all one task, which we, I don't know about you but [normally] we have to have different kinds of task; we've got to have visual, got to have kinaesthetic, and this is just one task for one lesson.

–Janet: I couldn't stand listening to my group not playing in time. I just had to show them. I just couldn't listen to it. I was getting their hands and fingers and showing them the notes.

–Denise: You knew you could show them how to do it but you had to watch them struggle.

–Brian: It's not in our nature.

Of the 'laid-back' teachers, Sandra was the prime case:

–Sandra: … the aspect of self-directed learning and the risk-taking in teaching is one of those things that I've focused on a lot in my own teaching, and just wondering how far pupils will go on their own before you have to input. Now normally we have to put some input in there to make the progress that's expected to be seen. But, you know, out of personal interest to me I've chosen to take a kind of, a non-interventionist approach almost to it, just to see how much they can come up with …

It became even harder for the teachers to stand back when the pupils began to deteriorate, which, as we will see in the next chapter, began to happen around the second or third lesson:

–Debbie: … about three weeks into it it took a real dip, and I was seeing all the evidence that I knew I would see. And it was actually quite, I felt there were no outcomes in the lesson, and I'm used to having really clear outcomes, and I know where every kid is up to, and I know that every kid by the end of the lesson can either do this, this or this, and I was missing that. And I felt I was failing them because they weren't producing that. … At least I would have got every single kid achieving something. And I thought that the outcomes were really low, not for every single kid but for a lot of the kids. And I would have pulled the plug on that …

However, to the surprise of all the teachers, this period was followed by the pupils finding their own ways out of difficulties. Debbie continued:

–Debbie: …but because I couldn't pull the plug on it, I'm really glad that I didn't, because over a period of about two weeks there was a huge change. The kids suddenly became, as they said to me, they started to panic: 'Oh, we haven't got anything, so we started to listen to each other.' And I was actually quite amazed by some of the results. I wasn't amazed at the kids who could achieve their outcomes, what I was amazed at was the low ability kids and what they were coming out with. … So they became much more focused by themselves. It was kind of a turning point that I didn't ever think they would get to.

All the other teachers confirmed the same, and this was also verified by those in the extension schools. For example:

–Richard: ... you know, if you sit in and listen to what they've actually got to do, you know, rather than being a teacher and getting involved, but actually stand back and just listen to what they're saying, they're talking about this and they're saying 'No, you should try that.' It's all anecdotal bits and pieces like that, where you think 'Yes, actually, they're discussing it and making a decision, a group decision, and then practising it.' Even if, through the practising, they get it wrong. But they're actually, the process is what ... you know, modern rock musicians, pop musicians would actually go through.

–Carol: ...it wasn't how we as teachers would think they would organize. They organized themselves in a different way. And I found that very interesting, and I already apply that in other lessons that I've taught – not to panic if it's not going quite how I perceive it's meant to. Because if you just watch it, they solve the problems for themselves, and they get themselves organized and they get on task, but not quite the road you would have expected them to go down. ... Oh, I've really enjoyed that [standing back], really enjoyed that. Because just to watch them you learn so much about the way they approach things. And as adults you think you can remember, but you don't, and it's a re-learning process.

–Sandra: So, for example, kids doing Coldplay were trying to work out some notes, and instead of trying to leap in and work out the notes, I just stood there while this kid tried the notes and then he just found them. ... And they will find the way themselves, and that came as a little bit of a surprise. I thought they would need a lot more input, a lot more guidance from me as a teacher, but I think they, in a lot of respects, have found the answers themselves, from the things they've asked. ... So within the space of two weeks, when I hadn't actually been able to put in any input and make any suggestions, they had done it themselves.

Many of the teachers began to feel that they normally over-paced and over-structured their lessons. For example:

–Brian: It's shown me that a lot of pressure and over-pacing of stuff isn't always a good idea. And I think leaving children to actually think and contemplate and listen and analyse, and then try stuff out and be able to do that without having a five-minute time limit, or a seven-and-a-half-minute time limit, or whatever time that you put on it, has certainly benefited a lot of children and there has been a sense of, sort of laid-backness with this, but which has still produced results which I've been impressed with really. ... I think, you know, you can learn a lot from that as a classroom teacher. We're so into pace and everything's going zap, zap, zap, zap and flashing lights and cartwheels and all the rest of it. And I think, especially with a subject like music, we need to argue our corner really as music teachers, because children need time to contemplate, think and consider, listen and try stuff out, and practise, and this is a word which is out of fashion in education, 'practice'. You need to practise stuff, and you need a lot of time to do that. And we don't give them time.'

–Debbie: I've learnt that things don't just last a lesson. And they sometimes, you know [pause] I'm very quick paced when I do things, and sometimes if I see one person off task I will stop it and bring everybody in, 'cause I want everyone to be focused the whole time. And maybe I'm stopping people from developing further by not giving them that time ...

Stage 1: diagnosing, suggesting and modelling

During the initial period of standing back for two or three lessons, teachers were asked to observe what goals pupils seemed to be setting for themselves, and to start diagnosing what the pupils needed in order to realize those goals. Pupils were of course free to ask for help at any point during the project, and had been told that teachers were available to offer help. However, it was not until pupils started trying to play instruments, and particularly to match pitches on instruments with those on their chosen recording, that they began to seek, or to really need, help. At that point, sometimes in response to a request and sometimes not, teachers began to offer some guidance in the form of suggestions and minimal demonstration, or what we referred to as 'modelling'. This approach was different from the usual instructional role, partly because it was based on the diagnosis of and response to learner-perceived, immediate need, rather than on pre-established teacher-set aims or objectives with long-term trajectories in mind. It involved teaching in a responsive, rather than directive way, metaphorically taking the learner by the hand, getting inside their head and asking: 'What do they want to achieve now, this minute, and what is the main thing they need to achieve it?' In this way, the teacher sits alongside the learner and is to a large extent a learner themselves. As Yasmin described the role: 'I'm learning to stand back I suppose, and I suppose it's teaching in a non-teacher-like way'.

One result was that teachers found themselves questioning pupils in a different way:

–Sandra: What I've been able to do is to go into groups, ask them questions, and then actually wait for them to come back with the answers themselves, rather than me having any particular input. ... I was in a group last week, went in, 'How did you get on today?' and they said 'Oh it wasn't very good.' So I was able just to say to them 'What, why wasn't it very good?' And they told me exactly why, and then looked for the next question. So I said 'What will you do about it?' And they came up with two almost, you know, perfect suggestions of things to try, and they've then tried it. And I think the effect that has on them is that they have found the way themselves, they know they've found the way themselves, and today they've done a performance which demonstrates how effective that's been, and that they can put together a piece of music from, from nothing. ... So I was questioning them in a completely different way, I wasn't leading them in any respect, I was just giving them the opportunity to speak out. It's a completely different way of questioning from when *you've* got the answer in your head, you want them to say the word 'dynamics' and you're going to get them to say the word 'dynamics' for as long as it takes you to do it. It's different – it doesn't matter.[8]

8　Interestingly, Sandra's approach here is commensurate with what is recommended by Edwards and Mercer (1987) in their discussion of the use of language in the classroom. It also

Some ways in which teachers provided help, and which we all felt worked well, included: showing pupils how to play something but only in rough, simplified or partial form, then retreating; showing them how to hold an instrument more comfortably, but without insisting on correct hold or posture; showing them where to find notes on an instrument, but without saying exactly what to do with those notes; playing a riff or a rhythm, but without expecting accurate repetition (as often the learner would be able to repeat, for example, pitch contour, but not the exact pitches); going along with pupils' choices, so that if a pupil wanted to play something on a glockenspiel which would be much easier on an electric keyboard, the teacher would avoid insisting on switching to the easier instrument, since (as we will see) the choice of instrumental sound is often vital to the learner's motivation. In general, teachers avoided standing over pupils to check that they were doing what they had been shown correctly, but instead left them to take the advice in their own way, or not to take it at all. A little help without seeking perfection gave a lease for further development by the pupils themselves, and enabled pupils to retain ownership over their musical products and strategies.

On some occasions pupils would take what had been shown, and change it in some way for the better. This could occur particularly since pupils were often more encultured in the relevant style than the teachers. Thus they knew what was more outstanding or distinctive about the aspect of the song they were copying, whereas those who are not encultured may tend to reduce the essential qualities down to a norm. For example:

–Connor: Well I asked Mr X to do it, and he showed me. He just went (plays beat), but I thought 'Nah that don't sound like the beat,' so I thought (plays beat, actually more accurate than the one Mr X had shown him).

In addition, not all the teachers were accustomed to copying music by ear, and they did not have proficiency on every instrument that the pupils chose to use. Their roles involved, to a large extent, becoming learners alongside their pupils.

Teachers also worked with *group* inter-relationships by, for example, suggesting that one person with a strong sense of rhythm should play an open bar, and others should then concentrate on listening to that person during the ensemble. As I will discuss in Chapter 6, the groups were composed of pupils with mixed ability and mixed prior musical experiences. Whilst it was part of the strategy for teachers to encourage certain pupils to help others, as will be seen, many pupils rose to take such roles upon themselves, and furthermore, they were not always ones who had been expected to do so.

Overall, the main approach was to help pupils, firstly through observing their actions and diagnosing their needs, then demonstrating, or modelling, in order to foster learning by watching, listening and imitation, rather than explaining, naming or insisting.

---

has much in common with the Brunerian concept of the 'scaffolding'. For a discussion and practical analysis of this concept within a music classroom see J. Wiggins (forthcoming).

The role of the teacher: Stage 2 and onwards

Partly because the Stage 2 task was more structured, the teachers were slightly more on demand at an earlier point. For example, many pupils were beginning to acquire basic technique on certain instruments, and hence looking around for more help in holding them properly, and pupils were quicker to ask for help in finding pitches. Teachers expressed some indications that they had:

> –Debbie: ... got used to now though, the fact that they ask you for help, and I've kind of got used to that now. And I do understand now that it's *their* work and they want to produce what they can. But I mean it is tempting to go in there and say 'Right, you could do this, that and the other.'

In Stage 3 (a repetition of Stage 1), although a few doubts continued to be expressed, the teachers had settled more comfortably into their new roles. They mainly demonstrated pitches and chords on instruments, and asked questions to encourage pupils to work things out for themselves. At the beginning of Stage 4 (composing), as mentioned earlier, there was a small upsurge of panic about the freedom and lack of structure, but this evaporated quickly. During Stages 4 and 5, in general teachers stood back at the very beginning, then took up roles mainly helping pupils to fit together parts. There were some cases where pupils created fairly sophisticated vocal or instrumental melodies, but were not always able to fit chords or a bass line to them; or they had put together a chord progression, but were at a loss to sing or play a melody over it. Teachers would help by, for example, suggesting a few notes or chords that would work, then leaving pupils to take the idea in their own direction. In Stages 6 and 7 it was agreed that pupils needed more help, and needed it sooner; however, the nature of the help that was offered continued along the same paths as the previous stages.

By the end of the project, as mentioned in Chapter 1, all the teachers in the main and extension schools unanimously agreed that, as phrased in the anonymous questionnaire, 'Using informal learning practices in the classroom has generally changed my approach to teaching for the better.'[9] The main respect in which this change had occurred, as indicated through interviews and discussions, concerned the role of the teacher, particularly as an observer and guide who stands back, rather than an expert who instructs.

One upshot of standing back, which was identified by teachers as the project developed, was that they were repeatedly surprised by their pupils. In general, their expectations had been too low. In response to the question, 'As an experienced Head of Music, what, if anything do you feel that you have learnt from the project so far?':

> –Janet: ... you can leave them and they will, they will sort of, I just [normally] think they don't know as much as they do, and I [now] think they actually know more than I give them credit for, and I've definitely learned that, and that they were able just to get on with it, and I was a bit wary of that. I wasn't sure that was going to happen. But they did.
> *(Interview at the end of Stage 2)*

---

9   Twelve teachers ticked 'Strongly agree'; the other five ticked 'Agree'.

–Sandra: It sounds cheesy, but what I think I'm learning all the time is just not having too many expectations at all. Because my expectations are consistently low of my pupils, because when they did their performances for Stage 3, judging by what had happened the week before, I didn't think they'd have anything ready, and they did really good performances. So my judgments are wrong; my judgment's always out. ... They're surprising me all the time. My expectations are too low.

(Conversation during Stage 4)

–Yasmin: I feel that I've learnt that pupils can take on more than I've given them in the past, in that they can listen aurally, and any pupil can pick out tunes given enough time and opportunity to do it. That's what the project has taught me.

(Interview at the end of the project)

Not only did standing back reveal new aspects of their pupils, but the teachers also felt that it gave pupils the opportunity to get to grips more immediately and directly with the stuff of music – its sonic properties and relationships, or what I will later refer to as its inter-sonic meanings. For example:

–Sandra: ... it lets you see things that you wouldn't see ...
–Lucy: Like what?
–Sandra: Like them making real musical progress I suppose. Which we don't give ourselves time to actually watch and see them do it themselves. ... It's a different set of skills from doing starter, plenary, pace, millions of worksheets that are all differentiated, and all those tricks, and everything else that you do. It's much more about *music.*

(Interview at the end of the project)

–Yasmin: That's been a big change for me, just standing back and letting pupils get on with it, and not constantly saying 'Come on, get on with it, come on, get on with it, you've got to do this by the end of the lesson.' The fact that there is no pressure on them, that they can just show what they've done, and that it is a positive experience, as much as we can make it for them. I suppose that's what is so different about the project than normal class teaching. In normal class teaching we have to have something at the end of the lesson ... This is more flexible, it allows the pupil time to absorb. I suppose that's it isn't it? It's the absorption of music and letting it come out again.

(Interview at the end of the project)

Many issues are suggested by these findings. They include the notion that pupils seem capable of progressing even when teachers do not help them; that progression may not always proceed in straight, upwards-sloping lines, but may involve a natural process of getting worse before you get better; that teachers seem to notice new qualities in their pupils by standing back and observing rather than teaching; that teachers tend to expect pupils to be unable or unwilling to work without structured guidance, whilst pupils can in fact show the opposite to be the case if given the chance, and many more. As the book goes along I will investigate these issues, and give examples of the role of the teacher in a variety of contexts. In Chapter 5 especially, I will discuss how pupils described their responses to this way of teaching.

The start of Stage 1: chaos, its aftermath and the questions it raised

Below is a transcript of a representative group of five boys in 'Deansgrove', a (fictitiously named) inner London school, at the beginning of the second lesson of Stage 1. The class had just been reminded that the task was to go into their practice space with their own CDs, choose a song (if they had not already fixed on one in the previous lesson), then copy it aurally from the recording, using instruments of their choice, and structuring their learning in whatever way they wished. One of the boys, Luke, had taken piano lessons for about two years, and was amongst a small minority of pupils in the project who were able autonomously to match pitches from a recording on an instrument by ear. None of the other boys in the group (or indeed, in the whole class) had taken instrumental lessons, and according to the class teacher, no others in that group had shown any particular signs of musicality or interest in music lessons previously. Although they later gave permission for its use, the boys had no knowledge that this recording was being made, and there was no adult in the room except where stated.

I have provided an extended transcription, as it gives a good idea of the kinds of chaos that seemed to characterize pupils' early approaches to the task – exactly as feared by the teachers – before going on to show how that chaos gradually gave way to something relatively organized and focused. (I have not provided the part in which there was teacher input, as indicated within the transcription, since the role of teachers is discussed elsewhere.)

> 3:30 The groups are starting out. The radio is on [since the CD player had an internal radio]. There is apparent chaos. 5:00 Some more organized work appears to be starting. 6:00 Mucking around, 'Radio One' is on [British pop music station]. 7:15 Still the same. 7:28 Again it sounds like more organized work is starting, but then it peters out all the time. 9:00 some more organized work is starting; humming, but then playing East Enders [TV theme tune] on piano. Apparently complete chaos and nothing going on at all. 9:45 They make more of an effort to get going on something. The CD starts in the background; i.e. this is 15 minutes after the class were first told to get into groups. Talking, random drumming and maracas, all completely out of time. Bit of swearing.

–I'm going to play it again.

> A girl from another group comes in and starts trying to tell the boys what to do. A different CD track goes on. 11:40 Still apparent chaos, no organization at all! CD goes off. Random notes on piano, some not so random now but formed into a short tune with a five-note scale and a repeated note. Possibly learnt from a previous piano lesson. Drums. Talking but can't hear what's being said. Someone says 'You're getting on my nerves' (?) to the boy playing the piano [Luke]. 12:38 Another effort to get going and organize each other. But random notes on piano continue. Some swear words again. 13:20

–Wait, is this alright? (followed by some more rhythmic drumming).

> Instrumental sounds.

–You play the guitar beat, right.

–Wait, wait.

> Sounds very chaotic but more on task. 14:20 The boy on the piano, Luke, says 'Cameron, is this OK?', then plays some of the previous notes on the piano, which

I can now hear are not so random but remembered from the notes on their CD (Red Hot Chilli Peppers). Now there is singing and drumming.

—It will take a fucking hour to get this together.

15:40 V. difficult to hear what's going on. 16:15 the CD goes back on. Discussion of use of keyboard. 17:30 Now some playing along to CD is taking place, some of which is in time, and some not.

—Hit that, hit that as a finish (demonstrates on cymbal) and I'll play this.

Continues up to 18:20 LG enters room. From 19.10 to 24.04 there is teacher input from me, listening to what the piano boy, Luke, had done and showing three notes of the guitar riff to Cameron. LG then leaves.

—Turn it off, I need to practise this.

CD goes off. Some drumming heard. 25:20

-Luke is really good.

-Luke is really good.

-You're not really good, you're excellent.

More talk all about this.

—Let's hear it again.

-Miss said we're not allowed to do that.

26:31 CD starts again. Drumming, maracas and guitar for the opening. CD goes off.

—How many beats are there?

Inaudible discussion.

—Hey you guys, I'm playing it now.

More talk.

—Hurry up.

-How many beats, how many beats are there?

—Sixteen.

—It's either sixteen or thirty-two.

CD goes on. Hugh [class teacher] comes in.

—Sir, this string down here, it doesn't make any sound.

—Hey Luke, you don't know (inaudible).

—There's thirty-two, thirty-two beats!

CD goes off again. Lots of discussion, all on task. 29:09 (There is a clear recording here of working out notes.)

—Oh, I found it out! (Notes being played on guitar). Listen, listen. I'm going to, I've got a good idea, listen.

—That bit at the end.

—It's just D E D E D E D E.

These are the correct pitches, matched against the recording with the correct rhythm. 30:16

—You're not doing anything.

—I don't want to sing. I have no high pitch. 30:40

—Three, two, one, go.

—It might be easier if you put on the music.

—Cameron can you just stop so –

—Wait a bit, der der, der der, der der (rhythmically).

—Play it with the music.

—OK.

—Music is starting very shortly.

—Are you actually playing the piano on this bit?

—Is it alright if I do this?

CD starts up
–Luke, start.

> Playing along is happening. 32:00 Still playing along (quite well). 32:50 Noise of other pupils coming into the room, having been told to do so for the end of the lesson.

–The chorus goes (plays on piano); no, I play this (plays) …

> *(Deansgrove School; Luke, Cameron, Mantsebo, Jared, and Kevin's group; Stage 1, lesson 2; concealed field recording, no teacher/researcher present, LG's transcript)*

At the end of the lesson, the group gave a performance to the rest of the class, in which Mantsebo played a 16-beat opening in a quasi-rock style, using a ride cymbal and a floor tom, and finishing with a crash on the cymbal. Along with this, Cameron played a melody of the song's opening notes on the guitar. At the cymbal crash Luke entered on the piano for a repetition of the melody, now played in unison with the guitar. There was hand percussion provided by Jared and Kevin, with pauses at appropriate structural moments. There was a sense of vitality in the playing, and Hugh, the class teacher, and I observed an air of serious concentration on the faces of the performers. There was also apparent fascination on the part of the listeners, who, as Hugh said, '… were listening a lot more closely and a lot more attentively compared to ordinary music lessons'.

The main questions I wish to address for the remainder of the following chapters all arose from the very beginnings of Stage 1 of the project, and are embedded in the above example. They include:

- How and why did those boys move from an apparently random and chaotic set of activities, to something musically ordered, organized and relatively focused?
- What, if anything, might they have gained from the task in relation to musical skills and knowledge, both as creators of music and as listeners?
- Did the task affect their motivation, enjoyment or application, and if so, in what ways?
- How did they respond to being left on their own to direct their own learning, and how did that affect the interpersonal relationships within the group?
- To what extent was the task able to reach pupils in all ranges of ability and prior experience?
- Finally, would pupils be able to transfer this way of learning to music that was unfamiliar to them, and with which they did not identify?

These are the central issues on which I will attempt to shed some light during the remainder of the book.

Chapter 3

Making music

Some musical practices involve the direct production of musical sounds, pieces of music or musical events. Other musical practices are centrally concerned not so much with production as with reception, that is, with listening to music, and the use of music in various contexts. The most primary and ubiquitous reception activity is that of listening, whether or not it is done while sitting in a chair or an auditorium, driving a car, dancing or anything else. Producing music and listening to music are of course intimately bound up. Musical production always includes listening, although listening does not always include musical production. Whereas it is therefore in many ways false to separate out the concept of musical production from that of music listening, I have done so here for the purposes of analysis, and merely as one way of attempting to consider the complex phenomenon of music learning in detail. Thus the present chapter focuses on how pupils approached informal learning practices that directly involved producing and manipulating the sonic properties of music and their inter-relationships: that is, *making* music. The next chapter considers those aspects of their learning practices, whether productive or receptive, that centrally concerned *listening* to music. As already mentioned, my main focus will be on Stage 1 of the project, but at various points I will consider aspects of the later stages.

Social distinction and the emergence of 'natural music learning practices'

It seems reasonable to suggest that certain music learning practices are liable to arise naturally, or in other words, to come about instinctively or intuitively, without the intervention of a particular cultural or educational system, across a wide variety of social contexts.[1] However, that suggestion demands a distinction between a learning *practice* and the *content* of what is being learnt. Clearly, if young teenagers from a society in which no one had ever heard any Western popular music, for example, were asked to aurally copy a Western pop song from a recording, using a drum kit and an electronic keyboard, we have no grounds to assume that those children's learning practices would be at all similar to those of children living in and around a large European city. But to stop there would be to miss one of the crucial aspects of the learning task under consideration here. For what I am suggesting is that the practices

---

1   There has been much interest in the connections between music learning and language learning as two quite parallel natural learning processes, although relatively little systematic research has investigated this as yet. See, for example, McPherson and Gabrielsson (2002, pp. 102f.), Kohut (1985) and Barrett (1996). The Suzuki method is founded upon the principle that children pick up music naturally in the way they pick up language; although the method itself is highly structured, and in that sense formalized.

of children across different cultures and contexts might be fundamentally similar if they were all given a fundamentally similar task – and this particular task centrally involves copying music that they have chosen *for themselves* from within their own culture. They would be likely to approach the task in ways that are fundamentally similar, even if on the surface their approaches are articulated in a variety of ways depending on the nature of the music being copied, the instruments, and the social practices and values surrounding music-making and music reception with which the children are already familiar.

Within the project, a number of learning practices seemed to emerge and take broadly similar forms, without teacher intervention or guidance, across all 21 schools. These learning practices can be seen as 'natural', in so far as we can assume that they would emerge in similar ways and take similar forms whenever a group of young teenagers was asked to go into a similar situation and carry out a similar task. However, within that broad base there are bound to be a range of differences reflecting issues of nationality, religion, locality, class, ethnicity, gender, age and many other social distinctions.

Amongst the seven schools considered in detail in this book, two of the London ones were ethnically very mixed. One of these, Deansgrove School, contained large numbers of refugee and newly immigrant children from many countries. One other London school, Westways, was relatively mono-cultural, with approximately 75 per cent of pupils from the Indian sub-continent, mainly from Hindu families, and 15 per cent Black pupils. The four main-study Hertfordshire schools contained pupils who were mainly, but not entirely, of indigenous white ethnicity. The pilot school in London was ethnically very mixed, and amongst the extension schools there were greater numbers of ethnically diverse pupil populations. There were three single-sex schools in the project: the pilot school, which was for girls, and the two EBD schools, which were for boys. All the schools contained a mix of children from different social classes.

Although I will mention gender and ethnic differences to a small extent as I go along, the project did not aim to investigate such issues, or those of social class, which would demand a different piece of research. There are, indeed, various research projects that could investigate differences between gender, ethnicity and class, as well as age, nationality, religion and many other social distinctions in relation to both formal and informal music learning, inside and outside educational institutions. However, my focus here is on some fundamental aspects of music learning practices that, based on our findings, we can reasonably suggest most young people of this age are likely to pass through if given certain tasks within a classroom context, and from which we may be able to learn interesting things about their needs and potential in relation to music education. For now, it seems fair to suggest that amongst the particular socially and culturally varied population of the London and Hertfordshire schools where the project took place from 2002 to 2006, there were indeed many practices which seemed to be held in common.

Listening, choosing and beginning to copy: an example from the first lesson

Below is a transcript of a group of five girls in an outer London school, Southover, taken during the very first lesson of the project. Like Luke's group cited at the end of Chapter 2, the recording was made without their knowledge, and there was no teacher in the room except for occasional monitoring. Again, the girls later gave permission for the recording to be used in the research. I want to consider it in relation to the learning practices and processes that were going on, specifically in relation to music-making. I have quoted it in full because it fairly represents the approach of the majority of groups, from which other shorter examples will be taken throughout the book; and it also raises a number of details that I will be examining in the current chapter:

> They had some trouble getting the CD player to work, then started listening to a Jennifer Lopez CD.
>
> –That one goes quite high. It goes quite high.
> –But 'Love Don't Cost A Thing' stays kind of at the same –
> 08:45 First play-through of song 'My Love Don't Cost A Thing'. Some singing along and talking at the same time:
> –What are we doing?
> –Nothing, just listening.
> Music plays.
> –And you can use that, er, for the beat bit, you can use the little, what's it called?
> –Yeah, you can use a glock, what's it called?
> Music plays. Some of them start singing along. 10:15
> –People could get instruments.
> –That wouldn't go well with the beat.
> –And the drums.
> –Yeah, we could use the drums, so …
> –And the keyboard.
> Inaudible talk.
> –How are we going to do this bit?
> Inaudible talk.
> –So right, are we using the agogos, right, for that bit?
> –Agogos.
> –But what are we going to use for this bit?
> Inaudible talk.
> –You can use the scraper.
> –The drum.
> –Is that the drum, that [inaudible] bit?
> –Yeah, the drum. And like a violin bit [inaudible].
> This sort of talk continues right through the song, while it's playing. 11:50 Some playing along begins, on the drums.
> –Is this the drum thing?
> Teacher walks in.
> –Hey Miss, can we use the drums to make it go along with this?
> Inaudible. Presumably teacher replies then leaves the room. Track stops. The next track starts.
> –Ooh, I like this song.
> –I love this song.

–So, just see, is there another one, or are we definitely doing that? Are we definitely doing that?

–I like this song.

> Various speech, largely inaudible. Track starts up again.

–Wait, put it back on the other song. Ow!

> Largely inaudible talk continues.

–You shouldn't – where's the words?

–It's there.

–Where? Oh right.

> 12:40 The song starts up again for the second time. There is playing along with the drums, plus talk, going on all the way through.

–No, we could do that thing (crash on cymbal).

–OK, we could do that in the chorus.

–Yeah.

> Music plays. Interesting to hear the drummer is playing the vocal rhythms at this very early stage. Up to 14:00.

–OK are we going to use the agogo here?

> Music plays.

–Shall I count to three?

> Music plays. 14:50.

–I've heard you singing before.

–I have.

–You have?

–Yeah, at [inaudible] party on Saturday night.

–Oh God, that was awful.

> 15:30 Music plays; playing along and talking (about the music) continue.

–Turn it up for a second.

> The drumming is getting completely out of time and random.

–Everyone, why don't we all, like sing it?

> Track stops.

–Shall we try again, maybe without the drum this time? (Laughter)

–(Drummer says) Sorry!

–Right shall we try again, without the drums this time?

> They search for the beginning of the track again.

–Altogether now.

> Song starts for third time. The singing along is much stronger than the first time through. There is continuing talk about what they're doing. Several voices can be heard singing along. 18:00 The drummer begins to join back in.

–Just go back on the drums.

> No talking now, just singing and some drumming along. Inaudible talk.

–What?

–Shut up!

–Think we're going to sing the whole thing to the class!

> Laughter. Song comes to an end.

–Shall I put it on repeat? ...

> The song starts for the fourth time.

–How does it go?

–Doesn't matter, just do what you want.

–Oh great (slightly sarcastically).

> Talk, drumming and singing along continue. At times it gets chaotic; at other times it comes together. No talk about extraneous things. Some hand percussion is

now joining the kit. Song ends. Listening to a different song to see if it would be
better but decide it wouldn't. 'My Love Don't Cost A Thing' starts up for the fifth
time. Playing along (drums) and singing along. 30:49.
–Turn it off. I'm getting into this now.
–Right, start again, Jacky it's your turn to sing.
–Can I have the words please?
–Don't you know the words to J-Lo?
–I know the chorus but not the other bits.
–Are you singing this?
  Inaudible talk.
–Pause.
  Music stops.
–Oh my God, you got a big, bonger thing there.
–That's supposed to be one of those big, you know –
–Bong the gongs.
  The CD starts again, with gong-like sounds.
  31:28 Clear recording of one girl singing along with others doing backing.
–I don't know where we are. Where is it?
  Music carries on with singing-along attempts.
–Sorry I done it wrong, I can't get these words right.
  (Southover School; Stage 1, lesson 2; Jacky, Amber, Gemma, Kayley and Grace's
  group; concealed field recording, no teacher/researcher present; LG's transcript)

Listening and choosing the song

Once in their friendship groups, pupils applied themselves enthusiastically to listening
to their CDs and choosing a song, as can be seen in the group above. For many
of them, especially in the initial moments, listening included moving their limbs,
jumping around, dancing or singing loudly. Most groups took about one lesson to
choose; a few came to the lesson with a song they had already selected, having heard
about the task beforehand; some were still choosing well into the second lesson. All
the groups chose songs that they could agree they liked, but as can also be seen in
the transcript above, they paid little heed to what might be musically more or less
approachable in terms of the song's demands on vocal, instrumental or aural skills.

  Choice of song threw up an interesting cultural difference that can be considered
here. As already mentioned, one school had a large majority of pupils from the Indian
sub-continent, who were mainly of Hindu ethnicity. It was situated in a suburb which,
during the 1990s, had been the source of Bhangra-beat, a highly popular fusion of
traditional Bengali music and Western pop music (see Bennett 2000, pp. 103f.).
The pupils listened to Bhangra at home and on their local radio, and in the past
some of them had taken lessons on the *dholak* and/or *dholki* drums which are used
extensively in Bhangra, as well as the Indian *tabla* drums, and in Indian singing.
However, only one out of the five groups, a group of girls whom the Head of Music
considered to be not particularly diligent or committed to music, chose a Bhangra
song to copy. They told me they had only chosen it because they had left their 'other'
CD behind; despite which, they did stick with Bhangra for the rest of Stage 1.

It is important to recognize that even when giving pupils apparently 'free choice' to select a song, there are of course many restrictions on what they are 'free' to choose. One problem is that there has to be group agreement, and therefore possibly some compromise from individuals. Another is that school pupils, especially under the age of 15 or 16, often feel under pressure to conform to mainstream definitions of mass culture. In particular, young people in ethnic minorities are prone to hide their 'true' musical tastes in certain situations such as the classroom (see, for example, Green 1999b and Bennett 2000).

It was interesting to notice that, by Stage 3 of the project, when pupils were given a second opportunity to choose a song to copy, their choices were more informed by musical considerations such as the suitability or approachability of the inter-sonic properties and relationships of the song, rather than subscribing so readily to the mass market. I will return to this theme later; but for now it is worth bearing in mind that 'freedom' is always a limited category, and that in this project its limitations were reflected in the fact that pupils' initial interpretation of their 'freedom of choice' was largely to restrict themselves to a selection from mainstream popular music.

Overall, the ways pupils approached the listening and choosing task involved trying out a variety of songs, sometimes listening to only the first few bars, and sometimes to a whole song. While listening, they began to discuss aspects of the music's sonic properties, especially textural features and instrumentation, in ways that teachers considered were more detailed and attentive compared to how pupils normally talk about music in class.

Singing

For about two thirds to half of the groups the next stage was to start singing along with the vocal line, sometimes using lyrics that they had taken from the Internet, their CD cover or a magazine, or that they had transcribed from the recording before the lesson. Otherwise, they either already knew the words, picked them up as they went along, or transcribed them during lesson time. Some groups organized two or three singers in unison; others had a lead singer with two or more backing singers in unison; others had only a solo lead, and there were various mixtures of these. In the pilot school, which had a very strong singing tradition, one group arranged a lead singer with backing singers in two-part harmony.

Most evidence concerning the role of gender in relation to singing within formal music education suggests that girls join choirs and show an interest in singing, much more readily and numerously than boys, who tend by contrast to actively avoid choirs and other vocal ensembles in many (but not all) schools. This situation also corresponds with the relatively high involvement of girls and women in singing above all other musical roles throughout the history of music.[2] However, there is some evidence that this situation does not necessarily apply to the singing of popular music, which is an area that boys are indeed willing to associate themselves with

---

2   As examples of literature referring to a range of musical styles, see: Bowers and Tick (1986), Dahl (1984), Gaar (1993), Green (1997) and Koskoff (1987). In relation to gender and singing in schools, see Koza (1994).

(see, for example, Green 1997). This was confirmed in the project. Some teachers expressed surprise and pleasure that some boys, particularly ones whom they had never seen participating well in music before, were willing to 'stand up and sing in front of the whole class':

> –Janet: I had boys singing who I would not have put money on ever singing in class – it was unbelievable – solos! Abdul stood there singing about whatever and not caring! And everyone else in the class just accepted it 'Yeah, it's a pop song, it's alright for him to sing, that's fine', but if it was me imposing that, it would never have happened.

> –Debbie: I was completely gob-smacked to see Scott singing in front of the whole class. I wouldn't have got that. I mean, I've got boys in my choir, but, you know, they're not that kind of Year 9 kid who will just not have a care and just sing. We were really thrilled with that actually.

However, many teachers were equally impressed with girls' willingness to sing: 'I was really thrilled with the girls as well just singing' (Janet).

It was notable that in the predominantly Asian school, Westways, there seemed a particular willingness to sing on the part of boys. One group of seven boys started off their practical work as six singers and one dholak player. Also, in response to the question 'What did you enjoy most, and what did you enjoy least, about the project?' during interviews, pupils in only 3 out of the total of 40 groups who were interviewed mentioned that they had enjoyed singing: all three were in Westways. Whether there is any ethno-cultural significance in that would form an interesting project requiring further research; I strongly suspect that there is.

Overall, approximately a third of the 40 groups did not go in for any singing at all, although it is difficult to estimate the proportion since all groups experimented with a variety of approaches at different times. Possibly the groups who did not sing at the start encountered difficulties sooner, as they were forced to move more quickly into matching pitches from the recording onto instruments in order to sustain a melody line – a task which is for most people harder than matching pitches in the voice, since it is one step further removed from the body. I will consider the strategies of these groups in a moment.

A note on the availability of instruments in the classrooms

Whilst most pupils were fairly accustomed to using hand percussion and keyboard instruments from their previous curricula, most of the schools in Hertfordshire bought additional instruments for use in the project. These mainly involved electric guitars, bass guitars, drum kits and synthesized drum pads. However, in the schools considered in detail here, the instruments did not arrive until the third or fourth lesson of Stage 1, due to delivery problems with the supplier. For most of the pupils in these schools, and some teachers, the project was the first time they had attempted to play these instruments. The grip and hand position for guitars and bass guitars were particularly challenging. Many of the schools had a drum kit in the classroom before the project started, but it had never been used by the pupils.

All the schools had computers in the music department, and one had a suite with enough ICT consoles for pupils to work in pairs. I decided not to use computers in the project, as this would have introduced logistical difficulties, as well as making findings difficult to compare across schools and across different groups of pupils. However, there would be nothing to stop a teacher undertaking informal learning in music using computers since, as I mentioned earlier, the learning involves a set of *practices* which are not tied to any one particular musical style or type of equipment. In the third year of the project, Richard's school integrated and alternated the project strategies with ICT.

An interesting issue is that no teachers elected to buy twin decks for scratching. This is probably because scratching is that much further removed from the popular music into which the teachers were themselves encultured than guitars and drum kits. However, so long as MC-ing and scratching continue to be popular using twin decks, or the newer technological substitutes for them, there is every likelihood that in time such instruments will become common in classrooms. In an extension school one boy brought in his twin decks from home. Overall, no doubt the readier availability of twin decks would have inspired a number of pupils.

However, the pupils in the project had to make do with whatever instruments were available in their schools. For the London schools, this did not involve any additional instruments over and above the normal range of tuned and untuned hand percussion, electronic keyboards, and in two cases a couple of electric guitars, bass guitars and a drum kit. For the four Hertfordshire schools studied in detail here, as stated, the additional rock instruments did not arrive until Stage 1 of the project was well under way. I will consider various issues concerning how the types and availability of different instruments affected pupils' responses in further parts of the book. As Cutietta (2004) well illustrates, the nature and role of instruments in relation to any style of music in schools is a crucial pedagogical as well as musicological issue. Unless teachers can provide the right instruments for the style of music their pupils are trying to play, they will be wrong-footed from the start, although compromises have always had to be made.

Playing untuned percussion

Simultaneously with, or very soon after, starting to sing, pupils began to experiment with untuned percussion. Those groups who did not go in for any singing went straight into this activity. In the schools where drum kits were available there was a lot of excitement. Shouts such as '*I* wanna do drums!' and 'Cool! Are we using *that*?' were to be heard. (I will examine how the availability of rock instruments increased motivation in Chapter 5.) However, even in the schools without such resources, teachers agreed that pupils seemed unusually highly motivated, and applied themselves to the task with more commitment than normal.

An interesting early finding arose from pupils' use of percussion at this point. Some pupils, when using a drum kit or other percussion at the very start of Stage 1, did not attempt to play a beat similar to the beat of their chosen song, but rather sought to replicate the rhythm of the song's main *melody* part (whether vocal or instrumental). We collected audio-recordings of this happening in five different groups, including Jacky's group cited above, and Luke's group cited at the end of the previous chapter, and we observed it happening in three other groups across the 40 studied in detail. Given that we only had one audio-recorder for each class in each school, and two observers taking field notes, eight groups seems to be quite a significant number to have caught adopting this practice, and it is reasonable to suppose that it is something which occurred in other groups when there was no recorder or no observer in the room.

There are no grounds to suppose that this tendency is a mere accident or an unconscious reflex. For example, we found three instances in which pupils quite deliberately practised their 'melody rhythms' on percussion, separately from the recording or from ensemble activities. Also, the idea of practising seemed to come about spontaneously and without any reflection, rather than being a hang-over from previous class music lessons. For, as will be seen in Chapter 5, the pupils portrayed the informal approach to learning as something very different to how they normally learn in class. Quite soon after such occurrences, our recordings and field notes contain examples of progression towards something more like a beat. This often involved an amount of conscious and unconscious peer-directed learning and group learning, the nature of which will be considered in Chapter 6. Also, in Chapter 4 I will suggest that part of the explanation for this progression was that, by their own accounts, pupils' listening skills improved as the task went on. To begin with, they approached listening in their 'normal' way, which meant they could hear only the lyrics and, in some cases, the main melody lines of songs. Gradually, as they worked on the music, they began to discern what they described as 'the underneath parts' or 'the background music'.

The tendency to play the rhythm of the melody line on the drum kit or other percussion instrument gradually gave way to a more 'correct' use of percussion by the end of the second or beginning of the third lesson. It then reappeared when a new song was approached in Stage 2 of the project, where we have only two recorded instances of it. From Stage 3 onwards, we have none.

This scenario might seem to cry out for a teacher to help pupils play more 'correct' drum patterns. Conventionally, a teacher will enter a room, see and hear a 'wrong' approach, and step in to correct it straight away. However, by sticking to the principles of the project in these early lessons, and standing back to observe rather than teach, the project team enabled some discovery learning and peer-directed learning to take place. As I have to some extent illustrated from teachers' views in Chapter 2, and as I will go on to show in relation to pupils' views in Chapter 5, there is evidence from both teachers' and pupils' accounts that the learning was somehow 'deeper'.

One further issue worth noting about pupils' approaches to percussion, concerns a cultural musical difference in Westways, the school with a high proportion of pupils with Indian sub-continental ethnicity. Even though, as already mentioned, all but one group in that school chose a Western mainstream pop song, the rhythms played by pupils in nearly all of the groups, especially but not exclusively the male ones, had many stylistic traits in common with Bhangra music. This is no surprise since, as already mentioned, the pupils were deeply encultured in Bhangra as well as mainstream pop music; and also they had dholaks and tabla in the school, which they used in their tasks. Again, it would be interesting to study the ways in which such enculturation and such regional, as well as other cultural and social differences impact upon different groups of pupils' approaches to the task, but it was not possible in the present study.

Finding pitches on instruments

Around the middle of the second lesson to the end of the third lesson, pupils started trying to match pitches from their chosen song onto a selection of instruments. Again, the Hertfordshire schools which provided electric guitars and bass guitars witnessed particular excitement at the prospect of using them, once they had arrived; but pupils in all schools were, so far as teachers agreed and so far as was observable, more than usually motivated from the start.

Matching pitches from a recording onto an instrument is more difficult for most people than matching pitches vocally. We only observed one or two pupils in each class who could do this without help, and in nearly all cases these were pupils who had taken or were taking additional specialist instrumental lessons. Dealing with pitches in general quickly became the area that called for the most teacher support and guidance. Unsurprisingly, it was also the point when pupils, on beginning to experience difficulties, started looking around for help. In some cases pupils became frustrated, and boredom threatened to overtake their initial motivation.

We have some field notes in which a bored, inactive pupil was apparently brought to life simply by being shown how to play a few pitches from their chosen song. Then everything changed, and the effect was sometimes quite surprising.

> There is no scientific way to monitor the light coming into someone's eyes. It seems that just locating a few notes that are in the song, and playing them on a keyboard can have a transformative effect. Today in Courthill School I went into a room of girls. Lauren was sitting on the floor looking completely bored and miserable. The others were listening to the CD; one was singing; one was playing a rhythm; two others were kind of half-engaged. I started looking for some of the song's notes on the keyboard and found a three-note riff, I think it was A-flat F E-flat F, and just played it along with the song. Lauren got up and craned her neck to see what I was doing. She looked into my face with an expression of amazement, as though the pitches I was playing were somehow magical. I taught the riff to a girl who was sitting at the keyboard, and asked her to teach it to someone else in the group. By the end of the lesson Lauren and another girl were playing the riff in octaves whilst two girls sang enthusiastically, and one played percussion. They did a performance to the rest of the class.
>
> *(Courthill School, Stage 1, lesson 3, LG's field notes)*

Whereas teacher input can of course have a positive effect in any lesson, there was a difference in the project which is hard to put into words. In a 'normal' lesson, simply showing a bored pupil how to play two or three pitches on an instrument would be unlikely to have quite the same effect. I will back up this claim further in Chapter 5, when I consider how pupils described 'normal' lessons in terms such as:

–Annie: In the other music lessons it's quite boring, you don't get a lot of work done. Most of the time you're just on the keyboards, playing notes that you've been told to play.

or:

–Chris: We would hear a song and it wouldn't matter, because at the end of the day you were playing 'A, B' wait five seconds 'A, B', and it's repetitive …

For now, I would suggest that if any claim to a difference elicited by the project strategies can be made here, it must derive from a combination of two reasons. One is that many pupils are so unattentive to the music they normally listen to at home, or indeed to any music, that not only are they unable to *hear* basic components of the music lying underneath the surface – again, a claim that I will back up later – but the idea that they could actually find and play the music's pitches and melodies themselves is quite novel to them. The other reason is that the pupils had chosen the music themselves, and therefore it was music that meant something to them, rather than being 'notes that you've been told to play'. This will also be examined in more depth later.

Another issue in connection with finding pitches on instruments was as follows. On one hand, many teachers felt at this point that the progress was slow. On the other hand, pupils themselves did not seem to mind if they could only play a tiny part of a song, and were prepared to repeat the activity for longer than many teachers would have wished. For Sandra, this was not a problem:

–Sandra: I've always found with Year 9s that they expect instant being-able-to-do-stuff in music, so if you were doing the blues with them, they expect to be able to do the blues straight away. And there's been none of that. And they don't seem to mind that it takes them a long time to learn something. This whole idea of 'I can't do it, it's too hard' and giving up, I haven't really seen that much. … They don't give up.

This again contrasts interestingly with pupils' attitudes to 'normal' lessons, in which 'you are just given notes' and have to play them in a way that was so often characterized as 'meaningless' and 'boring'. Why are three notes out of a song they have chosen for themselves not 'meaningless' and 'boring'? The answer has to do with issues of identity, cultural belonging and ownership. The three notes given to Lauren in the scenario above were completely nondescript and in themselves could appear in virtually any music from Monteverdi to contemporary pop. But the point was that they did not: rather, they were part of a song that meant something to her.

In seeking and matching pitches in order to demonstrate them to pupils, teachers were themselves often hard pressed to hear the recording against an extremely noisy and busy background. In addition, as I mentioned earlier, many of the teachers were not accustomed to playing the instruments that pupils had chosen. Rather than being the one who is in control and the one who knows, the requirement to listen to a song, perhaps one that was not previously known to the teacher, and find its pitches on an unfamiliar instrument while pupils watched, placed the teacher in a role which was much more similar to that of a learner. We considered that pupils benefited by observing how teachers went about finding and matching pitches, and it was one of the most fruitful ways in which teachers acted as musical models. Having observed this process, pupils gained an understanding of it and were more able to go about it on their own.

Progression: getting worse before you get better

I will consider the issue of progression specifically with relation to how well pupils were able to play in time with each other and with their chosen recording. At the very start of the project, pupil groups often exhibited a 'natural' sense of ensemble which seemed to be spontaneous. Some teachers noted that this appeared to be different to what happens in 'normal' lessons. For example, some performances in the first lesson were surprisingly confident and well in time, even if the pitches bore little relation to those in the song. However, many groups then seemed, in retrospect, to have been merely experiencing a kind of 'beginners' luck'. For, as I mentioned in Chapter 2, around the second or third lesson their music-making began to deteriorate badly, and they got 'worse' in various ways. These included singing out of tune, making only a sporadic input, playing the 'wrong' pitches, or playing out of time. With or without a CD in the background, some children were liable to play in the wrong part of the bar, so that although their beat was in time, their riff or melody would be displaced by one or two beats, causing them to be 'out' with everyone else. Some played in a way that seemed out of control, and could be almost, or exactly, twice the tempo required. At other times everyone in the group seemed to operate in their own time zone and play totally out of time with everyone else.

Such deterioration caused a lot of concern on the part of the teachers, as we saw in Chapter 2, and when it was occurring they found it particularly difficult to hold back. However, they managed to do so most of the time, and were quite soon surprised to find that pupils righted themselves without help, or with only minimal help. By the fourth or fifth lesson all groups produced a performance that was in most cases well in time, and the teachers indicated that the standards were better than usual, and better than expected.[3] (The same dip was noted also in Stage 2 of the project. In Stage 3 we reduced the number of lessons and it was not particularly noticeable, nor was it commented on in the remaining stages.)

It is interesting to consider why the pupils seemed to go through this cycle of success, deterioration, then improvement. Possibly in their first attempts motivation exceeded fear of error, and confidence allowed a rendition of something – anything – whose very conviction carried the players over what would otherwise be stumbling blocks. Group ensemble at that point was also novel, and participants would have been looking around to communicate with others, thus ensuring a certain amount of cohesion by default. Such a start may then have given way to anxiety and frustration

---

3   In the anonymous questionnaire, teachers rated the statement 'Overall achievement of musicianship and skill development of final Stage 1 performances': 5 of the 17 teachers ticked 'well above normal expectations', 6 ticked 'above average', 3 ticked 'average' and 2 'below average'. Of these, the two EBD schools ticked 'average' and 'below average' respectively. For the statement 'Ensemble skills (playing as a group, listening to each other's parts etc.)', 7 ticked 'well above normal expectations', 5 ticked 'above average', 3 'average' and 2 'below average'. The two EBD teachers both ticked 'average'.

as each player realized that their skill and knowledge levels were way below those needed for an accurate rendition of the song. At that point, lack of confidence would set in, leading to hesitation, which in the performance of music has disastrous consequences. Players would be likely to start concentrating on their own individual weaknesses, and thus group ensemble would suffer even further.

In an email communication, the composer and educationalist David Stoll suggested the following persuasive interpretation, focusing on 'the direction of listening':

> When playing along with something, at first you are 'passive': listening mainly to it (rather than yourself) and being part of its world. As you begin to learn it, you become more 'active' and attend to getting your bit right, which can be trickier. In fact, you probably are improving, but now that your contribution is from the outside, it can sound temporarily less well integrated. For example, you can leave difficult bits out at first because the original is carrying the impetus; later on, you need to include them and therefore might lose the beat.
>
> *(Dr David Stoll, email communication, 2006)*

It is also relevant, of course, to consider what might have happened if, instead of standing back, the teachers had stepped in to help. Would progress have been faster, better, longer-lasting? Such a question could be examined through a controlled experiment, and again it would be interesting to pursue it in further research. However, from the present research it is reasonable merely to suggest that if the teachers had not stood back and observed progress (or its lack), but had instead jumped in to correct mistakes or take control over ensemble playing, the tendency exhibited by the pupils to go through this apparent cycle of success, deterioration, then improvement would have been masked, as would their capacity to improve independently of teachers' help. In addition, as I will substantiate in subsequent chapters, not only performance skills, but also listening skills, motivation and group co-operation are all likely to have been affected.

Many pedagogic methods, curricula and theories of learning, especially those which have been officially sanctioned by government departments or other bodies, implicitly or explicitly assume that progression in learning occurs, or should occur, in a series of logical, incremental steps.[4] Tasks and curriculum content tend to be devised in ways that reflect this notion, usually by incorporating a gradual increase in perceived difficulty. Teachers and learners are regarded as failing if the latter are not seen to be progressing incrementally towards ever more difficult or complex operations. However, as Moore (2000) discusses, not in relation to music but to the curriculum in general, the intuitive sense and experience of teachers often suggest that progression does not necessarily occur in steps that gradually improve one upon the other. From a different perspective, Houssart's work in Maths (2002), and Voss and Wiley's in History (2000) are fascinating to compare with the project findings.

---

4   See Moore (2000) for a historical overview and a helpful discussion of a range of developmental and learning theories from Skinner through alternative perspectives, including those of Piaget, Vygotsky and Bruner. He also considers the relationships of different theories to contemporary perspectives and to teachers' everyday experiences.

Houssart found that too much over-structuring of the task in Maths lead to loss of motivation and a fall in pupil attainment. Voss and Wiley found that pupils' understanding of history was more sophisticated after they had grappled with a variety of conflicting perspectives, rather than being given a clearer, teacher-directed route through information.

I will return to the question of teachers' roles in fostering progression in Chapter 5, when I examine pupils' and teachers' expressed views of the project's teaching and learning strategies. For now, it seems reasonable to form two related hypotheses, based on the above observations of pupils' progress: firstly, that at least in music, 'getting worse before you get better' might be a natural or normal part of progression, and secondly, that leaping in to offer 'help', and thus attempting to stop learners from 'going backwards', could actually be detrimental to their learning.

As the project went on, teachers began to feel more secure that progression was in fact occurring, although it was harder to discern, and slower, than many of them would have liked.[5] In Stage 2 there was evidence that pupils were themselves aware of progression via the greater structure provided for them, along with the greater clarity of the task:

–Pritpal: Yes, we know how to build it up a stage at a time, not all at once ... because before we were like, like everyone do this at the same time, but let's do one stage until it's all finished.

–Andrew: We all started with big ideas. We should start with small and then build up.

–Emily: And everything that we done in Stage 1 that we like messed up, we can make it work for Stage 3.

–Connor: First of all I didn't [think Stage 2 was going to help]. I thought 'Oh it's another waste of time'; but then like when you get onto your third one then you start realizing what you've done it for.

(End-of-Stage 2 interviews)

During Stage 4, Head of Music Debbie asked Connor which stage was the pupils' favourite so far, and why:

–Connor: The last one, [Stage 3] 'cause like first of all [Stage 1] we started off blind really, we didn't know nothing, and then we went to the one you gave us [Stage 2] and we had all like information and stuff, and then the third one we knew what to do, 'cause we'd had the information in the second one.

The authority of the CD as distinct from the authority of the teacher

There was a general tendency for all the groups to play along with their CD at first, then those who gained enough autonomy seemed to drop it, often apparently without noticing that they had done so, and without making any conscious decision to do

---

5   In the anonymous questionnaire, the teachers rated the statement 'Overall, for the project as a whole, pupils' progress has been better than usual.' The results were: 8 'strongly agree', 5 'agree', 4 'neutral'.

so. A pupil at Grange School came up with an interesting view of what it means to play in time, when Abigail asked his group if they would like to try playing their song without the CD in the background: 'Yeah,' said Ian, 'Just to see what it sounds like. That way we don't have to do it in time'! Later we will see that many pupils reported responding well to learning from a CD rather than from a teacher. As one pupil, Lakmini, put it: '... you can't do nothing wrong, because it's just the way you wanted to do it'.

The question of the teacher's role within the project is particularly interesting when one considers that, in the position usually occupied by a human teacher, here we have a CD as the ultimate authority and model of what the pupils are trying to achieve. Ironically, although the CD is a much more inflexible, and in that sense tyrannical, teacher than any human being, pupils seemed to find it less threatening to work with, and in many ways, as we shall see later, it seemed to produce more fluent, 'musical' results.

One major difference between learning with a teacher and learning with a CD concerns speed. In some musical styles and cultures such as Gamelan, teachers do not slow down the music in order to make it easier for learners to pick up. The learners simply have to watch, listen and do their best to imitate the teacher at full speed. Likewise, when music is learnt mainly through enculturation, such as in African drumming, children acquire their skills simply by joining in with adult music-making, which carries on without any compromises.[6] Similarly, in popular music's informal learning practices, playing along with a recording is always up to speed. Such approaches to music learning have perhaps, each in their different ways, held on to an understanding which we in Western formal education may have lost. Learning this way is more like sketching the broad contours of a picture holistically than painstakingly tracing the details one at a time. From our observations in the project, learners will firstly stab at a note or two as the music flies past in time, then on repeated attempts they will try to fill in what goes between to the best of their ability while the music unrelentingly goes onwards. In many cases this approach lead to results which may have been less accurate in detail than more conventional Western classroom methods would have elicited, but which had more 'feel', and which were able to contribute to an ensemble straight away, even in the hands of players who had no previous experience of such activities.

An example from a field note taken during Stage 2 of the project can illustrate this:

> I go into the drum room at the end of the corridor. A boy in there is trying to get the riff GGG D B-flat on a keyboard. He has got the pitches from the sheet, but he's playing a completely different rhythm to what's on the recording. I show him the rhythm and ask him to imitate mine; he watches and listens, then tries but still can't get it. I suggest he plays along with me; again he tries, but stops every time he makes a mistake, then has difficulty picking it up again, so the whole thing grinds to a halt, then we try again and the same thing happens. I put the CD on and suggest he plays along with that. This has a different effect. As before, he stops after the first three notes because he has made a

---

6   See, for example, Dunbar-Hall (2000) on teaching and learning in Balinese Gamelan, or T. Wiggins (1996) on teaching and learning in Ghanaian drumming.

mistake, but this time he then waits, listening, and picks up the riff again when it comes round. Again he makes the mistake, stops and picks up. Next time he plays the whole riff, but not in exact time. After a few bars like this he gets it in time. When he was playing along live with me he didn't seem able to pick up and carry on like this but kept stopping. Maybe it is to do with the unrelentingness of the CD, its total reliability, i.e. he knows it will just keep on going, whereas another person is likely to stop, tell him he's getting it wrong, act unpredictably. Also a CD is non-judgemental.

(Heath School, Stage 2, lesson 1, LG's field notes)

The apparent fluidity of learning by aurally copying a recording became more pronounced during Stages 6 and 7, when pupils were learning to play more extended classical melodies, and I will mention it again in Chapter 7.

'Flow' and 'play'

We have recordings of pupils singing and playing together for periods of time which are very long for the classroom, especially for the kind of classroom work that involves directing their own rehearsal in small groups. Whilst a normal expectation might be that pupils would produce something lasting a few bars, in the project many groups would persist in singing and playing together for the length of an entire song, including extended versions. The longest uninterrupted playing that was caught on a recording was during Stage 2. It lasted over seven minutes, at which point there was a short stop, then the group started again. The group in question will become known to the reader later on, as Bobby's group at Southover School, who were assessed by both the teachers and myself as having problems accessing the task, and were known in the school as 'disaffected'.

A factor that particularly interests me in this is that unlike an ensemble of classical musicians, the groups did not stop to correct problems, but would carry on playing, either oblivious to or regardless of the fact that one or more group members might be totally out of time or playing the wrong pitches. Sometimes, if they were out of time they would phase into time more by serendipity than anything else, then phase back out again; but they never showed any concern about this, and whether in or out of time, they would not stop because of it. Only one pupil, Hana, reflected on this tendency, when she said in an interview: 'Yeah, and if you do it wrong, you sort of like, just carry on.' Carrying on over mistakes is often urged by classical teachers, especially when their pupils are sight-reading or playing in a group. But it is very difficult to do if stumbling over notes that are being read.

The tendency to keep going and avoid stopping, even to correct faults, suggests that pupils were having some kind of enjoyable experience, which made interruption to their music-making unattractive or unnecessary. Whilst I will consider the issue of enjoyment in Chapter 5 more generally, here I wish to isolate it specifically in relation to the experience of making music. Csikszentmihalyi's well-known concept of 'flow' (1990, 1996) is helpful in offering a theorization of the pupils' apparent sense of enjoyment. He developed the concept to identify an optimal state of psychological engagement, or a 'phenomenology of enjoyment' (1990, p. 46), which was reported by a range of over 90 people, who described what happens to them mentally when they are experiencing their highest levels of enjoyment. He conceived of flow as a result of both an activity and of the individual's attitudinal state. On one hand, some activities, especially games and the arts, are more likely to induce flow than most, and are actually designed to do so. On the other hand, some people have 'autotelic personalities', that is, they tend to orient themselves to whatever they are doing as ends in themselves, and thus to get flow experiences more often or more fully. Clearly, education could, in this analysis, put flow experiences in the way of pupils, so that even those who do not have autotelic personalities would stand more chance of experiencing flow than otherwise. Csikszentmihalyi, however, along with many other colleagues, laments the fact that schools too often fall short of doing so.

He does not investigate the grounds for making enjoyment a part of educational aims, or for suggesting that enjoyment is a good thing. Schoolchildren may well enjoy doing all sorts of things, such as taking drugs, having sex, eating fatty foods and watching horror films, few of which are likely to be regarded as educationally worthwhile by the government, their teachers or parents. However, he is careful to distinguish the notion of enjoyment from that of mere pleasure. For him, pleasure involves various bodily and mental gratifications which occur without much effort, and which add no 'complexity to the self' (1990, p. 46). By contrast:

> Enjoyment is characterised by this forward movement: by a sense of novelty, of accomplishment. ... None of these [enjoyable] experiences may be particularly pleasurable at the time they are taking place, but afterward we think back on them and say, 'That really was fun' and wish they would happen again. After an enjoyable event we know that we have changed, that our self has grown: in some respect, we have become more complex as a result of it. (Csikszentmihalyi 1990, p. 46)

This argument still does not establish any grounds for making enjoyment an educational aim. But, for the present, it gives sufficient grounds to further the discussion under way. This is because, if it can be accepted that we become more complex as a result of something, and assuming that the complexity involved is a healthy one, as is implied by Csikszentmihalyi's position, then that should at least be *compatible* with the aims of education. I will consider the question of how far enjoyment should be an educational *aim* in Chapter 5, where I will also illustrate how pupils responded to a question about whether they enjoyed, or did not enjoy, the informal learning approach. For the present, I wish to point out that all the elements which Csikszentmihalyi establishes as characteristics of enjoyment seem to be decipherable in the pupils' approaches to music-making.

He isolated the main elements which were mentioned over and over again by his subjects when they described 'how it feels' when an experience is enjoyable (1990, pp. 48f., 1996, pp. 111f.). These included having clear goals, immediate feedback, a balance between challenges and skills so that we feel 'our abilities are well matched to the opportunities for action', and a high level of concentration on a task, without distractions getting in the way. The pupils' goal was clear: simply to copy the music. The feedback arose immediately out of the match between the player's intention and the CD. Whereas it could be supposed that there was a huge imbalance between the challenge and the skill of the players, that is only so if the goal is to make a perfect rendition of the song. However, during times of uninterrupted flow, the pupils tended to base their goals, not on what seems to have been demanded by the CD, but on what they felt able to achieve. As already argued, they did not see the authority of the CD as being tyrannical, and when they failed to match up to the CD they did not regard themselves as failing. Another way to think about this is to say that the task was 'differentiated by outcome'. I will return to the topic of differentiation in Chapter 6.

More important for the present discussion are three further factors identified in flow. One is the disappearance of self-consciousness. In everyday life, Csikszentmihalyi suggests:

> ... we are always monitoring how we appear to other people; we are on the alert to defend ourselves from potential slights ... Typically this awareness of self is a burden. In flow we are too involved in what we are doing to care about protecting the ego. Yet after an episode of flow is over, we generally emerge from it with a stronger self-concept; we know that we have succeeded in meeting a difficult challenge. We might even feel that we have stepped out of the boundaries of the ego and have become part, at least temporarily, of a larger entity ... Paradoxically, the self expands through acts of self-forgetfulness. (Csikszentmihalyi 1996, pp. 112–13)

In the following three chapters I will present arguments and evidence which would support the notion that such an expansion of self occurred from time to time as a result of the project activities for many pupils. The backing for this statement relates to issues concerning identity, enjoyment and autonomy that will be examined in due course.

Csikszentmihalyi also suggests that in flow, the sense of clock time becomes distorted:

> Generally in flow we forget time, and hours may pass by in what seem like a few minutes ... clock time no longer marks equal lengths of experienced time; our sense of how much time passes depends on what we are doing. (1996, p. 113)

Again, such forgetfulness of clock time seems to be suggested by the pupils' tendencies to keep going for long periods while they were playing. It was also alluded to by several pupils in interviews, especially pupils at Grange School, who repeatedly requested that their 50-minute lesson time should be extended, and Abigail (Research Officer) noted a group at Grange who carried on working through break, apparently without noticing or caring that the bell had gone. This tendency to forget clock time was also alluded to by teachers, as when Janet said:

> –Janet: I think they loved it, they really, what I found was that it, coming to the end of the lesson, and we all, we didn't *know* it was the end of the lesson – we were all involved in the work, and then the bell would go and some of them would moan, 'Oh I don't want to go' ...

In connection with the concept of 'flow', it is also worth considering music-making as a form of play. This is particularly relevant to the notion of pupils finding the CD a less threatening authority than the teacher, and their corresponding apparent lack of concern with 'getting it right'. The educational psychologist J.S.

Bruner suggested that 'engagement in play involves reduction of the consequences of error or failure' (1979, p. 57). Although it is a serious activity for the child, play is 'without frustrating consequences' (Bruner 1983, p. 91), and does not involve an excessive attachment to accurate or correct results. In play, children will often:

> ... change their goals *en route* to suit new means, or change the means to suit new goals. Nor is it that they do so only because they have run into blocks, but out of the sheer jubilation of good spirits. It provides not only medium for exploration, but also for invention. (Bruner 1983, p. 91)

Keith Swanwick argues that the most crucial aspect of play lies in the imagination, and connects this with the processes of learning, from the initial 'transformation of pure sensory delight in sounds into an urge for mastery; an emphasis on the exploration and control of the materials of music' (Swanwick 1988, p. 71). He puts forward an understanding of musical development, and the arts in general, in which the concept of play is intertwined throughout the learning process (1988, pp. 50–51). Similar emphasis is placed upon the connection between the arts and, implicitly, the notion of play as 'the absence of rule' by Elliott Eisner when he states:

> ... the arts teach students to act and to judge in the absence of rule, to rely on feel, to pay attention to nuance, to act and appraise the consequences of one's choices and to revise and then to make other choices. (Eisner 2004b, p. 5)

Tendencies towards treating music-making as play, defined in the terms suggested above, can be discerned in our observations of pupils within the project. This is the case, both in relation to play as involving an absence of concern about the consequences of one's actions and in relation to the role of the imagination in play. As we will see later, these tendencies can also be found in the ways pupils talked about the project strategies.

Again, because a learning activity can be turned into a playful activity does not automatically qualify it for a place in an educational enterprise. In addition, critics might suggest that 13- to 14-year-old teenagers are not children of the age that Bruner or Swanwick had in mind, and in any case, should not be encouraged to play when they are supposed to be learning in class. However, what I am suggesting is that a playful approach to music-making is indeed a part of and a desirable precursor to musical learning. Within the project, such an approach can be argued to have unleashed some aspects of pupils' musicality which may have been missed out of their experiences when they were young children, or which may not have had sufficient nourishment. These aspects may be necessary for musical growth to take place, yet may be obscured by too many demands, too soon, for observable progression towards specified outcomes.

'Feel' and 'musicking'

In the first induction meeting for the main-study Hertfordshire teachers, on listening to audio-recordings of the London pupils playing their musical products, two teachers were at first wary and nervous of the possibility of 'dropping standards'. However, at the same time they noted that the elusive quality of 'feel' was discernible in the recordings, to an extent over and above what would normally be expected of groups of pupils at this age and level. 'Feel' is something that is both hard to define and, as the teachers agreed, hard to teach. It is connected partly with the ability to keep going in a perpetual 'flow', playing or singing each note at a precise point on or around a beat according to the style of the music, manipulating textural and dynamic qualities of the sound in fine ways, and many other aspects. In the case of a novice player it is rare, not only because the novice has insufficient control over the instrument or voice, but also because 'feel' requires confidence and, amongst other things, the ability to pick up and carry on regardless of stumbling. As I suggested above, and will argue from a different angle below, 'feel' is particularly difficult to induce if notation is the only or the main medium through which music is transmitted.

In listening to the pupils' musical products, it was agreed by all the teachers that pupils seemed to display less hesitation and fewer blocks than normal. This not only accords with the earlier concept of play as involving less concern with 'correctness', but it also corresponded with the notion that the performances had better 'feel'. In general, many pupils went straight to the sound they were aiming for, without the normal amount of hesitation. One way to understand this tendency is through John Shepherd's (Shepherd et al. 1977) and Trevor Wishart's (1997) concepts of musical 'immediacy'. Shepherd suggested that in pre-literate societies humanity had a more aural bent towards the world, and an 'immediate', rather than a 'mediated' relationship with music. The introduction of writing, of which musical notation is one variant, interrupted this immediacy, inducing a more alienated, 'mediated' or distanced relationship with the world, and more of an emphasis on the visual rather than the aural. This interpretation is helpful in providing an understanding of why aural learning and aural copying in music could lead to less hesitation; which can in turn be connected with the concepts of 'flow', 'play' and 'feel'.

The project teachers did not use these expressions, but many of them invoked the concept of 'being musical' or similar notions. 'Being musical' brings to mind Christopher Small's (1998) concept of 'musicking' and David Elliott's (1995) one of 'musicing'. These notions accord with a central theme in the current book, in that they place music-making at the heart of the musical experience, and also involve a passionate argument for music-making to be at the centre of music education. As against the notion of music as an object to be contemplated, music is understood primarily as an *activity*.[7] From the ways teachers spoke about pupils' practices within the project, we could say the pupils were seen to be 'musicking', or behaving less like novices and more like 'proper musicians', as Sandra put it. The implication was that this occurred in ways that teachers did not usually witness:

---

7   Also see Goehr (1992) on this, and a number of debates within ethnomusicology and the 'new musicology', such as Talbot (2000).

–Kenneth: The thing is, in every single group, they are all behaving as *musicians*.

–Barbara: I wouldn't like to measure national curriculum levels at the moment, but I think pupils were being very musical.

–Yasmin: Because it's an exciting way for the children to work. It starts to make music come to life … and not just 'Oh yes, we've got to learn this tune, let's learn it.' They're doing something really musical.

–Sandra: I think their performance today was great, they took a huge risk, they turned off the CD and they just played along, which I'm not sure how many times they've done that, but I think that was quite a risk to take in front of the whole class. But they managed to play in time, they managed to play so that it actually sounded like the song, the song was recognizable from it, and they gelled as a group, and just to watch them sharing, looking at each other, and sharing, you know, the kind of cues that you get as a proper musician, is fantastic, and I think for once was successful.

Some examples where the notion of 'musicking' came to mind during observations are as follows:

This is Marissa's group doing the Kevin Lyttle song. … They are much more confident [than last week]. Also the voices are better organized, with backing and lead. … The percussion players are moving freely to the beat, the singers are slightly swaying. I would say this group in particular is really 'musicking'!
(Westways School, Stage 1, lesson 4; Marissa, Sabrina, Lakmini, Rashi and Xena's group; LG's field notes and transcript of recording)

Deepak's group, who have not yet been recorded. I had thought they were off task in previous lessons; however they really got things together today. There were three vocalists, and who-sang-what had been well-organized; one boy playing the hi-hat with his foot, and a Chinese block with his hands (which you can't hear); and another boy playing an audible cow-bell. At certain places the percussion drops out, and this was signalled by one of the vocalists, who momentarily took a leadership role, gesturing frantically at them to stop and then start again. All the boys were looking around at each other to ensure they came in and went out at the correct time. They did the whole song. They knew all the words, which they had written down. The singing is out of tune. Again, I don't think it matters – getting it in tune would come at a later stage. The first thing is to get them 'musicking'.
(Westways School, Stage 1, lesson 4; Deepak, Jaspinder, Declan, Indulal and Sanjay's group; LG's field notes and transcription of recording)

Track 1 goes back on and the playing continues. This is also quite a good recording actually. You can hear that the steel pans and the keyboard are changing to the same riffs as each other *at the same time*! This has happened without any discussion between the players concerned! These boys have not stopped playing yet.
(Southover School; Bobby, Drew, Liam, Austin and Danny's group; Stage 2, lesson 2; LG's field notes and transcription of recording)

Not only were the pupils often seen to be behaving 'as musicians', but some teachers extended that to their own activities as well:

–Barbara: Something that this approach seems to do is to make you teach as musicians, rather than as teachers. You use your musical skills to demonstrate, rather than say, 'This is the theory, this is what you have to do.'

–Debbie :… somewhere along the line I feel we're being a little bit more musical than we would probably be being before.

–Richard: I've learnt something about them [pupils], I've you know, I've learnt something about teaching music, you know. It's basically it's been quite enjoyable. By doing this, teaching music *musically* if you know what I mean. You know rather than a set of instructions they must follow.

From some of the pupils' point of view, there were indications that they, too, felt more like 'proper musicians' and 'band members' than previously:

–Connor: Well, you're becoming a musician I suppose…

–Justin: It's the start of a rock band isn't it!

–Ian: I think I might have progressed a bit on the piano, learnt how to play the guitar, and just working in a band.

Possibly such a perspective was *verbalized* more by boys than by girls; further research on this issue would be interesting. However, field notes indicate just as much *observable* gelling as a band amongst girls as amongst boys.

A note on musical composition, improvisation and creativity

Pupils did not only copy music aurally within the project, but as already explained, during Stages 4 and 5 they composed their own music. Whilst, as indicated above, I do believe that music-making should lie at the heart of music education, it is important to remember that music-making includes both listening to music and creating new music, as well as playing or singing existing music. A certain amount of creativity, including improvisation and arrangement, was involved in all stages of the project. However, creativity had a central place during those stages that focused on composition. Whereas the following chapter is devoted to the area of music listening, restrictions of length and time make it impossible for me to delve into the many fascinating issues and challenges that arose in connection with creativity in this book. I hope to publish a separate article on that theme in due course.[8]

What counts as learning in music-making? Pupils' and teachers' views of the learning outcomes

When we interviewed pupils at the end of Stage 1, the biggest category in their estimations of what they had learnt was 'how to play instruments'. Pupils in 23 of

---

8   For work on creativity, especially in relation to composition in the music classroom, see for example, Byrne et al. (2003), Faultley (2004), Jorgensen (1997), MacDonald and Miell (2000), Paynter and Aston (1970), Webster (1992), J. Wiggins (2006) and many more.

the 40 groups mentioned this without any prompt, in response to the question: 'What, if anything, have you learnt from the project so far?'[9] What interests me most is that, with the possible exception of one or two newly immigrant pupils in inner London, all of them had played instruments in their previous music classes. Yet somehow they did not seem to have counted that as learning how to play instruments. By contrast, they seemed to regard the informal approach, with all its haphazardness, lack of guidance, and challenges, as somehow enabling them to acquire basic instrumental skills more effectively. Listening to them talk about this, one could be forgiven for not realizing that they had been playing instruments in their classrooms since they were five years old:

–Balpreet: I learned piano a little bit. … I knowed about – I just know now the keys of the piano. Because before I wasn't learnt how to play piano and I didn't even know where C and D is or anything. And now just when Sir helped us to, where's C and where's D, I'm a bit better; C, and where's C where's D.

–Mahamed: I think, I did, I knew the order of the piano's, A, B, C, D, E, F, G, but I didn't know how to place them. I didn't know where they would be. You know the blank part, mix them up, and everything will be different. So I think I learnt that as well.

–Cameron: I learned how to use a guitar *properly*. Like, for instance, I learned how to play the tune.

It is worth considering what is meant when pupils or teachers talk about 'being able' to 'play an instrument'. Olivia had learning difficulties. She found it hard at first even to play three repeated, slow-moving, step-wise notes with one hand on a keyboard, in time with the rest of her group or with a CD. During Stage 2 she progressed enough to play such a melody in both hands a sixth apart, including asymmetrically placed black notes. When asked what she had enjoyed or not enjoyed about the project at the end of Stage 2, she said:

–Olivia: I enjoyed when I was playing on the piano.
–Lucy: You enjoyed that?
–Olivia: Yes.
–Lucy: You played on the piano with two hands, didn't you?
–Olivia: Yes.
–Lucy: You were playing in harmony.
–Olivia: Was I?
–Lucy: You were, yes. What did you enjoy about that?
–Olivia: I don't know. Because I never used to play piano and now I can.
–Makayla: She learned a new skill.

---

9   The anonymous questionnaire given to pupils in both main-study and extension schools at the end of Stage 1, asked the same open question as that in the interviews; 358 evaluation sheets were filled in, four as group responses and the rest as individual responses, by pupils in nine of the schools. The highest number of responses all referring to one area concerned learning how to play instruments, which was volunteered by 28 per cent of the pupils; 13 per cent indicated that they had learnt a musical skill, without specifying what.

This 'new skill' clearly counted as something worthwhile to Olivia, and was also recognized by her colleague Makayla.

Although many people might be tempted to scoff at the idea that Olivia could 'play an instrument', to my mind the kind of positive self-image that she was developing as a person who *can* play, rather than one who can't, is a necessary component of motivation and self-confidence in learning to do so. Even advanced young musicians often hesitate to refer to themselves as 'musicians', as illustrated in studies by Lamont (2002), O'Neill (2002) and Pitts (2005). They show that many school pupils, university music students, amateur singers and instrumentalists, both within and outside education, tend to shy away from referring to themselves as that lofty ideal, a 'musician'. As Pitts says, many 'aspire to "musicianly" status, rather than feeling securely located within it' (2005, p. 14). I believe that as a society we are too reticent about identifying people, including children and amateurs, as 'musicians'.

Another aspect of our findings concerning learning outcomes was a corollary of this point. For a number of pupils reported that the aural learning experience, whilst making them feel more confident about playing an instrument, also increased their understanding of the difficulties involved, and along with that, their respect for musicians:

–Michelle: Yeah, and like I think the drums are a lot harder to play than it looks. You're just 'Oh you just hit the thing.' But you've kind of like, got to co-ordinate your foot with your hand, and it is a lot harder.

As time went on, some pupils learnt to play more than one instrument, often because they used a different one for each stage of the project, and it became evident that many of them valued being able to try different instruments:

–Ian: What's good about it is that you can learn different instruments as well, like I, the first time round I did piano, now I'm doing guitar, and I'll probably go onto drums and then bass. Have a go at everything.
(End-of- Stage 2 interview)

By contrast, in music education we seem to want pupils to specialize, a view which was implicit in one teacher's words below:

One pupil actually had swapped from drum kit to guitar, and I was a bit disappointed, because he had spent time up to this point really battling on and learning drumming styles, so it was disappointing to see him switch to guitar ...

In the UK the government has recently mounted campaigns to widen opportunities and increase entitlement (see, for example, DfES 2006) which give primary school children the opportunity to try a range of instruments. I am sure many teachers would agree that we should lay more emphasis on the old conception of music as a craft or trade, in which a musician acquires basic skills on a range of different instruments from an early age, rather than introducing specialization too early.

In the next chapter we will see that listening was the primary learning outcome throughout the project, as identified by teachers. There was also agreement that instrumental skills, singing skills and ensemble skills were above normal expectations, or at the very least were, in most cases, not below them.[10] Overall, by the end of Stage 1 the teachers' views of the approach had already undergone a fairly radical shift, and from that point they became increasingly positive during interviews and discussions. Whilst some doubts continued to be expressed that certain music-making skills were being left out, this was seen to be counterbalanced by the advantages:

–Yasmin: Yeah, and also they're learning skills on instruments that they haven't had before... There are still pupils in those groups that are picking up guitars and bass guitars – girls picking up bass guitars! – that are really enjoying learning and constantly asking for chords to be shown them.
(End-of-Stage 1 interview)

–Janet: I think it was really successful. What the kids were doing was really good, I mean they've never played together like that before, they've never performed properly, you know in such a big group, and it meant they had to listen to each other, listen to each others' parts, and they had to learn, memorize something and they had to choose themselves, then, what they wanted to do; and I think it made them aware, and they had to really think about it, not just go in and 'Oh I'll do that, I'll do that.' They had to really think about what they were playing and if they could play it or not.
(End-of-Stage 1 interview)

–Sandra: But then they did, you know, they did put together performances in a short space of time, which is a good achievement, and they all performed them, which is fantastic. And they all performed them with fantastic musical skills, with timing, with group work, and ensemble skills, and with listening skills, so, yeah, I can't argue with that really! ... They don't realize that they're actually playing really well in time together without a backing track to keep them, and they're actually developing really essential skills like that – ensemble skills, definitely, and also group work skills of listening to each other and having to put something together has really improved, dramatically.
(End-of-Stage 1 interview)

–Richard: What I have felt is ensemble playing, in terms of musical, of playing music within the group, that has developed. Even if the recording today wasn't particularly successful, I think there have been previous weeks where the ensemble playing has been good, keeping the same time with each other, maintaining that steady beat, and we had a very definite beat, a tempo which they could work to. I think they've, they did that much better than they did at Stage 1.
(End-of-Stage 2 interview)

This chapter has considered how pupils approached informal learning practices in relation to music-making, as inclusive of but distinct from music listening. Amongst other things, I have suggested that it is possible to discern certain learning practices which seem to come 'naturally' to many pupils without adult intervention. I noted how pupils started the aural copying task by focusing on rhythm, then moving on

---

10 In the anonymous questionnaire, 6 of the 15 teachers in mainstream schools ticked that instrumental performing skills were 'well above normal expectations', with 5 ticking 'above average' and 2 ticking 'average'. The 2 EBD teachers ticked 'average' and 'below average' respectively; 4 of the 15 ticked that singing skills were 'well above normal expectations', with 8 ticking 'above average', and 2 'average'. The two EBD schools both ticked 'below average'. Also see note 3.

to pitch, and gradually developed ensemble skills. They often underwent a dip in their observable levels of achievement, before righting themselves and progressing on. They seemed fairly unconcerned with any pedagogical notion of being 'correct' or 'getting it right', apparently preferring to engage quite haphazardly in what they were doing, with no particular sense of progression. Whether or not they were 'getting it right', they were liable to play together for relatively long periods of time, during which they seemed to be experiencing 'flow', along with a playful approach to music-making and music learning, high levels of enjoyment, and 'feel'. Pupils considered that they were learning to play instruments in ways that they cast as new; and teachers agreed that a number of basic instrumental and group performance skills were present, and in many cases enhanced.

Chapter 4

Listening and appreciation

Few subjects in the school curriculum, and indeed few activities in our lives, accord primary importance to listening as a skill. Probably of all curriculum subjects, the study of foreign languages is most similar to music education in its attention to listening skills. But even in language studies, as in music education, the components of the curriculum which involve some reading or writing have normally been accorded the highest status, and carry a great deal of weight in assessment practices. Music is an invisible entity, and its invisibility gives us difficulties when we try to apply names to its component parts. This is particularly so in the absence of any form of writing or notation through which we can externalize music and make it visible. Not only is music itself invisible, but its invisibility makes music listening skills particularly elusive. Music education has developed a sophisticated set of criteria and practices for assessing performance. Many of these are, in general terms, internationally, though not universally, recognized by musicians and music educators across all levels and many styles (Green 2000 has a fuller discussion of this). However, the assessment of music *listening* is generally much less developed. It has tended to rely on requiring learners to produce some kind of account of what is going on inside their heads while they listen. Such accounts can range from general descriptions of the music, to naming specific properties or relationships within it, to taking down music by dictation. All in all, it is hard both to enhance and to assess music listening through education, other than as an offshoot of other activities.

Yet music-makers and music listeners are immersed in a world of sound, without which there would be no musical experience at all.[1] Thus, despite the apparently lower status and importance accorded to listening within education, musicians and music educators value listening as an end in itself, implicitly regarding it as probably the most major musical skill that a person can have. Many aspects relating to music listening have already been alluded to in this book, because in considering school pupils as music-makers in the previous chapter, we have also unavoidably come across them in a variety of ways, as listeners. In the present chapter, however, I wish to isolate the topic of listening, in order to consider in more detail how the project affected pupils' music listening experiences in and beyond the classroom.

It will be helpful to distinguish between two main kinds of listening. One concerns how pupils approached listening to their CD when they were attempting to copy it instrumentally and/or vocally in groups, within the classroom context. This

---

1   In making such statements I am always conscious of the fact that many people with profound deafness can respond to music, and a few of them have risen to positions of international acclaim as composers or performers. None the less, it is sound that they respond to and manipulate, perceived in ways that are different to how hearing people perceive sound.

is what, in Chapter 1 and elsewhere, I have referred to as 'purposive' listening. I will also consider how 'distracted' listening featured during their listening-and-copying activities within class. The other kind of listening concerns how pupils listened to music when they had no intention to copy it, but were responding to it in receptive, rather than productive mode. This type of listening occurs both in and beyond the classroom when pupils listen to music on the radio, TV, personal stereo and so on. I will firstly consider what we gleaned from our observations of pupils working in their small groups, then I will focus on how pupils and teachers described the development of listening skills and experiences in interviews. Again, I will mainly discuss Stage 1 of the project, and its effects on listening beyond the school, mentioning how listening developed in some subsequent stages more briefly.

Before embarking on that discussion, however, it will be helpful to step back for a moment, and consider how pupils communicate to us and each other about the nature of their listening experiences, and particularly how they use language to describe music.

Pupils' musical vocabulary

As anyone who works in a school music department knows, and as must already be apparent from quotations of pupils talking in this book, their use of vocabulary to describe music ranges from general teenage slang to personal idiosyncrasy, and is usually very different from curriculum vocabulary. In particular, teenagers in the UK quite systematically use the words 'beats', 'beat' or 'rhythm' to cover all sorts of concepts, including 'accompaniment', 'backing' or even 'pitch' or 'harmony'; they often refer to a rhythm as a 'tune', as in 'the drum tune'; and they use the word 'song' to refer to both songs and instrumental music. At an individual level, some pupils in the project came up with idiosyncratic expressions such as 'We learned about how to put like different instruments into different beats of the music' or 'I learned how to put the keyboard inside the song.'

Formal music education normally demands that pupils learn the meanings of a range of technical terms. However, retention of such words is often poor, as indicated on occasions by some teachers in the project. For example, Debbie had introduced the term 'riff' and was making a teaching point to the class at the end of a Stage 2 lesson, hoping to forge a link with previous work on ostinati that the pupils had done as part of the National Curriculum in the preceding academic year:

–Debbie: What's another word for a riff? [She looks around the class for someone to put up their hand. No response.] It's a pattern that repeats. What other word do we use for a pattern that repeats over and over again in music? [Long silence. Everyone starts to look awkward. Debbie looks round at me and Abigail, and expresses disbelief.]
–Debbie: A word beginning with 'O' – a repeated pattern of notes.
–Pupil: Ostinato.
–Debbie: Ostinato! [To me and Abigail:] Oh my goodness me, that is a real worry.

Often, as with learners in the informal realm outside the school, pupils do not use words at all to communicate about music. Instead, they express themselves by singing or playing what they mean. This can be seen in many transcripts, such as the quote at the beginning of the book, with exchanges such as:

–Ross: I'll go (plays guitar riff).
–Michael: You don't need to play that, so when I go (starts to play) if you be silent (guitar plays) and then you go silent for (bass plays).
–Ross: I know! So I'll just go (guitar plays).

Possibly some of the reasons for pupils' difficulty with musical vocabulary relate to the invisibility of music, as already mentioned. Music is a thing existing independently of the knower or perceiver, not a 'mere' idea (as I argue more fully in Green 1988, pp. 121–36). But in most realms of our lives we tend to connect the names of things with visible items. The use of notation in formal music education has been one way around this problem, as notation gives a visual focus that affords a multitude of possibilities for naming components and their relationships. However, learners may be able to acquire technical knowledge through notation which they are then unable to use effectively when actually making, or listening to, music.

During the project, pupils did not acquire much technical vocabulary, but it was felt that their understanding of music had increased in other ways. For example, as time went by Debbie became less worried about the fact that her pupils did not produce the 'keywords' she was looking for. This does not mean she would have supported failing to teach them such knowledge altogether, but rather that she could see some benefits of a complementary way of coming to know about music, without using such technical vocabulary:

–Debbie: … with asking them questions, we're trying to get a word from them, and you'll go in every different direction to get that keyword, and I was finding I wasn't really doing that at all – and they were still learning.

A similar notion was suggested from a pupil's perspective by Luke, who was one of the few London pupils who had taken instrumental lessons, through which he had acquired a smattering of vocabulary. Below, he is discussing this issue with his peer, Cameron:

–Cameron: I'm not really sure [what I learned] actually, because, like, now that I think back on it, like it was, like I feel I've learnt loads, but I just can't really remember …
–Luke: Maybe it's just me, but I don't think that we learnt much. I don't exactly think that we learnt as much as we might have done, but I do think that we did get a lot of experience, sort of … I suppose in a way we have learnt a bit, but we just haven't learnt in the way that you can say, 'Oh, I know what, I know what pitch is, I know what tempo is'; we haven't really learnt that but … It will probably make our understanding of songs better, though we're not actually aware of it. … In something like this you haven't really learned anything because you don't get someone saying, 'This is what this word means, this is what this means', as in other lessons.

Luke's concept of learning here seems to be overtly restricted to fact-gathering, or nominalism; yet at the same time he and Cameron seem to be reaching for a way to express what it like is to learn something that cannot easily be named.

Pupils also 'picked up' vocabulary in the way very young children do, by simply using it. As one teacher said:

–Katerin: I think you get it in comments. If you say 'Oh that's a really good riff', and they learn what a riff is just by conversation.

Ideally, the acquisition of technical terms through informal learning would develop over years within the school environment. On one hand it would replicate the ways that young popular musicians outside schools gradually pick up conventional terms and technical knowledge through use and experience. On the other hand it would also develop through integration and cross-fertilization with more formal approaches, a topic which I touch upon in the brief final chapter of this book.

An interesting aspect of pupils' responses to the musicians' workshops in Stage 5 should be mentioned here. Some of the adult community musicians who came into the schools to provide workshops used a range of technical vocabulary in their demonstrations, including in just one session that I observed, the words 'middle eight', 'bridge', 'verse', 'chorus', 'D minor', 'C major', 'riff' and 'hook'. Surprise, and some dismay, were expressed by a number of the teachers that at the end of such sessions, pupils did not put up their hands to ask questions, but instead offered a rather pregnant silence. One reason is undoubtedly that, as already illustrated, pupils' knowledge and understanding of technical vocabulary was limited. Thus terms such as those above could have an inhibiting and possibly quite terrifying effect. But not only that, linked to this is an issue concerning pupils' willingness, as distinct from their ability, to talk about their experiences. A Head of Music in one of the extension schools reported that, in response to a question he put to the class after a peer demonstration, 'What did you think of the workshop?', there was no response at all until one boy put up his hand and explained, 'Sir, it's *music*!' Teachers were even more bemused by such apparent unresponsiveness, given the sense of excitement which they all registered during the sessions, and following on from them when the visiting or peer musicians began working with the small groups. Also, when asked if they had enjoyed and benefited from the sessions afterwards, in interviews and anonymous questionnaires, the response of pupils was overwhelmingly positive, including expressions such as 'that was amazing', 'superb', 'really good fun' and so on.

I find this conundrum interesting, because it suggests that through some amount of informal learning, the pupils had access to a sonic realm of music that was meaningful to them, yet free from linguistic concepts. By saying 'Sir, it's *music*!', I would suggest that the boy was not being dismissive, but rather questioning the need to talk about something that is essentially non-verbal. In formal music education, despite the oral-aural approaches and deep musical understanding espoused by educators from Curwen, Orff, Kodály or Suzuki to Paynter, Swanwick, Reimer, Elliott and many others at the present time, our syllabi and assessment mechanisms have long placed a high emphasis on the development of linguistic concepts, theory and notation. Perhaps our exam systems, and some of our teaching practices along with them, have over-leapt a necessary stage which should come *prior* to the acquisition of such knowledge, a stage when learners are simply allowed to immerse themselves in sonic musical materials and their relationships, without having to comment on them or prove themselves.[2]

Pupils' aural approaches to the task: purposive listening

Field notes and transcripts from the small-group observations contain evidence that several pupils had a great interest in small details which could be heard on their chosen recordings. As I mentioned in Chapter 3, pupils were often prepared to play just a few notes of a song, and to 'sit on them' for longer than their teachers sometimes wished. Now it is relevant to add that those few notes were not in all cases the most obvious or most audible ones. Yet often pupils seemed to have a fervent desire to play those particular notes rather than any others.

This issue of pupils' attention to detail is linked to another issue, which concerns the value that pupils placed on fine aspects of sound quality or textural properties of the music demanding intense, concentrated listening. Sound quality in relation to tone or texture has always been a central concern for music education. In instrumental or vocal tuition a great deal of time is spent trying to get learners to produce a 'correct' or conventional tone quality through minute manipulations of breath, touch and many other aspects. Sound quality is also one of those aspects of music that is extremely hard, or impossible, to codify in conventional staff notation. Thus young musicians who are brought up through notation none the less need to listen to a range of music, played on the instruments that they are learning, in order to be able to transform notation into sound qualities that are accepted and recognized within the social practices surrounding the relevant style of the music. Many approaches to instrumental and vocal training have tended to somewhat overlook that necessity, or have taken it for granted, relying mainly on the teacher to transmit such knowledge through relatively brief demonstration as well as verbal explanation. Thus young musicians can grow up without expert ears for the kinds of sounds they should be aiming to produce.[3] By contrast, those who acquire their musical skills and knowledge

---

2   This argument also brings to mind the well-known musical development spiral of Swanwick and Tillman (1986; also see Swanwick 1988, 1994), which suggests that in the early stages of musical encounter and/or musical development, learners are primarily immersed in the immediate sonic qualities of musical materials. As time goes by they develop an ability to organize sounds, or to perceive sonic organization at a fairly foreground level; and later still, they begin to control or perceive more abstract, background formal properties of music. This research suggests that the 'materials' stage of learning is not merely important, but necessary. If we move away from it too soon, or assume that older learners such as teenagers – and adults – can bypass it, we may be doing them a disservice. Also see McPherson and Gabrielsson (2002) for a discussion of evidence that too much notation can lead to decreased sensitivity to patterns in music and a restriction in overall musicianship.

3   This is one reason why the Suzuki method of teaching was such a revolution in the classical music education world: because he placed prime importance on sound quality through listening in the very first stages, only approaching notation much later. In this sense the Suzuki method has a major feature in common with informal learning; however, in other senses it is very different since it is highly formalized, teacher-led and structured.

primarily through aural copying start attending to fine aspects of sound quality right from the beginning of the learning process.

This tendency was evident during the first or second lesson of Stage 1 in the project. For example:

> Melanie was listening so intently she was asking me to hear first a very quiet piano part that she really wanted to play. I showed her the notes. Then she asked me to listen to an even quieter piccolo-like synthesized part which was so high that to begin with I found it very difficult to hear at all. She was listening to miniscule details. She asked me what instrument she could use to replicate that sound, and the best thing we came up with was a recorder, so she went off to get one.
>
> *(Southover School, Stage 1, lesson 1, LG's field notes)*

Another significant issue here is that, as with Melanie above, many pupils were particularly careful and attentive in choosing instruments whose sonic properties could match as nearly as possible the sounds on the CD they were copying. Most interestingly, the desire to match the sound often overrode any potential misgivings about the type of instrument which pupils were willing to use. Thus an instrument would be selected for its sound qualities, even if it carried cultural connotations that might in other circumstances have lead to its rejection. If for example, a group's CD contained a high bell-like or tingling sound made by a synthesizer, the group members might firstly spend time trying to match it on their electric keyboard. If they could not find a satisfactory match, they would go off and find a triangle, glockenspiel or some other instrument with suitable sonic capacities. Indeed, we have records of pupils in several groups going off to look for a glockenspiel (which they often refer to as a xylophone), and in different groups, a triangle, a scraper, a tambourine, agogos, a shaker, a cowbell, a recorder, 'a big bonger' and 'those little beaters'. Even in the schools that had electric guitars, basses and drum kits, if a suitable sound could not be made on the same instrument as that in the recording, as one girl said to another: 'We can add the xylophone to pretend it's something else.' A few orchestral instruments were also selected, notably by pupils who had never played them before, including a clarinet, a trumpet and a violin. (By contrast, all those pupils who took lessons on orchestral instruments outside the classroom avoided bringing their instruments in until the classical stages of the project, an issue that I will take up in Chapter 7.)

Not only are the kinds of instruments mentioned above rarely or never used in the pupils' chosen music itself, but most of them, as we will see through interview data later on, were *described* with derision. Pupils associated them with the 'normal' curriculum, with 'boring', 'terrible' lessons, and with younger children, rather than with the 'cool' music they had chosen to copy. As one pupil, Chris, portrayed the xylophone: 'It's the worst thing ever, I'm serious.' However, no pupil referred to any apparent contradiction between their collective voluntary *use of* and their expressed *attitudes towards* those instruments when they were interviewed, or showed any awareness of a disjunction there. Pupils seemed, in other words, more concerned about the quality of the musical materials, that is the sonic properties of the music, than about any social or cultural connotations of the instruments.

The further development of pupils' listening capacities

On one hand, the suggestion that pupils attended carefully to sound quality, texture and small details of the music flies in the face of critics of mass culture, many of whom would suggest that teenage popular music listeners are somehow impoverished in their listening capacities. But on the other hand, as I will go on to show, there was evidence to suggest that many pupils' ordinary listening stance was indeed, very passive, inattentive or undiscerning. If they had remained as passive listeners only, rather than engaging in informal music learning practices as music-makers involving *purposive* listening, then their listening would have been less incisive, and their attention to quality and detail more restricted. For many of them revealed, rather implicitly than explicitly, that when they started out on the listening and copying task they could hear little more than either the lyrics or the main vocal melody of the song. Many of them even expressed surprise to discover that 'there is more to it' than that! This suggests, indeed, that their listening was somewhat restricted, not only in the classroom, but since they had chosen their 'own' music to work on, in their lives outside school too. One graphic example of this restriction was given by Makayla at Deansgrove School:

–Makayla: When I listen to music at home, I don't learn, I don't really actually sit there and think about how the tune is going. I listen to the words. That's my point of music. I put music on, all I care about is the words. I don't care how he's singing it or how she's singing it. I just want nice words. Also, I like R'n'B songs, because it's loud. I like some loud songs. Very loud songs. And also I watch TV to get some dance off it. And I definitely don't watch it, I definitely don't hear it, to learn how to play it.
(End-of-Stage 1 interview)

We have several examples of how pupils' listening seemed to deepen as the task went on (including Makayla's, which will be illustrated in due course). In order to frame the following examples, it is helpful firstly to observe that pupils could be seen to engage in both 'distracted' and 'purposive' listening at school, as introduced briefly in Chapter 1 (and see Green 2002a). These concepts concern two aspects of aural copying which can be identified as opposite extremes along a pole, going from the virtually unconscious to the highly systematic identification of components of music, and their incorporation into musicians' own practice. Firstly, distracted listening goes on effortlessly, feeding into learning practices either unconsciously through enculturation or at occasional moments of spontaneous, dawning awareness. It was discernible in a few observations of pupils in groups who, whilst not apparently attending to anything in particular, would suddenly shout out something such as: 'There's a piano! Did you hear that?' (Fariba). Secondly, we also have field recordings of pupils apparently concentrating in a focused way on purposive listening, by consciously struggling to hear parts: 'I can't hear it. I can't hear the guitar properly. ... It would be so much easier if I could just listen to the guitar' (Simon).

In interviews, many pupils reflected on the difficulties of purposive listening, without using that term of course, through comments such as:

–Tanya: It was sometimes hard to hear the different notes, 'cause you could easily hear the tune, but it was hard to hear the second part.

–Valji: Trying to actually listen to the tunes in the background [was difficult], because sometimes you could only hear like one, and it was hard to hear the others.
–Sayeed: Yeah, the others get drowned out by the normal music.

There were also various ways in which pupils reflected on how their listening processes developed, enabling them to hear more of the 'background' music, and to identify different instruments or parts, as the task went on. They seemed to particularly struggle in finding words to express this:

–Indulal: We've learned how to like listen to the music carefully.
–Declan: Listen to the background and all the music.

–Amy: I learnt to like listen to the beats of music, and listen to what, what is actually happening in the background of the music.

–Rhona: Yeah, 'cause it's like they had more depth in the music.
–Nicola: There's more like –
–Rhona: 'Cause normally you just hear the top bit.
–Nicola: Yeah like we hear this instrument …
–Rhona: … Especially when you, you know like listening to CDs when people are singing and stuff, 'cause you normally listen to the words, but then when you have to, to do it, you hear the underneath bits as well.

As well as attending to accompanimental features and identifying parts, some pupils' listening also began to focus on form and structure. This included identifying simple background structures such as verse and chorus, (which were often marked in the group performances by percussive up-beats):

–Kimberley: Yeah, like we've learnt about the different stages in a song, like.

There was also some evidence of more foreground structural listening through counting beats or bars. For example, in an excerpt in Chapter 2 Luke's group counted through a section of their song, finding that the music was organized in groups of either 16 or 32 bars to a chorus. They had no previous knowledge that this was a standard way for popular songs to be organized, or that the apparent difference in the number of bars identified merely arose from how fast they were counting. Other examples of how pupils found their own ways into structural listening include:

–Teacher: What were you listening out for when you were copying the drumming?
–Pupil: The seconds, to know which second you were on – there were 16 seconds and then you had to come in.

–Ian: Right, I've got to learn where I stop playing the piano. Right, where do I stop? I start here, wait, wait, wait.

In Stage 2, some of the separate riffs were arranged so that if played together they would form three-part parallel harmony. Thus as pupils worked on their music-making they gradually came to discover how chords are built up, from an experiential rather than a theoretical point of view. This would then, in turn, enable them to hear how harmonies change:

–Oh look, look, look, look, look, look, look!
–Look, D and B-flat!
     Demonstrates.
–Then B-flat and G, yeah?
–Where's C and E?
–Oh yeah!
     They continue playing the two tracks, now in 3-part harmony, out
     of time.
–I know, it's easy to play it together.
–Yeah, but what two are we playing together?
–Or, or, we two can play together.
–Look, I can play it together.
–Simran, Simran, listen, we two can play it together, like quadruple!
–Yeah!
–Yeah!
–Play it!
        (Westways School, Stage 2, lesson 1; Andrea, Rashi, Simran and Masooma's
        group; field recording, no teacher/researcher present, LG's transcript)

A number of pupils also identified purposive listening as an explicit learning outcome of the task. The quotes below were in response to the question, 'What, if anything, do you feel you've learned from doing the project so far?':

–Tomash: The rhythm.
–Will: Beats. [Pause.] Of the music.
–Lucy: Beats. How to listen to them or how to play them, or both?
–Will: Listen. And play.

–Kayley: Yeah, I think I have [learnt] with the drums. Because I picked up the kind of beat
    of it. And I wouldn't have been able to do that before, because I don't really do that, I
    just listen to the song. But because we had to try and um –
–Jacky: Break it down –
–Kayley: Yeah, break it down. And I thought I learnt that.

–Olivia: I learned how to put the keyboard inside the song; how to put the music – I tried
    to figure out if it really suited the song or not, and then, I also think it's hard as well to
    do the project. [Inaudible] In future I'd sit down, listen to the tape, or CD player, play
    and try to figure it out, and especially when the song is very fast.

Listening beyond the project

As explained earlier, I was interested not only in how the pupils' distracted or purposive listening skills were affected *during* the lesson, but also whether their listening experiences were affected when they were listening to music outside school. We asked each group the question: 'Since you've been doing the project, have you noticed any differences in the ways you listen to music, say if you're listening to music or watching music-TV at home?'

It is only possible to identify about 20 out of the approximately 200 pupils who clearly stated that the task had not affected their listening.[4] Of these, most just shrugged, looked bemused, or simply said 'no' without any further elaboration. Some of them were ones like Melanie, who was discussed at the beginning of this chapter, and who had revealed through observation that her approach to listening was already highly attentive to detail. It may be that pupils such as her were already listening carefully to music before the project started; or that they simply did not notice any enhancement in their listening which might have taken place during the project. One or two others who said in response to that particular question that their listening had not changed, none the less made statements during other points in the interview which suggested that in fact it had. There were a few more substantial negative responses, revealing clues about the limited ways in which many pupils normally approached listening. I cited one such response, by Makayla, earlier. Another example is this exchange:

> –Ameera: I don't really listen to the music in the background really, I just like listening to the song, and I don't really pay attention to the instruments playing, I don't think about that really.
> –Kaylee: You just listen to the person singing don't you? And then you sing along sometimes if you know the words.

Some pupils said their listening had improved whilst they were working on their chosen song in the classroom, but that they had not noticed any changes outside of school. For example:

> –Liam: Yeah. When you're listening at home you're just listening, you're not listening properly, but when we were in here, we was listening to it properly.
> –Lucy: Oh yeah? In what sense were you listening to it properly?
> –Liam: More carefully.
> –Ian: Yeah, I tend to, when I'm at home I just listen to other things, but when I was here I was actually listening to like individual parts.

---

4   Out of the 40 groups interviewed there were 3 groups who were not asked or who gave evasive answers such as 'I like music'; 5 groups in which all members said no; 11 in which some pupils said yes and some said no; 16 in which everyone said yes, and 5 in which everyone or some pupils said yes, but only when they are listening in the classroom. All these categories will be considered and illustrated in more detail during this chapter. We also asked the same question in the anonymous questionnaire at the end of Stage 1; 358 pupil evaluation sheets were filled in, four as group responses and the rest as individual responses, by pupils in nine of the schools; 44 per cent of the pupils indicated that their listening had changed. However there were subsequent uncertainties as to whether they had understood what was meant by the question. The interview data of pupils in the other schools, allowing exploration of their views, is more reliable. Seifried (2006) also found that school students reported improvements in their listening skills and appreciation during a guitar programme with a strong popular music and informal component.

–Abigail: Why do you think that was?
–Ian: Probably because we were trying to learn how to play it.

More significantly, a number of pupils indicated that not only had their listening skills been enhanced within the classroom, but this had spilled over into their leisure time. As the responses are quite individuated, and I think interesting in themselves, I have supplied excerpts from a number of them, although it must be said that this is none the less only a small sample of the available data. The comments were made in response to the same question as before, that is: 'Since you've been doing the project, have you noticed any differences in the ways you listen to music, say if you're listening to music or watching music-TV at home?'.

Many pupils indicated that they were now able to hear what was going on 'in the background', whereas previously they listened mainly to lyrics:

–Mantsebo: Like, usually in a song you listen to the words and the rhythms, but after this you started to learn the beats and the basic instruments they're using …

–Kimberley: Yeah, 'cause I used to just hear the beat and the lyrics, but now I can hear more stuff that actually sounds really good in the song. 'Cause it used to be like just a block of music.

–Isabelle: I've learned to listen to music, like actually learning –
–Vicky: We never really like listened to the proper beat did we?
–Isabelle: No.
–Vicky: We just like –
–Isabelle: In the music we just listen to the words [normally].
–Ava: The melody.

–Alyssa: At the moment I've actually been listening to the background, to the drums.
–All: Yeah, yeah!
–Harry: Yeah, like the song, you realize there's actually more to it.
–Stacey: Yeah the bass line thing.
–Sofia: You realize there's more to it than just the words, and you listen to the different instruments in it.
–Annika: There's more to it than just someone singing…

–Kayley: I listen to more of the beat of the music than the lyrics. … I think we're, like before we were really concentrating on the, like, rhythm and the beat of that song, and now, to me, like, in songs, the rhythm and that stands out more than, I don't really take any notice of the words.

Other pupils simply indicated that they heard more of the accompaniment, without mentioning any previous focus on singing and lyrics. Particular attention was paid to instrumentation:

–Sara: Yeah, it's like when you hear it, you can like, identify what instruments like –
–Jordan: It's like, 'Oh, that's a drum, that's a drum.'
–Danielle: 'Oh no, there's a little piano going "Eee".'
–Jordan: 'Sounds good with that, or that', yeah.

–Danielle: Yeah.
–Sara: You listen to the beat a bit more.

–Trishanker: A bit yeah, and you start noticing what instruments they're playing, and you can notice they're playing the guitar, and they're playing – if you're listening to a radio or CD you can tell what they're playing more than before.

–Aaron: Yeah, when I listen to music I like, I listen to like the different keyboards, like all the notes and stuff, like the pattern, and like the drums and stuff. I listen to them more.

–Jason: I can hear like the background music a bit better.
–Michael: Mmm.
–Abigail: Right OK. What do you mean by the background?
–Jason: Like they have like instruments playing in the background.
–Michael: You can't really hear –
–Jason: That you don't normally hear.
–Michael: Barely.
–Jason: You can hear them better now.

A small number of pupils indicated that they had been listening particularly carefully through headphones, including in some cases, manipulating the balance of sound:

–Tomash: I put my bass thing up, up, now. Because I used to have it down, because I didn't like the bass, but I do now.

–Gabrielle: I listen to, I think, in particular because I have this special thing on my Walkman so I can listen to things [inaudible]. I usually put it on that so I don't hear the vocals so much, but this thing in particular, I play it quite a few times, and I listen to electric guitar, then I listen to drums, and then if I want to I listen to vocals.

Some pupils reflected particularly perceptively on how they held lines aurally in their 'mind's ear':

–Madeline: Yeah, the other day I was listening to my CD Walkman, and before I didn't really notice the background instruments, but as I was listening to it the other day I actually brought it into my head and I can tell what instrument it is …
–Maria: I found that when the music starts with the instrument, that's much better, 'cause then you can hear the instrument and you won't lose it.

–Kayley: I find that when I listen to music the first thing I hear is the drum, if there's a drum in it, and then I go down and I think like, 'Oh have I played that instrument before?' and then, 'Oh yeah we done that in the project we done' or whatever.

Music appreciation

The concept of 'music appreciation' first made a prominent mark on educational circles during the early twentieth century. It developed in the USA after the work of W.S.B. Matthews, and through the efforts of the Victor Phonograph Company, amongst others, and was spearheaded in the UK by Stewart MacPherson, the BBC and others.[5] The movement had echoes in many countries, and its presence within music education can be felt to this day. Its main aim was to improve the musical understanding, taste and enjoyment of children, as well as the public at large, through an educated exposure to good music. This involved guided listening to the music of the 'great' classical composers through a range of classroom activities, educational materials and radio programmes. The implicit or explicit assumption of the movement, whether coming from the left or the right of the political and ideological spectrum, was that the education of the masses, for their own sakes, involved the need to fend off mass culture, and with it, popular music and jazz.

The history of music education and the inexorable rise of the music industry since then have, of course, singularly conspired against that ideal. Sitting and listening to music, it seems, with or without structured guidance, is not on its own enough to change the listening habits and tastes of most children and young people; and this is particularly the case when the music they are requested to appreciate is already far removed from their lives.

There seems to me a happy irony in the relationship of the music appreciation movement to the project that is under discussion in this book. For the project brought into the classroom a set of informal learning practices that were drawn, precisely, from the world of popular music and mass culture; yet, by requiring pupils to listen to their 'own' music with the express purpose of playing it themselves, it seems to have enhanced the ability of many of them to listen analytically to musical detail, sound quality, texture, accompaniment, instrumental parts and structure. All these aspects of music are exactly what the appreciation movement had in mind, except that the music was intended to be classical.

Not only that, but according to pupils' own accounts this listening enhancement was often accompanied by a rise in their general musical appreciation, and indeed some of them autonomously used that very term. Their descriptions of how their appreciation developed ranged over three main areas. One concerned appreciating the technique of the performers, including how difficult it is to play their instruments:

–Michelle: I think that now I understand more how it's, like, harder for the groups that play it like. Before we'd be 'Oh wow, they're so good', but now we're like 'That must have taken ages to sort it out and get it', like.

–Craig: I think you can hear more of the instruments that are playing, and appreciate how hard it is.

Another area concerned gaining some insight into the processes of composition, including group composition:

–Janine: I've learnt how hard it was to actually get a music piece together, now I actually appreciate like what other people are doing.

---

5   See Martin (1995, pp. 230ff.), Rainbow with Cox (1989/2006, pp. 276ff.), Scholes (1972, p. 48) and Simpson (1976).

—Joshua: Rather than just a noise while you're doing your homework on the radio or something …

—Janine: They've had to write it as well as learn to do it all. Instead of just learning to do it –

—Abigail: So you appreciate how difficult –

—Janine: Yeah, I do appreciate it more.

—Sean: And now we can, like, we know a lot more about how you, you like make songs and everything. And how they did it. … Yeah I just didn't, like realize how, how –

—Anthony: Difficult.

—Sean: How they can do it and everything, and how –

—Ava: It shows you how to hear a piece of music and listen for all the riffs, the notes, and to try and, it shows you how music is made, so you can start making your own.

The third area related to the quality of the inter-sonic relationships and the structure of the music itself:

—Kimberley: I learnt more about music and what's in a song, like I learnt about all the different things in a song not just like the lyrics.

—Tomash: Yeah, because you see how hard it is, to actually, you don't appreciate the music [previously].

—Steve: Yeah, there's, like more to a song than just lyrics and the singer. Like, you get to understand that a song isn't just lyrics, 'cause if you take away the music then there's not really a song there anymore so –

The progression of listening and appreciation through Stages 1–5

At the end of Stage 2 of the project we asked the same question as at the end of Stage 1, about whether pupils' listening experiences had changed outside of school; 13 of the approximately 20 pupils who had *clearly* reported no change at the end of Stage 1 now said that it had changed.[6] Their comments were rich, but similar to those above. I will provide only one example, as it indicates perhaps the most radical change. I cited Makayla's denial earlier, thus:

---

6   In the anonymous questionnaires at the end of Stage 2, 45 per cent of the pupils gave an affirmative answer to the question. There is no way of knowing what overlap this included with those pupils who had answered affirmatively at the end of Stage 1. The question was specifically whether their listening had changed as a result of Stage 2. Therefore, those who had answered affirmatively at the end of Stage 1, but for whom no further improvement had taken place during Stage 2, should logically have answered negatively. We do not know whether they did in fact do so. However, it is reasonable to suggest, based on the interview data as discussed in the main text, that some pupils who had answered negatively at the end of Stage 1 did answer affirmatively at the end of Stage 2, but unlikely that this applies to all 45 per cent of them.

–Makayla: When I listen to music at home, I don't learn, I don't really actually sit there and think about how the tune is going. I listen to the words. That's my point of music. I put music on, all I care is the words. I don't care how he's singing it or how she's singing it. I just want nice words. Also, I like R&B songs, because it's loud. I like some loud songs. Very loud songs. And also I watch TV to get some dance off it. And I definitely don't watch it, I definitely don't hear it, to learn how to play it.

(End-of-Stage 1 interview)

At the end of Stage 2, in response to the same question she said:

–Makayla: I have. As I listen, as I listen to the instruments what's playing in the background. Before I used to watch the musicians, see how they dance. That's all really. [Laughs]. Now as I listen to it, the instruments, how they're playing in the background, I try to figure out –
–Chantelle: What instrument they use.
–Makayla: Yes. Like what instruments they use really, and see if it's nice kind of. I listen to the instruments and the songs more instead of just watching the dance.

(End-of-Stage 2 interview)

Overall, our qualitative data strongly suggested that there continued to be an increase in pupils' self-assessments of their listening skills as the project went on. After the composition work in Stages 4 and 5, we posed the same interview question about listening to 12 groups in three schools, comprising 50 pupils. All but one of the pupils gave affirmative replies, indicating an increase in both listening and, as I will now go on to discuss, appreciation.

As with specific listening skills, there was evidence that pupils' appreciation also continued to develop during Stage 2 of the project, and if anything, to increase. This was probably owing to two main factors. The first is that the Stage 2 funk track which pupils were listening to and copying had been broken down into its constituent parts, revealing its inner workings one riff at a time. Therefore, it was easier for them to hear the parts. For example:

–Michelle: Yeah, and it's like, with the second stage, I think more for me it's the second stage [that has improved my listening], 'cause when you had the sheet you had all the different riffs, so you saw how much, how many different like set like pieces of music there were to make one whole song sort of thing really. ... Yeah, showed you how much work went into it really.

(End-of-Stage 2 interview)

A second possible reason why appreciation continued to develop further during Stage 2 concerns the longevity of the task. Indeed, if such tasks were built into the curriculum over a longer period than the few lessons involved here, it seems reasonable to suggest that further improvements would occur, mirroring the ways that popular musicians' aural skills continue to improve, according to their own testimony as well as other evidence, in the world outside the school (for example, Green 2002a). By the end of Stage 2 pupils were expressing themselves, if anything, more confidently and forcefully on the topic of appreciation:

–Susan: [I've learnt] how to analyse music.
–Lucy: Right. Anything else?
–Melanie: How to listen closely to it.

–Andrew: And now I understand how hard it is to [make] a piece of music.

–Pritpal: We're more sensitive to the music and what it means to the author.

–Simran: Before you thought it was like, somebody that thinks of some words they're singing and that lot, but now I realize there's a lot of like, work and thinking about the tune and the background and how to put the music together.

–Rob: It's a bit like inspiration, 'cause you can see and learn how to do it.

–Daisy: 'Cause like there's loads of different parts to it, and before we were just like thought there was just like one big thing.

(End-of-Stage 2 interviews)

At the end of Stage 2 we asked some of the groups how they would feel about the prospect of repeating Stage 1 again. (Those in the London schools were answering hypothetically; those in the Hertfordshire schools knew they were going to repeat Stage 1 a few weeks later, after the Christmas break.) All the responses indicated that they would plan, or were planning, to think more carefully about what song to choose. Most of their answers focused on choosing something that would be easier to play or to hear, either because it was slower or simpler in some way. These considerations contrasted starkly with the approach they had taken to choosing songs in Stage 1, which had been oblivious to anything other than whether they *liked* the music or not. For example:

–Aidan: … we can work on our mistakes that we made before. Make sure that it doesn't happen again.
–Lucy: So what sort of mistakes would you be working on?
–Aidan: Like, listening to the music. Listen to the music, pick easier music, pick easier notes, so we can play fast and finish early.
–Elias: You would learn the notes easier.

–Jacob: I think yeah, because we've chosen an easier song …
–Lucy: OK, so tell me first of all in what way is it an easier song?
–Jacob: 'Cause –
–Rob: It's more calmer.
–Daniel: Steady. It's not like, we ain't like gone in for something which is like really hard.
–Rob: It's not loads of tunes it's just basically –
–Jacob: One tune going –
–Rob: Doesn't change, one tune that just goes all the way through, and it repeats itself quite often.
–Jacob: It just sounds, it just sounds so easy to play.

–Michael: Er, the song, I think we should choose a different one, because the first one, it wasn't really the right song for playing guitar on.
–Stephen: We just kind of got it 'cause we liked the song, we didn't really think about it.

–Ian: You'll learn, you'll learn your lesson. And you'll get more appreciation if you can actually play the song than trying to go, jump yourself in the deep end and choose a really hard song and you can't play it.

(End-of-Stage 2 interviews)

During Stage 3, the teachers noted that, true to their plans as expressed above, pupils had indeed thought more carefully about the music they chose, and selected songs with strong, clear melodies and riffs. In addition to choosing 'easier' songs, many pupils now moved outside the immediate sphere of contemporary culture, choosing 'old' songs going back to the 1960s. I mentioned in Chapter 3 that their original interpretation of 'freedom' to choose their own music actually consisted in limiting themselves to the narrow sphere of contemporary mainstream mass culture. Now, for example, out of five groups at Heath School, four chose songs by Nirvana, Bob Dylan, Aerosmith and The Jackson Five, with The Darkness being the only current chart-topping hit. In this sense, it would be reasonable to suggest that the pupils' sphere of musical appreciation had widened, and they had gained some critical distance on the immediate hot sales of the music industry. Rather than responding to music largely on the basis of cultural connotations and extra-musical references, including lyrics, the images of performers and other associations, they were now responding to, and taking into consideration, the inter-sonic properties and relationships within the musical materials.

Music appreciation and the development of 'critical musicality'

The concept of music appreciation tends, for historical reasons, to carry connotations of a struggle to impose a superior, complex, autonomous classical musical taste upon the 'masses'. Rather than that concept, for today's world I would suggest the notion of 'critical musicality', which I have already alluded to in earlier parts of this book. It relates to the linked concepts of 'critical literacy', 'critical pedagogy' or 'transformative pedagogy' and other similar terms that are associated particularly with the work of Paulo Freire (1972, 1974), and that have been developed by educationalists with reference to many curriculum subjects. In the field of Media Studies, Buckingham's (2005) interpretation of 'critical literacy' includes the need to help pupils attend critically to visual, audio-visual and digital literacies as well as those related to print. He argues that we should confront contemporary technologies and cultural media within education, rather than attempt to bypass them. For only by confronting them do we stand a chance of making pupils more critically aware of the underlying messages they contain. As Moore explains (2000, pp. 86f.; pp. 151ff.), 'critical pedagogy' invites pupils to recognize and discover power relations and symbolic violence both in and through the curriculum, by presenting alternative ways of viewing the world, and challenging commonsense or hegemonic views. By necessity, this also involves bringing contemporary mass culture and students' own existing knowledge into the educational environment, rather than excluding it.[7]

---

7   Other educationalists across a range of subjects who also advocate including mass cultural objects within formal education include Bentley (1998, pp. 80f.); Kress (2006), Moore

In the case of music, the concept of 'critical musicality' includes the idea that *all* music can be listened to more or less analytically, with more or less understanding. On one hand, this would involve increasing aural musical understanding and appreciation concerning inter-sonic musical properties and relationships, as illustrated throughout this chapter. On the other hand, any such increase could also lead to a greater awareness of how the music industry works. For example, pupils began to decipher the hand of the music industry in manipulating musicians' outputs. As Cameron volunteered:

–Cameron: Yeah, when I watch 'Top of the Pops'[8] or something [now], I notice that they don't actually sing, like, they just mime.

Similarly, pupils can be brought to question why the musicians playing the instruments they can hear on recordings, and see on videos, are sometimes withheld invisibly behind the scenes, unnamed and unknown to the fans. As Luke described it:

–Luke: Also, since we started to emulate the 'Can't Stop' song, when I heard it again it sounded a bit different, because you could hear like the guitars behind the main one. So all the stuff in the background, you kind of noticed that after you've been listening to it again and again and tried to copy it. And also, there's this song I've heard for quite a while and it got to Number One, and I heard her afterwards and it sounded quite strange, I don't know why ... I don't know why because there's, when she's singing there's this constant violin sound. Yeah and I only just noticed that ...

Through informal, aural learning involving their own choice of music, pupils seem to be in a better position to make more informed judgements about the quality of performances, of compositional input and of musical products themselves. They can also begin to develop their understanding of how 'talent' is selected, primed and marketed. They are, by the same token, a little better placed to discriminate and recognize those musicians whose performance, improvisational or compositional skills are justifiably held to be above the norm as a result of technical and/or musicianly qualities. Rather than 'dumbing down' or pandering to pupils' existing levels of knowledge by allowing them to bring their own music into the classroom, I would suggest, informal learning practices that require them to listen purposively to the music and copy it as music-makers, are more likely to raise their heads, and help them to develop a more critically aware musicality.

(1999), Osler (2006), Sefton-Green (2003) and Somekh (2006). Within music education, such sentiments are echoed by many teachers as well as scholars and researchers such as those cited in note 10 in Chapter 1 and many other parts of this book.

8   'Top of the Pops' used to be the most well-known pop TV programme in the UK. During the year of the London interviews it was still on prime-time television and a number of pupils were watching it; but it was axed shortly afterwards.

Teachers' views on listening

By far the strongest learning outcomes of the project overall, as identified by teachers across all 21 schools, consistently concerned listening skills. The teachers who were interviewed were unanimous that pupils' listening improved, and listening was in all cases the first skill that they mentioned in response to the interview question: 'What, if any, skills and knowledge do you think the strategies have enhanced?' We saw at the end of Chapter 3 that teachers identified an improvement in ensemble skills, particularly in relation to listening to each other during performance and rehearsal; and also it was noted that pupils' approach to listening 'in audience' to each other's live group performances was considered to be more attentive.[9] Below are some examples of how all eleven of the teachers interviewed across the seven main-study schools talked about pupils' approaches to what I have called purposive listening and copying in relation to their chosen music. As before, these quotes come from Stage 1 of the project only.

Barbara, Yasmin and Sandra compared the project's approach with the kind of whole-class listening work that they normally do:

–Barbara: Definitely the listening. … Because they're really focusing their listening in a way that they probably don't – if you just play something in the classroom, you know, they may or may not take it in, and you have question and answer, the same few people put their hands up. And you don't really know what other people have really heard. It's very hard. Unless you do a directed listening sheet.

–Lucy: Yes. So are you saying you think a larger number of them are listening more carefully?

–Barbara: Definitely, I would say, without question. Because there's a purpose, isn't there? There's a purpose to them listening, hearing sounds, doing this, because they want to learn how the song goes, and copy it, so they've got to listen. … Because otherwise, it's just 'Why are we listening to this piece of music? Just because we've got to learn about music.' You know, It's kind of a bit unfocused, isn't it?

–Yasmin: They're learning to use their ears a lot more – aural skills, differentiating. A lot of students are able to do that aren't they? Listen to bass lines and pick out, and listen to percussion parts. But they are doing that more than I ever dreamed that they would.

–Lucy: And why do you think that is basically?

–Yasmin: Because we're asking them to do it for whole lessons rather than for just five minutes at the beginning or ten minutes at the beginning. We often use listening activities to prompt composition exercises, as a composition tool. But we're asking them to listen a lot more carefully in this project.

---

9   In the anonymous questionnaire, the 17 teachers rated the following statement: 'Overall standard of skill development in Stage 1 in relation to aural skills (listening carefully, hearing independent parts, etc.).' Six ticked 'well above normal expectations', 6 'above average' and 5 'average', including the two EBD schools. For 'Ensemble skills (playing as a group, listening to each other's parts etc.)', 7 ticked 'well above normal expectations', with 5 ticking 'above average', 3 'average' and 2 'below average'. However, in conversation, improved listening was always stressed as the main learning outcome. For 'musical appreciation and understanding', the results were: 4 'well above normal expectations', 7 'above average' and 6 'average', including both EBD schools.

–Sandra: And also the fact that they're working, almost, their listening skills are so integrated in what they're doing, it is almost unique in that respect. Because normally listening skills are sat behind a desk where everybody listens at the same time, and in this they can listen as many times as they want, with a focus on any particular aspect of the music that they want to do. And I think that that is as integrated as listening can be, really. … I think their listening skills are developing in a different way. I think they're having to focus on layers of music in the background which they might not necessarily be able to do already. And in [normal] classes I do find that they, they can hear something in the background but they can't always identify what it is. And if this project enables them to have to focus on a bass line or a rhythm or on a guitar chord pattern or something like that, which they wouldn't normally do when they listen to pop music, I think that has just got huge implications for improving listening across the board.

Many of the teachers expressed an amount of surprise about pupils' listening abilities. On one hand, they were surprised to find that pupils had more *latent* ability than they had previously supposed:

–Brian: Quite frankly I was very surprised with the level of listening skills they actually demonstrated. They were able to discriminate between the rhythm, the harmony, the melody and various other sort of aspects and elements of the music, features of the elements. … Well, generically obviously it's a listening skill. And there's a certain amount of musical analysis going on, because they're having to subdivide what they're hearing into different strands and different things going on within the music. And to a greater or lesser degree they're processing that information in order to do the task. So, you know, listening and musical analysis really. Focused listening and musical analysis.

On the other hand, they found it revealing to observe how pupils went about the task of listening and copying:

–Katerin: Yes, and they've been picking up the parts from the CD, and have been listening for more detail. … And they're starting today to sort of see what it's really about. It's so interesting. They're sort of twigging, 'If I listen, I can pick out things,' and it's started to go beyond choosing a CD now, and it's the detail in the CD that is perhaps the reason why they've chosen the CD.

Many of the teachers considered that enhanced listening skills would be transferable to other music beyond the classroom:

–Carol: Well I think the aural skills seem to be developing, because they're really having to listen to this CD and they're having to listen to hear 'where's the lowest part', 'where's the highest part', 'what's the rhythm of the percussion', so they're having to draw out. I certainly think the aural skills are developing, and I'm sure that can be applied when they come to listen to other music, so they can apply that to other music.

Overall, the -teachers' collective identification of listening skills as the main learning outcome continued consistently throughout the project.

Listening, musical meaning and experience in the classroom

From the findings above it seems reasonable to suggest that, despite being avid listeners to popular music, and despite the fact that popular music has been a part of the school curriculum for many years, school pupils of this age do not tend to listen to it with a great deal of perceptivity, awareness, or even appreciation. The main question that I now wish to address is: why?

I will firstly take a step back in order to consider how we experience music as listeners. The topic of musical experience has for some years been entangled with that of musical meaning, for musical experience usually involves some kind of meaning-making processes that go on in the mind of the listener. Although there are many ways to conceive of these, most commentators tend to locate two broad aspects.[10]

One aspect concerns what I have already referred to earlier in this book, as the sonic properties and the inter-sonic relationships of musical material. In order to have a musical experience, the listener must be able to mentally pattern music so as to make it recognizable *as* music to him or her. In forming mental musical patterns, listeners attend to the sonic properties and their inter-relationships. These properties are only meaningful, and their relationships are only decipherable, in so far as listeners know how to, or are able to decipher them. In other words, listeners must have a certain level of competence or familiarity with the *style* of the music. Otherwise, listeners would not be able to notice any inter-sonic properties and relationships; and if that was the case, they would not be able to have a musical experience. For short, I will refer to the inter-sonic properties and relationships of music, construed in the mind of a perceiver, as 'inter-sonic musical meaning' (or what I have elsewhere referred to as 'inherent musical meaning').[11]

The other main aspect of experiencing music, concerns what I have so far been referring to as the cultural associations of music, or what I elsewhere call 'delineated musical meaning'. This refers to the extra-musical concepts or connotations that music carries: for example, its social, cultural, religious, political or other such associations. These may be conventionally agreed, such as the connotations of a national anthem or a famous TV theme tune; but they can also be unique to an individual, such as when someone associates a particular song with a memorable event in their personal life. All music must carry some delineated meaning, arising possibly, although not necessarily, from the original context in which it was created, and, certainly, from the contexts in which it is heard, or put to use in whatever way.

The main difference between inter-sonic meaning and delineated meaning is that the former involves mentally constructing relationships between one part of musical

---

10   See, for example, Martin (1995) for a helpful sociological discussion of this. My own theory is available in Green (1988, 1997, 1999b, 2005a, 2005b and 2006), although I have introduced a slight change in terminology here, as explained below.

11   I have given up using the term 'inherent meaning' as in the texts in note 10, and replaced it with 'inter-sonic meaning', since the former has lead to some confusion. I hope the new term will be clearer. However, there is no difference in the theory I am putting forward: both terms refer to the same meaning-making musical processes and practices as each other. The following paragraphs are a re-written version of Green (2005a, 2005b, 2006).

material and another part of musical material; whereas the latter involves construing relationships between musical material on one hand, and other things existing outside the music on the other hand. In all musical experience, both the inter-sonic and the delineated aspects of meaning must occur, even though listeners may not be aware of them. For we could not notice any inter-sonic meanings without simultaneously being aware that what we are listening to is a recognized cultural object, that is, a piece of music of some kind which exists and takes on meanings in relationship to a social setting. Vice versa, we could not conceive of a piece of music unless we were already also ascribing some inter-sonic meanings within it.

We may have positive or negative responses to either inter-sonic or delineated meanings. Positive responses to the former are likely to occur when we have a high level of familiarity with, and understanding of the musical style. Positive responses to the latter occur when delineations correspond with issues that we feel good about in some way. By contrast, negative experiences of inter-sonic meanings arise when we are unfamiliar with the musical style, to the point that we do not understand what is going on in the music. We have difficulty recognizing inter-relationships between the music's sonic properties, or understanding them in relation to the norms of the music's style, and are likely to find the music 'boring'. Meanwhile, negative responses to delineations occur when we feel that the music is not ours, for example, it belongs to social groups that we can't identify with, or it upholds beliefs, values or actions that conflict in some way with our beliefs and identities. What I refer to as musical 'celebration' is experienced when we are positively inclined towards both inter-sonic and delineated meanings; musical 'alienation' occurs when we feel negative towards both.

Our responses to inter-sonic and delineated meanings usually correspond, so that if we are negative towards the one we will probably be negative towards the other, and vice versa. However, although I have suggested that inter-sonic and delineated meaning must always co-exist, we do not always feel the same way about each of them. A person may be negative towards one aspect of musical meaning, whilst being simultaneously positive towards the other, engendering what I call 'ambiguity'. It is helpful to distinguish two types of ambiguity.

In one type, the experience of inter-sonic meaning is negative, whilst that of delineated meaning is positive. For example, a person might be unfamiliar with the inter-sonic meanings of Mozart. Perhaps she has never played or sung any Mozart herself, and listens only rarely to his music. Therefore, she is relatively unable to recognize sonic detail, inner parts, formal, harmonic or rhythmic change, or other inter-sonic relationships, and hears the music as frilly, dull or superficial. But at the same time she can enjoy the delineations, because she loves the spectacle of opera, or the social event of going out to the opera with friends, and so on.

In the other type of ambiguity, the experience of inter-sonic meaning is positive, whilst that of delineated meaning is negative. We can think, for example, of a Mozart opera-goer who is totally familiar with the inter-sonic meanings of the operas because of his classical training, having performed Mozart's music and listened extensively for many years. But he is critical of the operatic plots because he thinks they are sexist, and dislikes going to the opera because he finds it 'stuffy'.

Most music educators would probably agree that encouraging young children to have 'celebratory' experiences of as many styles and pieces of music as possible would be a legitimate and indeed, a highly desirable aim. As children grow up, and especially for those who go on to study music in Higher Education, we would certainly want to encourage some critical distance, or what I have referred to as 'critical musicality', so that celebration could give way to a more balanced judgement, allowing considered responses and evaluation of different musics in relation to a variety of criteria. Achieving such criticality is more likely to occur if pupils' ears have already been opened through positive experiences of a variety of musics, in relation to both inter-sonic and delineated meanings; that is, through what I have referred to as musical celebration. However, not all pupils do have celebratory musical experiences in the classroom. Many have experiences that, using the terms I have suggested above, would fall into the category of 'alienation' or 'ambiguity', resulting from negativity towards the inter-sonic and/or the delineated meanings of the music. The reasons for this are not straightforward.

First, let us consider delineation in the classroom. In the post-second world war period, it was unthinkable that popular music, jazz or any other vernacular form, apart from Western folk music, could be brought into a classroom in which a Western style of music education prevailed. This was partly because the delineations of such music were, and continue to be, associated with issues such as teenage rebellion, sexuality, drugs, and so on. Pupils were educated in Western classical music and folk music, mainly through singing and musical appreciation classes. Thus, they were required to study music with whose delineations they largely had no point of identification.

Second, let us consider inter-sonic meaning in the classroom. Pupils tended, and still tend (as we will see in Chapter 7), to be unfamiliar with the inter-sonic meanings of classical as well as folk musics. Whilst folk music in some countries has a stronger presence in family and social life across the generations, folk music in many other countries has more negative delineations in the social and political climate. For many children, as well as teachers, it has taken on the mantle of a museum culture (for example, Green 2002b and Endo 2004). Overall, listening to classical and/or folk music is simply not a part of the cultural practices of most school children. Further, as I have argued above, without repeated listening, stylistic familiarity cannot develop, and without some stylistic familiarity, positive experience of inter-sonic meaning is unlikely to occur.

Therefore, in general, pupils in the post Second World War period were likely to be in a negative relationship to both the delineated and the inter-sonic meanings of music in the classroom, and thus, alienated. As discussed in Chapter 1, in response to this situation educators began introducing music which pupils could be expected to welcome. Popular music and jazz, along with 'world music', were accepted into the curriculum gradually from the end of the 1960s until their formal inclusion within a number of countries towards the end of the century. One could therefore suppose that pupils should no longer be particularly negative towards the delineations or the inter-sonic meanings of music in the classroom.

But the situation is more complex than that. As I have suggested, music always carries some delineated meanings relating to its social contexts of production, reception or both. As soon as any music is brought into a *new* context of reception, its delineations are, therefore, liable to change. Thus, when popular music has been introduced into the classroom, its very presence there has often meant that it ceased to be considered as 'pop music' by the pupils at all. As we will see later in the book, pupils often don't seem to relate to music in the curriculum, even when it includes a wide variety of upbeat popular, jazz, traditional and world musics. Further, even teachers who use up-to-date popular hits cannot reasonably change their curriculum materials at a speed which reflects pupils' changing allegiances. So in short, music which carries positive delineations for pupils inside the classroom is hard to come by, and even harder to sustain as curriculum content.

Not only delineations, but inter-sonic meanings are also affected by the classroom environment. As I hope has been abundantly clear throughout this book, the informal learning practices that go into the making of popular music are very different from the usual pedagogic methods of formal music education. Yet once inside the classroom, popular music has tended to be *approached* largely as though its inter-sonic meanings warranted the same kinds of attention as those of classical music. In the words of one pupil in Paula Jackson's doctoral research, 'It becomes like classical music when we do it in school' (Jackson 2005). This is bound to miss the mark in relation to either any authentic reproduction, or deep understanding of popular music's inter-sonic meanings.

Another way of putting all this is to say that once inside the classroom, both popular music's delineations and its inter-sonic meanings tend to be affected. The music is likely to take on new, problematic delineations, and even pupils' familiarity with the inter-sonic meanings is likely to turn sour if those meanings are approached in formal educational ways. On top of that, approaching popular music's inter-sonic meanings through formal methods will undoubtedly end up with a musical product that does not resemble its original. In short, while popular music, broadly defined, has been present in the classroom for many years, identification with its delineations, and familiarity with its inter-sonic meanings have not been leading to experiences of 'musical celebration' for overwhelming numbers of school children. Thus, many pupils have tended to find themselves in an ambiguous or even alienated relationship to much music in the classroom, even including music which 'celebrates' them when they are outside school.

Within the classroom project discussed in this book, this issue was addressed, not by the obvious aspect of allowing pupils to choose their own music; but by allowing them to approach the inter-sonic materials and meanings of whole pieces of music directly, in ways that were derived from the 'real-life' informal learning practices of popular musicians, as these occur in the world away from schools and classrooms. As I have attempted to show in the current chapter, this approach seemed to enhance the listening skills and musical appreciation of many pupils, or to promise a form of 'critical musicality'. Further, informal learning practices seemed to have revealed to pupils themselves, that their previous approaches to music-listening were, relatively speaking, somewhat limited.

How pupils put distracted and purposive music listening practices into action within the project was, of course, idiosyncratic, as is the case with informal popular music learning practices outside the school. There, skill and knowledge are initially derived primarily from experience, usually in a haphazard way. Later on, such informally-acquired skill and knowledge may, or may not, become related to more theoretical, abstract understanding, linked to a technical vocabulary. Clearly, in the case of informal learning practices that have been adapted for an educational setting, the role of the teacher would come to the fore at such later stages. Teachers can then make connections between what has been learnt informally through experience, and what can be learnt in more abstract, technical ways through structured progression. A longer time period and further development of the particular project considered in this book would be needed to forge those links. The crucial thing, I believe, is not to try forging them too soon. That tendency, which goes down a road that music education has been following for many years, can, if too precipitous, interrupt the flow of learning and prevent meaningful connections at a deep level. Again echoing the cries of many educators from music as well as a range of other curriculum subjects, I wish to suggest that we are too concerned with speed and the narrow assessment of progress, focusing too much on only those areas that are susceptible to measurement. Thus we have overleapt the need of the learner to dwell in the quality of experience and develop an idiosyncratic, but for that very reason, deeper aural understanding and appreciation of music over time.[12]

I believe that through direct engagement with the inter-sonic meanings of music via informal music learning practices, pupils can come to a realization which complements the learning they undergo through more formal approaches. This realization includes the idea that inter-sonic musical meanings are subject to interpretation according to the existing knowledge and competence of the listener. Through this realization, learners can also come to understand that the delineated, cultural associations of music are not fixed either. One way to express this is to say that pupils' engagement with inter-sonic musical meanings enables them to recognize the *arbitrariness* of delineations; or in other words, the notion that delineations are not fixed entities belonging to sonic musical properties and their inter-relationships, but are socially constructed associations that arise from the ways music is *used* in different cultural contexts. Although 'celebration' might be one aim of music education, it is, as I have suggested, a more critical response to music that we should aim for as educators. Critical musicality simply means being able to listen to music more attentively and knowledgeably; hearing more synchronic parts and/or diachronic relationships within it; being more aware of how it came to be made; and having a more informed, percipient, and a less alienated, biased response to both its inter-sonic and its delineated meanings.

---

12 Again, such sentiments are echoed in a range of educational fields today, dating back to the philosophy of John Dewey (1916), up to the work of Howard Gardner (1983, 1999) and his colleagues, and others such as Csikszentmihalyi (1990, 1996) and Eisner (2004a, 2004b). Also see theorists such as Alderson (2003, 2004), Watkins (2005), and others within music education cited elsewhere in this book.

Chapter 5

Enjoyment: making music and having autonomy

This chapter considers how pupils described their responses to the project in terms of how much they did, or did not, enjoy it. The topic of enjoyment revolved around two main areas. One concerned music-making. The other concerned the project's pedagogy, particularly the relative autonomy that pupils were granted to direct their own learning. It became apparent that these two areas – music-making and autonomous learning – were deeply connected in relation to enjoyment levels.

As discussed in Chapter 3, there is no necessary reason why, if pupils are enjoying themselves in a classroom, that should mean that they are simultaneously becoming well educated. However, assuming that the activities *through* which the enjoyment occurs are themselves considered to be educationally worthwhile, then that would form reasonable grounds for suggesting that enjoyment is a desirable and helpful aspect of an educational experience. For if learners enjoy learning, it follows that they will be more highly motivated towards it; if they are more highly motivated, they will be more likely to apply themselves; and if they apply themselves, they will be likely, at least in the long run, to learn more. As O'Neill and McPherson tell us:

> An important outcome of [research in motivation] is that motivation is no longer viewed as a distinct set of psychological processes but as an integral part of learning that assists students to acquire the range of behaviors that will provide them with the best chance of reaching their full potential. (O'Neill and McPherson 2002, p. 31)[1]

This chapter will consider these and other related issues in connection with the views of pupils, and later on, those of teachers. Again I will focus mainly on Stage 1 of the project, but towards the end of the chapter I will give an overview of how participants' views developed as the year went on.

---

1   They also provide an overview of research on motivation in the psychology of music. Also see the case study by Renwick and McPherson (2002). There is a quantity of literature in the psychology of education generally to support the claim that enjoyment enhances motivation and learning. See, for example, Gardner (1993), Csikszentmihalyi (1990, 1996), or for an overview, Bentley (1998). It was concluded by Harland et al. (2000, p. 8), from a three-year study of five secondary schools, that enjoyment was a key factor in determining the efficacy of learning in the arts.

Bobby's group: ''cause it was boring'

At the end of Stage 1 we asked pupils the question: 'Can you tell me what you have enjoyed most, and what you have enjoyed least about the project?' Only one out of the approximately 200 pupils interviewed, Bobby at Southover School, had nothing positive to say in answer to that question, although he did make one or two positive comments at other points during the interview. Two others among the six boys in his group were also relatively lukewarm. In the interests of representing these dissenting voices, I have quoted Bobby and two of his colleagues on this subject below.

–Lucy: First of all, I want to know if you would please tell me what you enjoyed most and what you enjoyed least about the project.
–Drew: I know what I enjoyed least.
–Lucy: OK.
–Drew: Working in the cupboard.
–Lucy: Working in the cupboard. It was unfortunate that your group had that change. Why did you find that problematic?
–Drew: 'Cause it was too squashy.
–Lucy: Too squashy.
–Drew: And, like, the music weren't that loud.
–Lucy: Mm-hmm. Does everyone feel the same way about that?
–Group: Yes.
–Lucy: So you enjoyed least of all working in the cupboard. If you had been working in a nice room, would you have enjoyed the project more?
–Group: Yes.
–Bobby: [Shakes his head]
–Lucy: You wouldn't.
–Bobby: No.
–Lucy: No. OK.
–Bobby: 'Cause it was boring.
–Lucy: It was boring.
–Bobby: Yeah.
–Lucy: OK. Do the other people feel it was boring or –
–Danny: Working in the cupboard was boring.
–Drew: Yes.
–Lucy: Or if you weren't working in the cupboard?
–Bobby: No.
–Drew: It wouldn't be that boring.
–Bobby: No.
–Lucy: It wouldn't be that boring?
–Bobby: No.
–Drew: When Miss X was there it was boring.
–Lucy: Why?
–Bobby: 'Cause when we put the music up, like, half way we thought, 'Oh right, this is alright,' but she come in and turn it down and went, 'What's all that about?'

This level of negativity was higher, and in most cases much higher, than that of all the other 39 groups who were interviewed. However, it is worth noticing that the two main *reasons* given by Bobby and his friends for their negativity corresponded with two central strands that also ran through the other pupils' discourse. Firstly, rather than the informal learning task *itself* being described negatively, Bobby's group reported frustration at having insufficient space to carry it out. Similarly with the other groups, those aspects that were named as least enjoyable also involved practical impediments towards engaging in the learning practices, rather than the learning practices themselves. These impediments included lack of space, time, equipment, and in a few cases disruption from other pupils. Secondly, Bobby said that his group were just beginning to enjoy what they were doing when the teacher came in and, the implication is, ruined things. As will we see shortly, the notion that the teacher and his or her pedagogical approach could be impediments, rather than aids towards learning was also articulated by numerous other groups. But in their cases this was said, not in connection with the project strategies, but with what they referred to as 'normal' lessons. By contrast, they implicitly or explicitly placed a high value on the autonomy they were granted in the project.

Enjoyment, 'fun' and the 'normal' curriculum: learner autonomy and curriculum choice

As already mentioned, the above negative responses were massively outweighed by positive comments from the other 39 groups.[2] Many of these comments were made in direct answer to the question, 'What did you enjoy most, and what did you enjoy least, about the project?', but a number of them were also made in response to other questions or during discussions between pupils in the course of the interviews. A large number of the pupils indicated high levels of enjoyment, including, to illustrate the opposite extreme from Bobby's comments, statements such as the following.

–Lucy: What did you enjoy *least*?
–Marissa: Nothing.
–Lucy: Nothing. Other people? [Everyone shaking their heads.] There wasn't anything you didn't enjoy? OK.

–Will: There wasn't really anything–
–Tomash: There's nothing really bad that we can say about it.

–Christian: My motivation has increased tenfold, 'cause I just want to get out there and make songs.

–Ella: I reckon we should do it till like we leave school.

–Kaylee: It's an experience … it's just better for everyone really.

---

2   In the quantitative results from nine schools at the end of Stage 1, 358 pupil evaluation sheets were filled in, four as group responses and the rest as individual responses; 74% of the sheets showed an above-centre positive response to the question: 'How much did you enjoy the task?' The breakdown of results was: 'a huge amount' (24%); 'it was good' (50%), 'it was OK' (19%), 'some of it was OK' (7%), and 'didn't enjoy it' (2%).

–Hana: I really, really, thoroughly enjoyed it.

–Abdul: I enjoyed every single bit of it …

The 'normal' curriculum

The project did not set out to make a comparison with other classroom approaches. However, an unsought comparison ran through the responses from pupils in 21 of the 40 groups across all seven schools, and is intertwined throughout this chapter. It concerns the ways in which pupils spontaneously and unexpectedly compared the project with what they often called 'normal' lessons. Preference for the project approach in these and the extension schools was overwhelming, running at over 90 per cent, and in some schools as much as 97 per cent.[3] As a preliminary example, the word 'fun' cropped up in 25 out of the 40 group interviews, and in some cases it was contextualized thus:

–Joseph: It's a lot better 'cause it's not like usual lessons. And you're having fun.

–Rebecca: I liked it, 'cause like, I used to really hate music, but since we've been doing this I find it really fun.

–Ava: Yeah. It's a lot more fun than like normal music lessons. Yeah.

–Jack: Because it's really fun. It's unlike any other lesson, like, we've done before.

These unsought opinions about 'normal' lessons are all the more fascinating, because as we will see, many of the ways in which pupils described their previous lessons, bore little obvious resemblance to what most teachers would recognize as the National Curriculum for Music in England. This curriculum, which almost all the pupils in all the schools had been following for the preceding two years at secondary school, as well as previously in primary school, is highly practical. It involves a range of activities, including listening, playing instruments, singing, composing and improvising, much of which is done in small groups. It places little emphasis on theory or notation, although teachers often use worksheets with some guidance or stimulus such as a collection of notes or a film, to aid performance or composition work. Such aids may or may not be presented using staff notation, but very few teachers make serious attempts to teach staff notation across the whole range of ability and experience in the classroom. All the tasks involve a wide range of musics, covering classical, traditional, jazz and popular styles of the world.[4] Listening to

---

3   In an anonymous quantitative questionnaire returned by 189 pupils in nine schools at the end of the project as a whole, 91% said, via a tick-box, that they preferred the project's approach to traditional music lessons; 8% preferred the traditional approach; 1% said they liked both equally.

4   For details of the National Curriculum for Music in England, see <http://www.qca. org.uk/>. For general discussions of the nature of music education in the UK today, see, for example, Welch (2001), Mills (2005), or for historical perspectives, Cox (2002) and Pitts (2000). The approach is similar in many other countries in relation to the diversity of musical

pupils' unsought verbal descriptions of their previous lessons, however, an outsider would be forgiven for not realizing that such a varied and practical approach had ever been in place.

Curriculum content: 'pieces of paper'

A large number of pupils implied, without any prompting, that previous lessons involved a great deal of theory and writing things down on pieces of paper, which was 'boring'. In their minds, the time and emphasis allotted to such tasks seemed to have far outweighed the practical activities:

> –Kimberley: It [the project] was really good 'cause like normally in a music lesson we have to like follow a sheet and it's really boring. ... It was like, 'cause all last year, all I remember was being given a worksheet saying 'Do a certain amount of notes on the keyboard,' or something like that. Or 'Make up a note.' That is all I remember, worksheets. And it was really boring.

> –Barjarji: It's better than normal work ...
> –Lucy: In what way?
> –Barjarji: Like normal lessons you just like –
> –Abdul: Most of the time you just write.
> –Hardeep: The teachers are doing most of it sometimes.
> –Abdul: They're on the board, the keys and everything on the keyboard.
> –Valji: We're doing something we like [in this].

> –Dylan: Also it was different to just like sitting in a room and doing nothing. Just copying off the board or something all day. [This involved] playing.

> –Vicky: It's more fun than like, being just given a piece of paper and saying 'Go and write this out and do that.'

There was an indication that some pupils had found previous lessons relatively passive, such as the two girls below, who seem to be describing an echo of the music appreciation movement discussed in the previous chapter:

> –Rebecca: And I'd prefer music if it was like this for like the whole of school ...
> –Maria: 'Cause we can't learn anything just sitting down and hearing stuff.

Overall, the project was contrasted to the 'normal' curriculum, as a much more enjoyable approach, partly because it bypassed worksheets and went straight into practical activities. Although pupils hardly ever mentioned listening in connection with what they enjoyed, we have already seen that their approach to listening was, by their own accounts, also distinctly more active than normal.

---

styles and practical activities that are involved; although some countries currently place less emphasis on composition in the classroom, and many are only just beginning to systematically include up-to-date rock and popular music.

Curriculum organization: choice of instruments

Overall, 17 groups, as always unprompted, mentioned how much they enjoyed playing instruments in the project. Again they often placed this activity in contrast to 'normal lessons' and written work:

–Abigail: So, how much did you enjoy working on the project?
–Ian: Loved it, loved it.
–Abigail: Can you explain why?
–Ian: It gave me a chance to get into the piano, and other instruments, and learn how to play in a group, and it was really good. ... Because it was just like straight into the playing, there weren't really a sit-down worksheet –

–Cameron: I enjoyed just the fact we got to play instruments because, like, when we're in music lessons [normally] we have to do these pieces of paper, yeah, and like, he gives us questions, 'What is a parallel fifth?' That's just boring. You could actually learn stuff from practical that you can't, you can't learn practicals from writing.

Again there is something strange about these comments, given that the pupils certainly had opportunities to play instruments before the project started – indeed, playing instruments is a mandatory part of their curriculum. Several reasons why they seemed to contrast instrumental playing in the project with that in normal lessons, and why they seemed to get so much enjoyment out of the former, can be suggested.

One reason may be related, not to the mere *fact* of playing instruments, but rather, to the fact of being granted 'freedom of choice' over *which* instruments to play. Whether 'freedom of choice' is universally experienced as a good in itself, or whether it is merely portrayed as such within Western or Westernized societies would take a lengthy treatise to establish. It is always, of course, limited by what is possible. With those provisos, however, it seems reasonable to suggest that 'freedom of choice' is likely to be interpreted, by school pupils in many parts of the world, as a desirable asset:

–Gemma: I thought it was quite good, because we got to decide, like, what instruments we could use ...

–Jack: 'Cause you get to use more instruments and learn more stuff ...
–Craig: You get more sort of freedom really.

–Justin: Since I changed into this music it's been, it's been really good, 'cause I, I never would have thought in a music lesson they'd like let us get all the instruments out and try it for ourselves.

It was not only freedom of choice concerning instruments that pupils identified as an asset. In the Hertfordshire schools, as mentioned in Chapter 2, a number of new rock instruments were provided in the middle of Stage 1, mainly including electric guitars, electric basses, drum kits and electric drum pads. These instruments were identified as, in themselves, motivational spurs:

–Sofia: Yeah, it's been good …
–Stacey: We're not really allowed to use those sorts of instruments.
–Abigail: You're not normally allowed to use the instruments?
–Annika: Yeah, the electric drums …
–Harry: Yeah, and all the new ones, because before we had really crummy ones.
–Alyssa: Yeah, the old drum thing had a hole in the bass-y bit and it was naff.

–Jack: I've never actually been able to use the guitar or the drums in any lesson here so far …

All the teachers in Hertfordshire were also impressed by the motivational factor of the rock instruments:

–Debbie: I've got kids coming in at break to use them.
–Richard: Amps as well.
–Debbie: It's made a huge difference. It's made it kind of like a rocky school and the kids are –
–Richard: I call it a rock academy!
–Debbie: Yeah. They love the fact that we've got all these instruments and, you know, even from other years they're like 'Wow, look at that room full of amps and drum machines.'

This increased motivation surrounding the rock instruments can be understood in relation to both inter-sonic and delineated meanings, using the terms I introduced in Chapter 4. On one hand, these instruments enabled a more authentic replication of many of the inter-sonic properties, that is the sounds of the pupils' recordings. As observed in that chapter, accurate replication of sound quality and texture was a factor they valued highly and went to some lengths to achieve. On the other hand, the instruments carried cultural associations, or delineations of authenticity in relation to the images of chosen musicians which are visible on stage, screen and in photographs. These images include not only bodily looks, hair, clothing, gait and so on, but also the kinds of postures and gestures involved in playing certain instruments, and the shapes of the instruments themselves.

By contrast with this enthusiasm, in a number of responses, as already seen to some extent, the unpopularity of certain percussion instruments that were associated with previous classroom activities came richly to the fore:

–Daisy: And in [normal] music lessons if you're too noisy you sometimes have to do sheets and work and that. If you're OK you just have to do the xylophone or something. But in this you've got the guitar, the piano, the drums and that.

–Simon: Yeah. So we just like, liked [the project] more than –
–Joshua: Rather than like bongo drums and –
–Simon: Yeah, something like that.
–Joshua: Shakers and rattles.
–Janine: Yeah, like we normally have, you know, it's like, 'Here's a tambourine, make some music!'

These responses are again interesting in view of the fact that, as I noted in Chapter 3, when allowed to choose their own instruments for their own music, pupils on several occasions displayed an apparently unproblematic willingness to use the self-same instruments which they were so disdainful of in other circumstances. Again, the reasons for this can be understood in relation to their responses to musical meaning. For, as I suggested, their willingness to use xylophones and other classroom percussion occurred if those instruments were considered to provide the best possible match to the original sounds in their chosen song. In such cases, choice of instruments operated primarily in relation to inter-sonic meanings, and pupils' concerns over reproducing inter-sonic meanings as accurately as possible overrode the otherwise negative associations, or delineations, of the instruments. It must, therefore, ultimately be the sheer fact of choice *in itself* to which the pupils responded affirmatively, rather than merely the *types* of instruments available. Overall, the general opinion of both pupils and teachers was that the rock instruments helped to increase motivation, but were not essential to it or to the learning practices in themselves.

Finally, it is worth mentioning that, as discussed at the end of Chapter 3, many pupils identified instrumental playing as a learning *outcome*, in ways which again, surprisingly, gave the misleading impression that they had not played instruments in their lessons previously. In the present context it is possible to suggest that one of the reasons for this impression is the choice and autonomy they were allowed, not only over what instrument to play, but also over how to go about playing it. I will investigate the latter area in due course.

Curriculum content: choice of song

Connected with the unpopularity of certain instruments was the dislike expressed by many pupils concerning the styles of music with which those instruments were associated, and more generally, the music that pupils regarded as being part of the 'normal' curriculum. The very breadth which music education has striven to achieve over the last few decades, and its attempts to increase trans-national, inter-cultural and inter-racial understanding, appear, in the quote below for example, to have led to a narrowing down rather than an opening out of response:

–Janine: 'Cause I think that like, I think we've learnt a lot more than if, 'cause when we do bongos – we always do bongos nearly every year, we do it for like a term –
–Joshua: Yeah.
–Matt: [Inaudible] And samba.
–Ella: Like bongos, cymbals, maracas and shakers.
–Janine: Yeah stuff like that, and we never actually do music we like, so when we do bongo music or something like that, we don't like it. We don't really pay much attention 'cause like –
–Joshua: Yeah, no offence to the like African tribe who made it up [laughter] but –
–Janine: Yeah, but do you know what I mean?
–Abigail: It's not your music.
–Janine: No, so, so you don't, you don't remember it. I can not remember any other music I've done because of, because I don't want to remember it.

–Ella: Because like we worked in groups before, and it's kind of like you work something out one week and –

–Matt: It's not as fun as playing the kind of music you like as well.

–Ella: One week and then you have to change it because you just can't remember it.

–Janine: It's easier to do this.

Sixteen groups mentioned the importance of being allowed to bring in their own choice of song:

–Will: I think I enjoyed like, because we done music that we like.

–Cameron: Because, like, if you play something and you don't want to play it, you don't really feel the need, you don't want to learn.

–Jenny: It's better than doing, kind of like, normal school, like, it was open to what we could do. Like we didn't get told 'That's the song you have to do.' We got to choose.

Surprisingly, given the difficulty of the task and the number of lessons which pupils quickly realized would be required in order to carry it out, very few pupils expressed concern that they would get bored with their chosen song. The only examples of this that we heard were very early on in the first or second lesson. As they worked on the song, they seemed to get less, not more, bored with listening to it over and over again. This cannot be only because it was their own choice of song, for the same thing happened when they were copying classical music, as we will see in Chapters 7 and 8. However, for the moment I wish to consider some of the educational ramifications of allowing pupils to work on music with which they were already familiar and which they had selected for themselves.

Allowing pupils to bring in their own music, as I discussed in Chapter 4, overcomes the probability that they will have negative responses to both inter-sonic and delineated meanings in the classroom. For one thing, it is easier to aurally copy music whose inter-sonic meanings are familiar, as indicated by Janine above. The reasons for this are partly that the learner already has a level of competence with the style of the music, and partly that the musical details of the particular piece are likely to be lodged to some extent in the learner's memory. For both these reasons, the music can be called to mind mentally and heard by the 'inner ear', without having to replay the recording as much as would otherwise be the case. It is through inter-sonic meanings that pupils gain access to the material and practical elements of music-making and music listening. But it is through delineations that they touch upon issues of personal identity and social belonging. If learners' responses to both the inter-sonic and the delineated meanings of a piece of music are positive, what I have referred to as a 'celebratory' musical experience is likely to occur. The aural copying of music that is familiar and self-chosen, and whose inter-sonic and delineated meanings are positive for the listener, thus enables celebratory musical responses to be carried into the school, where they have so often in the past been overridden.

Through such responses, pupils are, furthermore, able to make connections between what they know and can do in their lives outside the school, and what they are learning within it. This connection was in itself regarded by the teaching team as motivational. Here is one teacher's observation:

> –Debbie: it has been highly motivational. I really believe that. What I'd also like to say is that, even though it's been motivational, the stuff that we usually do in class I think is motivational as well, because we do pick stuff which is very relevant to them, and I'm quite into relevancy with them – finding things that mean something. I think that the kids were already highly motivated, you know, the majority of them; 90 per cent were highly motivated in music lessons. But kids who wouldn't take that outside the classroom, if that makes sense, they have with this. It's linked into their lives, 'cause it's hit on their culture, their music culture, and what they like … What we were missing was them taking it outside, taking it a step further, discussing it in form time [that is, registration period outside music]. The lessons were very sort of in a box, very kind of 'in this lesson' and then go away and not talk about it. But they are taking it outside now, which they didn't do before.

It could be objected, again, that the point of education is not simply to affirm what learners already know and can do in their everyday lives. However, the evidence that I have so far provided is that although the pupils were already familiar with their own music outside the school, they were largely unable to engage in its inter-sonic meanings other than at a surface level, either as music-makers or music listeners. By bringing an adapted form of informal learning practices into the school, pupils were introduced to knowledge and skills that did extend their existing ones. As I argued in Chapter 4, for many of them the experience opened their ears to more details and layers of inter-sonic meanings than they had perceived before. In this chapter, the evidence from their own accounts also suggests that it enabled many of them to experience music-making as a more enjoyable activity than before.

Learner autonomy and pedagogy

The pupils' apparent pursuit of fun, and their unwillingness to engage in written work, play xylophones and study unfamiliar music, did not seem to be related to an unwillingness to learn, nor to any idea that they were having fun *instead* of learning:

> –Sara: You can learn by having fun, though.
> –Jordan: They [other pupils] won't listen, but if you make it fun for them, they'll enjoy [inaudible].
> –Danielle: If people are having fun then they'll listen.

Another main theme to emerge from pupil interviews was that the 'normal' approach was seen to be both less enjoyable and less pedagogically effective, precisely *because* it involved carrying out instructions given by teachers. In other words, one of the reasons why pupils indicated that they benefited from the project, in relation to both motivation and educational achievement, was that they were granted the autonomy to direct their own learning practices.

The value of developing 'personal autonomy' as an educational aim has been generally accepted within the philosophy of education literature for over thirty years, and has entered into the commonsense assumptions of educational policy and practice in a number of areas.[5] As Hand (2006) explains, the concept of 'personal autonomy' relates to a dispositional trait which involves an inclination to determine one's actions. However, the kind of autonomy that I am referring to here is of a different sort. For the pupils in the project were granted what Hand refers to as 'circumstantial autonomy'. In other words, they were afforded, or allowed, independence of action. Circumstantial autonomy, as he points out, cannot be an *aim of education* since it is not learnable. However, through what follows I would like to suggest that it can be a *means to education*.

We asked pupils: 'What did you think about the fact that the teachers didn't give you as much help as usual; and they were just letting you get on with it by yourselves?'[6] Only one pupil indicated that this was an ineffectual policy:

–Mantsebo: Yeah, but Miss, when there's teachers there you can actually learn stuff, but when you just leave us by ourself, we have to [do?] stuff and it's not really [inaudible] –

Out of the 40 groups, five seemed clear that they would have liked more help, although there were no cases amongst them of pupils saying that the lack of help prevented them from enjoying the project or from engaging in the learning practices. For example:

–Michelle: It was quite hard, but like, it was weird because we're used to the teacher saying 'Now we're going to do this, now copy down this,' where we were just like 'OK, what do we do first?' sort of thing. 'Do we work on the guitar?', or whatever really.

–Gabrielle: I think you kind of have mixed feelings, 'cause on one side of it you think 'Yeah, it's going to be really good 'cause we're going to learn how to play all of these really cool instruments,' but on the other hand when you get there you're like, 'OK, what do we do now?'

–Brendan: Well, I personally enjoyed it quite a bit, but I think we should have had more structure to it rather than so much freedom. 'Cause then, once you learn the bit that you've got to learn, you get a bit bored of it and you need something new to do.

---

5   See Peters (1978) for a seminal text, and Hand (2006) for a cogent rebuttal of the validity of the notion as an educational aim.

6   In 358 qualitative questionnaires from nine schools at the end of Stage 1, pupils gave prose responses to the same open question: 'How did you feel about the fact that the teachers didn't give you as much help as normal?'; 76% of responses were positive, of which: 48% said it was good/better than normal; 10% liked the independence/freedom; 4% said it was difficult, but good; 2% said they learnt more; 12% said it was alright; 17% were non-committal, of which 9% said it was more difficult, but without saying whether that was a good or a bad thing; 5% said they didn't know or didn't mind, and 3% said it was no different from normal; 6% said they wanted more help, and 1% said it was strange/weird. However, as we will see, in interviews, when pupils said they would have liked more help, this was often in the context of requiring help only when it was wanted, and not too much of the time.

'You learn more when you do stuff for yourself'

By contrast, in 15 out of the 40 groups, every member saw being left alone to direct their own learning as an unqualified good. This was, once again, linked with the notion of 'freedom of choice'. For example:

   –Billy: It's a lot better when you've got your own freedom to choose what you want to do.

   –Tom: I enjoyed the project loads, I think everyone did, because we just like could do what we wanted without any teachers' help.

   –Ava: I liked it because it was, you, you were independent.

However, what was valued was not merely the autonomy to select equipment and content, that is instruments and songs as discussed above, but moreover, to direct one's own learning in relation to pace, structure and progression:

   –Alex: I think it helps you learn more on your own because you can do it in your own time.

   –Jenny: You didn't have set things to do each lesson, it was like –

   –Craig: You get more sort of freedom really.
   –Jack: Yeah. So, all the other time we have to do exactly what she tells us to.

   –Lakmini: I thought it was good because you could do your own thing; no one telling you what to do, just do what you want to do …

This point relates again to the concept of 'flow' and the observation that pupils were liable to play together for long periods of time, as discussed in Chapter 3. For their comments seem to confirm that they were conscious of this tendency and that they valued it. By contrast, teachers' approaches were portrayed as involving too much 'stopping and starting':

   –Jacky: And usually, like, in the lessons we stop and start. And it was nice to just, like, have a blank amount of time, and do it when we want to do it.

   –Ava: And it was good 'cause we had more than one week to do it, and we were left on our own, to like to do it. We weren't having to show it every week, at the end of the lesson.

   –Leila: I learnt better than I did in Year 8 because we used to do all sorts, we'd, like one week we'd do something and another week we'd change. But with this music we stayed to the one thing till we learnt it.

Teachers' talk was often portrayed as a waste of time, as though pupils felt they had a better understanding of what they were supposed to be doing without it:

–Tanya: Yeah, it was good.

–Abigail: Why was it good?

–Tanya: 'Cause you didn't have the teachers lecture at the beginning, you just had to go in and get on with it.

–Abigail: And you liked doing that?

–Tanya: Yeah.

–Abigail: Are you the same?

–Daisy: Yeah, and like every lesson you know what you're going to be doing.

–Vicky: Yeah, and also I don't like it when everyone, all the teachers take up half the time just talking. I just like –

–Ava: To get on with it.

–Vicky: Yeah, to get on with it.

As we saw in Chapter 3, pupils were prepared to play the recording of their chosen song over and over again, and to repeat their actions in attempting to copy it for relatively long periods. It is therefore interesting that when referring to music that the *teacher* had instructed them to play, they described having found the need to repeat their actions as boring or irksome:

–Shaun: Yeah, [I enjoyed] not being told what to play 'cause –

–Abigail: Right, OK. And do you, so that's a good thing, not being told what to do?

–Shaun: Well it's not but, it's just because when you get told to play music on the keyboard then, it's like, you play it so many times, like during the half term it just gets really annoying.

–Alex: Because normally they give you like a piece of work, and they tell you how to do it, and you've got to do it for like half an hour.

Being given instructions of this kind was also portrayed as leading to arguments:

–Ava: You didn't have like, you didn't have a certain thing you had to follow. 'Cause you always get, it always causes, I don't know more arguments and stuff if you've got a certain thing you've got to follow, because there's, over like what, who's going to play what bit and things.

By a similar token, many pupils indicated a response that corresponds with some comments that I made on the basis of observations in Chapter 3. This is that autonomous learning gave them a relief from the demand to 'get it right' by teachers. Indeed, teachers were often characterized as hampering progress and putting on negative pressure which lead to lower performance:

–Ella: 'Cause we got to do what we wanted and we didn't have like, the teachers boss us around …

–Matt: I think it's easier than being –

–Janine: I quite liked it.

–Matt: Than being, like if there's someone there saying 'Do this' –

–Simon: More freedom to do what you want.

–Ella: At your own pace.

–Davinder: I thought it was good because it … gave us to do it our own way …
–Melanie: Because you got to do it your own way, you didn't have teachers telling you they wanted it this way or that way …

–Alex: You can do it in your own time, and you're not like being told what to do by the teacher, or, like being fussed around and stuff.

–Daniel: I think it's better, 'cause like the teacher is always behind you kind of thing, and you're like a bit under pressure, whereas teaching yourself is like a bit better.

In Chapter 3 I suggested that the CD acted as a less threatening authority than the teacher. Here now is an example of a pupil who seemed to have come to a similar conclusion:

–Hana: Like because Mr X, last time when we was doing it Mr X would sit like, Mr X would be able to do it, and he'd try and show us how to do it. But just saying to us 'Oh this is how you've got to do it' wasn't like making us learn it. Doing, letting us do it ourselves, like this, and letting us, like choose what bits we want to do and like listen to the song and work it out ourselves made it a lot more, like, yeah; and [to another pupil] you said, this time we've done it ourselves and not had to have a teacher going 'Yes, and this is how you play this,' if you know what I mean.

Both implicitly and explicitly, this freedom from pressure was often related to the corollary idea, that in self-directed, autonomous learning, 'you can't get it wrong':

–Lakmini: And you can't do nothing wrong because it's just the way you wanted to do it.
–Lucy: … So, does that mean you're learning, though?
–Marissa: If you do it well!
–Lakmini: In your own way.

–Harry: And not being given notes, like 'Oh you must do it like this' and then if you don't do it like that then you're wrong.

Pupils in 22 out of the 40 groups indicated that teachers' help was indeed valuable, but only so long as it was needed or wanted. Many pupils suggested that such help would be most valuable only if it followed on from an autonomous learning experience which involved an amount of self-motivated discovery. For example:

–Luke: let's say you're in a band and you have to do what we did, or create a song, or make a piece of music up, and you just send us into a practice room and give us some instruments, and we can get on with it ourselves; and then if we had any problems, he could tell us how to solve it, and then we'd learn stuff that way. By trial and error … Because you can learn from the mistakes you made …
–Kevin: I think that's a better way. So, we tried to handle it ourselves, but if we can't do anything someone will help us …

–Cameron: … if you were taught one time, you'd have experience, and you'd be prepared for the next.

–Danielle: It's like a teacher could be near the room and when you need their help, they'll come, but otherwise just improvise by yourself.

–Rebecca: Just say like, instead of saying 'do this', I find it better if we find it out ourselves.
–Madeline: Find it out ourselves, yeah.
–Shanice: And then they give us ideas.

–Nicola: Teachers should like, set you goals and like be there if you need help.

These perspectives are interesting to compare with a discussion by Bruner (1983, p. 96f). In a small-scale primary classroom project, he and his colleagues came across a finding which 'rather took us aback'. It was that whilst the presence of an adult had a positive effect on children's play, but: 'I do not mean an adult "over the shoulder" of the child, trying to direct his activity, but one in the neighborhood who gave some assurance that the environment would be stable and continuous, but would also give the child reassurance and information as, if, and when the child needed it.' Let the adult intervene brusquely and steal the initiative from the child, and the children's play would 'become duller' (p. 97). The pupils within the project seem to be pointing to a similar conclusion from their own experiences.

There were indications that overall, being granted autonomy was seen by learners to enhance their sense of personal responsibility and conscious awareness of how to improve their own learning:

–Lindsey: It was good because like … we were kind of like allowed to be independent and we were like able to teach ourselves …

–Leila: It was a good thing because we did it by ourselves, we didn't have no teachers helping.
–Lucy: Right. And why is that a good thing?
–Leila: So we can learn by ourselves. Learn it for ourselves.

–Matt: And you had the responsibility to do it yourself …

–Brendan: … you had to do a lot of work, to make it work.
–Steve: We had to pay a lot of attention as well. We had to make sure that we could produce something at the end that was worth doing as well … I've learnt how when you don't have any goals to aim towards like, setting some so that you can do it yourself as well
…
–Brendan: I learnt that, pretty much the same that, you know, if you haven't got any goals set for you, you've got to find some yourself, and work towards it with maybe not so much encouragement as you're used to getting from teachers.
–Abigail: Yeah, OK. And do you, do you think that there's some value in setting your own goals?
–Steve: Yeah because in life you're going to need to do that later on as well, when someone doesn't set you some, and it's quite an important thing to do.

Many pupils indicated implicitly or explicitly that they valued having to 'work stuff out for themselves':

–Lindsey: It shows us how capable we are.

–Amy: Because it gives you the chance to prove what you're capable of.

–Emily: It was quite good 'cause like then you learn to do things for yourself.

–Lindsey: It teaches you as well that you can learn it on your own, you don't need a teacher telling you what to do …

–Cameron: We had to figure stuff out by ourselves.

–Jordan: The lessons here [that is, a different room than the previous year], it was different to the music lessons, 'cause in the music lessons you're told what to do and you're given the notes and everything, but here we had to work it out ourselves.

A number of pupils also indicated that autonomous learning lead to a better sense of *satisfaction* than teacher-directed learning:

–Kimberley: Yeah. But like you feel like much more satisfied –
–Hana: Yeah.
–Kimberley: That you've actually learnt something. Rather than like, finishing questions or something, you think, 'Oh well I've done it.'
–Jenny: Yeah.
–Kimberley: But when you've actually done an entire song with yeah, help but you've actually learnt something, you feel much more satisfied than in a normal lesson.

–Janine: If you teach yourself you feel better, 'cause you realize that like –
–Joshua: You've done it.
–Matt: You've done it all by yourself.
–Janine: Yeah. You did it

–Rhona: 'Cause like, it's up to you, you've got sort of more control over it.

–Bobby: 'Cause we learned off our own back.
–Drew: Exactly.

A few mentioned a positive impact on self-confidence:

–Justin: Well it's, sort of, it's good in a way. Like so people can learn on their own what to do, so build up self-confidence.

Not only did pupils say they enjoyed autonomous learning, but also that they learnt *more* than in 'normal' music lessons where the teacher has the role of instructor:

–Emily: Um, you learn more when you do stuff for yourself

–Madeline: 'Cause that way we can actually learn more about music.
–Rebecca: Learn how to play things as well.
–Shanice: And you enjoy it more.

–Jenny: Yeah, it goes in better …

–Hana: Technically, I actually think the learning is better, not just what we think of it, if you know what I mean. Like I've learnt more in this than I did in the whole of music last year.

–Daisy: You learn more by doing it yourself.

The notion that they learnt more became particularly apparent, unexpectedly, in answer to the question, 'Do you think it would be a good idea for other teachers to do this with other classes, in this school or other schools?' The boy who had questioned the value of autonomous learning, Mantsebo said 'I don't think so'; and Bobby, whom I mentioned at the beginning of this chapter, said:

–Bobby: No. I think, well, I don't really care to be honest, but if you lot want to then, that's up to you.

Amongst other groups there were some concerns which mirrored those of their own teachers, that other classes might 'take advantage'. The project, they said, would only work with classes who were 'co-operative'; and only where there are sufficient resources. Pupils in four groups suggested that a good way forward would be to intersperse the project's approach with more formal ways of learning – exactly the approach intended, and that we recommended when the project became available to other schools.

There were pupils in every single group who gave a positive answer to the question about whether the project should be extended to other classes, and this was unanimous in 27 of the 31 groups for which there is data. Some responses focused on the fun element as a good reason for doing it with other classes: 'Yeah, I think they'd enjoy it as much as we did'; 'It's proper fun.' But most reasons given were connected with learning more, and that, in turn was connected with enhancing motivation. For example:

–Abigail: OK. Now final question. Do you think it would be a good idea for other teachers to do this with their classes?

–All: Yeah, yeah.

–Stacey: Yeah, 'cause they will learn more about music and stuff. Like high notes, low notes rather than just like –

–Harry: And it's fun.

–Alyssa: Rather than copying something on a xylophone.

–Harry: Rather than just a xylophone and it's just 'bing bing'. There's more to it.

–Abigail: So you think that you learn more this way than you do normally?

–All: Yeah, yeah.

–Alyssa: It's more like what you're going to need when you're older, sort of thing, like how to play an instrument rather than just how to read notes and stuff.

–Harry: You're more involved in what you're doing.

–Barjinda: I think the whole school should do it because that way they can learn so much more.

–Alex: I learnt more in this five weeks than I did in the whole of last year.

–Simon: More people would take up music.

It is of course significant that the content of the learning that the pupils were referring to above mainly involved psycho-motor performance skills, as distinct from what might be considered purely cognitive skills. Thus the findings here could apply particularly to performance skills in other subjects such as sports, drama or modern foreign languages which involve a listening and speaking component, as well as activities not usually included in schools such as driving a car and many others. It would, in addition, be interesting to consider whether other more theoretical subjects could also be affected in a similar way. For example, although the activity might be more obviously cerebral, the requirements of an educational context, and particularly of assessment, mean that when pupils are trying to solve a problem in maths, conduct an experiment in science or write a story in their first language, they are always, in a sense, performing. In such a light, it might be appropriate to understand education as requiring a performance out of the learner all the time, and to take this into consideration when planning pedagogy.

Overall, the pupils seemed to be identifying a learning experience which, although they did not use these terms, bears a close resemblance to the concepts of 'child-centred education' and 'discovery learning', the rights and wrongs of which have been debated by educationalists going back centuries. 'That education is not an affair of "telling" and being told, but an active and constructive process, is a principle almost as generally violated in practice as conceded in theory,' wrote the great educational philosopher John Dewey (1916, p. 38). Such perspectives echo back to Rousseau and beyond, and forward to the work of the constructivist educators and many others in the present day.[7] However, one thing that is important to bear in mind here, is that the learning practices adopted in this project were based, not on any theory of child-centredness or discovery learning, but on an empirical investigation and analysis of the real-life, informal learning practices of popular musicians as they operate outside the educational environment.

Stage 2 and on

The above responses were all given at the end of Stage 1 of the project. Because Stage 2 introduced a pre-selected song (which some pupils openly stated they did not like), a worksheet and a greater amount of instructions, teachers' expectations were that pupils would regard this as a return to the 'normal' curriculum and that their motivation would correspondingly drop – despite the fact that the role of the teacher, once the task was set up, continued to involve standing back. It was agreed that a slight drop in observable motivation at the very beginning was largely recovered by the end of the first lesson. As one class teacher, Barbara, put it: 'They got interested

---

7   See Rousseau (1762), and for a helpful discussion of the historical development of the concept, Moore (2000). For perspectives in contemporary music education, see, for example, Chapter 1, notes 8 and 10.

despite themselves.' In interviews, pupil opinion was divided as to whether they enjoyed and benefited more from Stage 1 or Stage 2. Most preferred the choice of song in Stage 1. Whereas some felt more supported by the greater amount of guidance given in Stage 2, others continued to prefer the greater autonomy invested in them by Stage 1. For many, Stage 2 lead to a higher-quality musical product, and there were, overall, more expressions of satisfaction and pride in what they were able to produce. However, all our quantitative and qualitative results from the main-study and extension schools show that, overall, pupils reported far more enjoyment in relation to Stage 1 than Stage 2.[8] In Stage 3, pupils were very pleased to once again have a choice of their own music, and findings in relation to enjoyment and motivation largely replicate those of Stage 1.

During the composition task in Stages 4 and 5, motivation was particularly high according to pupils' accounts. Expressions of having 'fun' were voiced many times, along with words such as 'superb', 'excellent', 'brilliant' and many other accolades. These were, again, often expressed in relation to the amount of 'freedom' pupils were given:

–Chris: ... it's fun, it's made me want to do music lessons, 'cause I'm the worst in the group, and it's better than all the other lessons because it's more freedom.

More strongly than in Stage 1, the fact that it was 'fun' was often linked with being 'challenging' (echoing Csikszentmihalyi's stipulation that flow occurs when the task is neither too difficult, *nor* too easy; Csikszentmihalyi 1990 and 1996, pp. 111ff.). Rather than allowing their autonomy as learners to run away with them, as teachers had feared they might, pupils seemed to become increasingly appreciative of the trust that was put in them as the year went by, and correspondingly responsible:

–Emily: We weren't being told what to do and the teachers put trust in us.

–Shaun: I felt the teachers finally put some trust in us. We got the chance to have a choice. The lesson was flexible and was really fun. We didn't have teachers bossing us around and watching us all the time.

The idea of being left alone without pressure was linked to personal creativity much more frequently and more forcefully than in Stage 1:

–Justin: It's really like easy when they leave you to do it by yourself, 'cause you, like you think, you think of something, like an idea springs to mind and you just, you go on the idea instead of all the teachers going, 'Oh no you got to, you got to do it this way,' and you can do it all by yourself, and it just sounds all good.

---

8   In an open-ended qualitative questionnaire returned by 269 pupils from 6 schools at the very end of the project, in response to the question 'What did you enjoy most about the project?', 29% of pupils put Stages 4 and 5 (composition), and 22% put Stage 1. Other responses (all from the same open-ended question) related to a variety of factors, such as being able to work with friends (20%), which will be discussed in the next chapter.

A lot of emphasis was placed on the fact that the composition was 'all ours', and this was strongly linked with the fact that they had not had much help:

–Harry: And it was good that we got to make up what we wanted and not have to copy another song, it was all ours.

–Jacob: If we had too much help then, like, we wouldn't really have done it ourselves.
–Michelle: It wouldn't have been our own.

–Joshua: It makes you feel proud 'cause it's all –
–Alex: It's all yours.
–Joshua: You've made the tune.

There were also some indications, particularly in these composition stages, that pupils valued the chance to 'be creative':

–Marianne: It was, we had a lot of freedom and we could be very creative, and when you're in school you can't really be creative a lot of the time, so it was nice to just have an hour where we could just chill out and do our own things and just experiment really.

In the anonymous questionnaires, 11 out of the 17 teacher respondents agreed with the statement: 'Pupils' compositions during Stages 4 and 5 were more musically interesting and sophisticated than usual.' The other four teachers were neutral. The topic of creativity is a major field of educational research. Unfortunately, I am unable to enter into it any further here, although I hope to write an article on this aspect of the project in the future.[9]

Overall, it is worth noting that pupils' positive responses to being granted circumstantial autonomy to direct their own learning had, if anything, strengthened and become even more vehement by the end of the project. This is particularly interesting in relation to the final two stages of the project, which involved informal learning with classical music. As we will see in Chapter 7, many pupils felt negative or extremely negative about classical music. Yet during the classical stages, even though the curriculum content was contrary to their wishes and tastes, they none the less continued to respond positively to the pedagogy. Although they had no choice of music, a number of other main characteristics of informal learning, as identified in Chapter 2, continued to be in operation. These were that they had a certain amount of group decision-making over what piece to choose from a limited range, they continued to have choice over what instruments to use, and most importantly, they continued to organize their own learning within friendship groups. All the themes concerning their responses to this that have come up so far were repeated, if anything,

---

9   Within education generally, see, for example, Craft (2001; 2005), Craft et al. (2001), Jeffrey and Craft (2001), Csikszentmihalyi (1996), Eisner (2004a, 2004b); Gardner (1983), Hartley (2006), HMI (2003), NACCCE (1999) and Watkins (2005). For work on creativity in relation to composition in the music classroom, see, for example, Byrne et al. (2003), Faultley (2004), Jorgensen (1997), MacDonald and Miell (2000), Paynter and Aston (1970), Webster (1992), J. Wiggins (2006) and many more.

more forcefully, and many pupils spontaneously generalized their responses to cover the whole year. As just one out of quantities of examples available at the end of the classical stages:

–Ed: I find it a bit boring when teachers tell you what to do.
–Peter: 'Cause teachers tell you, it's just like, 'cause they already know the answers, and when you figure it out yourself you kind of like, you're more like proud of yourself 'cause you're doing it. You're getting the answers yourself then, rather than getting someone telling you.
–Arlene: You learn about using your brain more.

The above quote comes full circle, to connect to some of the ways in which teachers found their approaches to teaching had begun to change as they became more accustomed to the project's strategies. I referred to this issue in Chapter 2, where I cited Sandra to illustrate the point:

–Sandra: What I've been able to do is to go into groups, ask them questions, and then actually wait for them to come back with the answers themselves, rather than me having any particular input. ... So I was questioning them in a completely different way, I wasn't leading them in any respect, I was just giving them the opportunity to speak out. It's a completely different way of questioning from when you've got the answer in your head ...

Enjoyment, motivation and application: teachers' expectations and views

Whereas we asked pupils the question, 'What did you enjoy most, and what did you enjoy least about the project?', when interviewing teachers the question was: 'How would you describe pupils' motivation and attitude during the project?' Both questions were intended to 'get at' similar issues, one from the pupils' perspectives, and the other from that of the teachers. The reasons for the change of terminology from 'enjoyment' to 'motivation and attitude' arose from an attempt to use language that would be meaningful and normal to those involved, rather than from any philosophical attempt to *distinguish* between the concepts. In addition, it seems more reasonable to ask teachers to make judgements about their pupils' motivation and attitude, based on observation and experience, than about their pupils' enjoyment levels, which are perhaps of a more personal nature only known to the individual. However, I do not wish to make fine distinctions between the three terms here, and hope it suffices to suggest that they are linked. For, as I indicated earlier, if a person is enjoying something, he or she is likely also to be motivated towards it, and their attitude is likely to be positive (see note 1 in this chapter). Whereas no pupil used the terms 'motivation' or 'attitude', teachers in the course of their conversation used all three terms. They are all, therefore, thrown into the debate here.

One way in which teachers tend to make judgements about pupils' motivation is by evaluating their degree of application to a task, or in the everyday parlance of the contemporary classroom, by evaluating whether pupils are 'on task'. Being on task means being focused on a given educational activity, and not 'mucking around' or talking about extraneous matters. The assumption is that if pupils are motivated, they are most likely to be on task, and vice versa. Research by Smith (1996), Jensen (1995) and others suggests that there are limits to how far it is desirable, or indeed possible, for pupils to remain on task. Our brain is 'not designed for constant attention', according to Smith (1996, p. 21), and with reference to Jensen (1995), he suggests that the maximum amount of time that adults can expect to remain on any one task is 20 to 25 minutes. These findings lead Moore to question the notion of 'on taskness' as a teaching aim and as an indicator of pedagogic and learning success. They inevitably force teachers, he says:

> ... to address the issue of what students are 'actually doing' – and what learning is actually taking place – when they appear, through all outward bodily signs, to be focused on a given task and in a fixed manner for longer periods of time than those suggested by Jensen and Smith. (Moore 2000, pp. 161–2)

On the other side of the coin, however, I would like to suggest that the project does seem to offer some examples of pupils remaining on task for periods of over an hour. For example, I have already mentioned some field recordings of pupils working together for long time spells, even though they did not know that they were under surveillance; that is, there was no teacher in the room for most of the time, and they were unaware of the presence of a MiniDisc recorder. When I returned home with the first field recording of the project in my bag I felt depressed and nervous about listening to it, since I expected to hear a lot of 'mucking around'. During the lesson I had not been at all sure that the girls in the group were motivated, or that they were on task, and I had strongly suspected that as soon as I or their class teacher left the room after each monitoring visit they had stopped making any pretence at doing any 'work' or applying themselves. I was astonished and very excited by what I heard. The recording, which was cited in Chapter 3, lasted 33 minutes, although the girls had been working for over 20 minutes before the machine was switched on. The song they had chosen was played six times during that half-hour period, unrelentingly, with only one break, during which they listened to an alternative song to see if it would be more suitable. The only comments that could be regarded as extraneous were:

–I've heard you singing before.
–I have.
–You have?
–Yeah, at [inaudible] party on Saturday night.
–Oh God, that was awful.

The talk then reverted to the task in hand, and the party was not referred to again.

As we saw in Chapter 2, one of the main anxieties about the project expressed by teachers, concerned the high level of autonomy given to learners. Their biggest fear was that pupils would not stay on task and would 'muck around'. Yet by the end of Stage 1, teachers were already turning away from this opinion. There was unanimous agreement that pupils' motivation rose quite dramatically from the start, and that they applied themselves to the task more than expected, and more than usual:[10]

> –Richard: I was also concerned by the very nature of informal learning, that the freedom that you gave the pupils, which they wouldn't otherwise normally receive in a traditional music curriculum, that they would take advantage of it and it would create chaos and ill discipline and misbehaviour. And I was very wrong. By the first lesson it was quite clear that pupils were extremely excited about the work, very highly motivated, and in fact worked on task throughout the entire Stage 1 process. They didn't mess around in practice rooms, they chose their instruments very carefully, they selected which parts they were to copy, and they worked in a sociable, informal manner, just as the project was initially set out. And so my very first fears were actually completely wiped away. … That was a big surprise. I thought they'd go wild, and that they'd be like rubber balls bouncing round the classroom. Um, but quite the opposite actually.

> –Janet: Again, the first lesson, I wasn't too sure. I was particularly worried about one girl's group, because they're not really that motivated in music lessons full-stop. But I was very surprised, they really got on with it, they were very interested, and that really pleased me. The second and third lessons I was far happier because every group was on task and they were all motivated, they all knew what they were doing …

> –Sandra: I think it really works in terms of the motivation of the students, of their enthusiasm, and it actually has had effects on the behaviour of students too. So I've seen really marked improvements in how many students stay on task, how you can actually leave students in a room, with instruments, and they will do the work that they are expected to do.

Teachers continued to identify improvements in enjoyment, motivation and application as the year went by. As just one example from Stage 2:

> –Janet: They love it! They just did it, they didn't even explain, they just, like the layering effect you know, one came in, the next one came in … They, I think they loved it … What I found was that it, coming to the end of the lesson, and we all, we didn't know it was the end of the lesson – we were all involved in the work, and then the bell would go and some of them would moan, 'Oh I don't want to go' and some of them would go off singing what they'd done, and I think you, you can tell they've learnt something when they go off and sing it.
>
> *(End-of-Stage 2 interview)*

Why is it that pupils seem to remain relatively well on task when involved in informal learning practices adapted for the music classroom? On one hand, music engages music-makers and listeners in an inter-sonically organized flow of time. The concept of experiential 'flow' and the enjoyment that is associated with it, as discussed in Chapter 3, can offer some explanation of how pupils managed to stay on task. Cutting up the lesson to accommodate shorter spans of concentration and

---

10 In the anonymous questionnaire filled in by 17 teachers, 11 ticked that pupils' enjoyment was 'well above normal expectations', 5 ticked 'above average' and 1 (an EBD teacher) ticked 'average'. For motivation, 11 ticked that it was 'well above normal expectations', 3 ticked 'above average' and 3 ticked 'average'.

provide a variety of learning activities – according to the pupils' own accounts cited earlier – tends to be interruptive and counterproductive to this experience. On the other hand, I have suggested that music's cultural delineations, when positive for the listener, can affirm a sense of identity and belonging. The pupils' familiarity with their chosen music's inter-sonic meanings, combined with their positive identification with its delineated meanings, according to the theory I put forward in Chapter 4, can together be understood to lead to a sense of musical 'celebration'. If we ignore pupils' relationships with musical meanings outside the school, we override the possibility of affording them celebratory musical experiences inside school. But not only that, for from the present chapter it seems that if we attempt to intervene too much in their learning processes, structure their tasks, set them goals and assess them at every possible moment, we may also be interrupting the possibility of celebration for them – and of enjoyment, 'flow', and even to some extent, of learning.

Many of the project teachers asked whether it was acceptable for pupils to include dancing as a part of their listening and copying activities. My answer was always yes, so long as some music-making practices were also going on simultaneously. Dancing is and has always been a fundamental, integrated aspect of music-making worldwide, and different kinds of dance are often particularly associated with the music that pupils had chosen. To enforce the separation of dancing from the activity of music learning in relation to such music, and where learners have shown an inclination towards their integration, would be to override some of the most trenchant musical delineations carried by the music, as well as the practices that are associated with its performance and reception. It also flies in the face of that imaginative side of music-making identified by Swanwick (1988), and discussed in Chapter 3. In the end, only 3 out of the 40 groups included dance as part of their final product. They all approached it in a way that was integrated with music-making, so that, for example, the dancers all played some hand percussion or sang while they danced. Their teachers agreed that the musical outcomes were of a good standard, and that the pupils were more than usually highly motivated and on task. The pupils confirmed this opinion in their interviews.

In the pilot school in London, a group of girls, described by Ken, the Head of Music as the 'lowest ability' pupils in the class, chose to copy Geri Halliwell's version of 'It's Raining Men'. Before their final performance they spent time making paper cut-out men to sprinkle over each other like a confetti of rain, and they procured two umbrellas from myself and Ken: 'It's all part of our act, Miss.' Again, according to the argument that I have put forward, allowing such an engagement with the music's delineations as a part of the learning experience is more likely to foster a celebratory relationship with the music, increasing motivation, opening ears, and ultimately allowing pupils to access the music more deeply, not only in relation to its delineations, but at the inter-sonic level. It also connects, again, with imaginative play, without which, musical experience would be impoverished (Bruner 1996, Swanwick 1988, Eisner 2004a and 2004b, as discussed in Chapter 3).

It is tempting for teachers and observers to regard pupils as 'off task' at times when, if viewed from a different perspective, the case might appear very different. What we as educators count as being on task does not necessarily correspond with the musical aims that pupils identify for themselves, nor the paths which lead most directly to the achievement of those aims. For example, a collection of apparently random notes heard on entering a room might suggest that a pupil is 'mucking around'. But the notes may in fact represent an experimental stage of musical play prior to the beginnings of a riff, as a pupil searches around their instrument for a particular pitch or group of pitches. An example of such a case was cited in Chapter 2, when Luke was heard playing some apparently random notes, followed by a melody that had nothing to do with his chosen song, which slowly and inexplicably turned into a riff from the song. Similarly, pupils will play 'wrong' notes, and may repeat them with further, apparently random, mistakes again and again, in ways that sound as if they are making no effort at all, and as if their minds are very far from the task. Yet later, and sometimes with a small amount of input from a teacher, as described in Chapter 2, it becomes apparent that they were experimenting in a playful, constructive way. As I argued in Chapter 3, and as has been suggested by many educationalists across a range of fields, play is a fundamental part of learning, and in the case of musical play, it is not likely to sound very organized. The case I am making here is that unless we can recognize, encourage and reward play as a legitimate part of musical learning, we are liable to leave large numbers of pupils behind.

The main reasons why pupils seemed to have enjoyed and been motivated by the project are that it allowed relatively high levels of autonomy over both the content and the strategies involved in learning. The rationale for allowing such autonomy derived from empirical observation and analysis of real-world learning practices adopted by popular musicians in the society outside the school. Their learning practices, being informal and self-governing, are therefore by default accessible to a wide range of learners who can work at their own pace and level, without reliance on a teacher or other expert to provide guidance and structure. Through adopting and adapting such learning practices in the classroom, not as a substitute, but as a complement to more formal teaching methods, we are making the autonomy of the learner into a *means* to becoming educated, not necessarily an *end* of education.

Another major aspect of enjoyment and motivation which was cited by pupils and observed by teachers concerned the types of group interaction that the project strategies demanded. This is the topic of the next chapter.

Chapter 6

Group co-operation, ability
and inclusion

> I came into the room and there were two boys at the back. One of them had the other in a
> head-lock. I went up to them and said 'Why are you doing that?'; and they said, 'Oh,' you
> know, 'Sorry Sir.' They took it as a rhetorical question. And they put their heads down:
> 'Oh, oh.' But I said to them 'No, no I really mean it; I mean why were you doing that – are
> you bored with the project?' and they said 'Oh no, sir, we're really enjoying it'; and I said
> 'Well why were you doing that then?' and they said, 'Sir, it's just that we couldn't agree
> on what we're going to do next.'
>
> *(Conversation with Brian, Head of Music, Deansgrove School, during Stage 1)*

This chapter focuses on how pupils related to each other during the project with
reference to group dynamics and individual differences. It firstly considers group
co-operation and inter-personal relationships between pupils, examining how they
organized themselves to approach learning collectively, and how leadership emerged.
Then it considers ability levels and prior experience, asking how individual pupils
of different abilities, and those who had taken extra-curricular instrumental tuition,
fared within the group. In so doing, it raises questions about pedagogic strategies of
'differentiation', and how ability and achievement reveal themselves in the music
classroom. Finally it considers issues of inclusion, specifically in relation to concepts
of ability, and in relation to pupils who were identified as 'disaffected'.

Group learning and peer-directed learning in the music classroom

Educational researchers and theorists distinguish many different types of classroom
groupings, ranging at one extreme from ones in which pupils may be merely
sitting together in groups while each works on their own individual task, to another
extreme in which every member of a group is integrally involved in a task which,
without their particular input, would disintegrate. For Bennett and Dunne, the 'truly
co-operative group' is one where the task 'cannot be achieved until every group
member has successfully completed their piece of work' (Bennett and Dunne 1992,
p. 23); and for Bielaczyc and Collins, group learning, in what they and others refer
to as a 'learning community', means that 'everyone is involved in a collective effort
of understanding' which, however, 'supports the growth of individual knowledge'
(Bielaczyc and Collins 2000, p. 271).[1] It is at this end of the spectrum that the

---

1   For discussions of the field, see, for example, Bennett and Dunne (1992), Slavin
(1995), Bielaczyc and Collins (2000), Kincheloe and Steinberg (1998), Watkins (2005), and

informal music learning project under consideration in this book lies. For whilst there is the possibility that a member of a group may make only a limited input to the group's music-making activities, the role of each group member none the less contributes an integral part to the overall musical product, whilst the choice of what to learn, how to go about learning it, how to assess the quality of the learning and how to improve the product, are in the hands of the learners.

As I mentioned in Chapter 1, informal learning in the popular music realm beyond the school places a central emphasis on group activity. I suggested that it can be helpful to understand this in relation to two main aspects. One aspect involves 'group learning', by which I mean learning that occurs more or less unconsciously or even accidentally, simply through taking part in the collective actions of the group. This includes unconscious or semi-conscious learning during music-making, through watching, listening to and imitating each other. It also involves learning before, during and after music-making, through organizing, talking and exchanging views and knowledge about music, such as deciding who will play what, sharing ideas about chords, rhythms or melodies, swapping parts, seeking each others' opinions, and so on. Although not directly *intended* to foster learning experiences, 'group learning' in this definition, both during and outside of music-making itself, tends to lead to the gradual refinement of the musical product.

The other main aspect of informal music learning that I wish to mention here is what I refer to as 'peer-directed learning'. This is not a distinctly different aspect, but is situated further along a continuum, from unconscious, implicit learning via group interaction, towards a more conscious approach in which knowledge or skills are learnt through being explicitly and intentionally imparted from one or more group members to one or more others. For example, one group member may explain a technical point, demonstrate how to play a bass line, take charge over how fast the group should play, and so on. As with group learning, the learning that results from peer-direction may arise from watching, listening and imitation; but the difference is that the learning is explicitly and intentionally guided and directed by a peer. Peer-directed learning is thus a form of learning through being *taught*.

This incidentally often involves a certain amount of leadership by one or more members of the group. Such leadership may be a constant feature of that group's interaction, resulting in a role that is always occupied by the same person or persons; or it may be a shared, informally rotating position, occupied for a few minutes by one person, then another.

---

for a philosophical examination, Lipman (1991). Group learning is variously referred to as co-operative learning, constructive learning, or more radically, co-constructive learning, in which 'responsibility for and control of knowledge becomes shared', and knowledge is built 'through doing things with others' (Watkins 2005, pp. 47–59 and 17). Various authors above, and many in Craft et al. (2001), for example, consider learning communities and group learning in relation to creativity. For discussions of the role of the group in relation to music-making outside the school, see, for example, Berkaak (1999), Cohen (1991), Davis (2005), Finnegan (1989), Green (2002a) and Pitts (2005). With reference to groups in relation to music education, see, for example, Faulkner (2003), Morgan et al. (1997) and J. Wiggins (2006).

Sefton-Green (2003) made a study of informal learning in children's uses of chatrooms and computer games. He observed that in teaching each other, children adopted many approaches which were parallel to formal teaching-and-learning situations, such as question-and-answer formats, 'master–apprentice' models, or other traditional pedagogic methods. Whilst recognizing that teachers have much to learn from pupils' informal approaches, their adoption of such pedagogic methods lead him to question the validity of the concept of 'informal learning'. However, I would suggest that rather than making the concept invalid, peer teaching and learning have some qualitative differences from an expert-to-novice teaching and learning relationship. These can be considered in three main ways. One is that learners in the informal realm seem to experience a qualitative difference between being taught by someone who is designated as a teacher and being taught by someone who is a peer, regardless of the particular teaching method. This difference relates to issues of power and expertise which frame the teaching and learning relationship. Another is that, at any rate in the project under consideration in this book, observers and learners reported that peers *did* use different methods from teachers. Thirdly, informal learning for many learners *includes teaching* one's peers, and in such cases there is evidence that learning takes place through teaching.

Group co-operation and the importance of friendship within the project

At the end of Stage 1 we asked each of the 40 groups of pupils the question: 'How well or how badly did your group cooperate during the task?' Only five groups indicated that they had experienced problems. For example, they said they had found it 'difficult to agree on a song', or they 'took too long to settle down'. Even amongst these five, however, there was agreement that overall co-operation had been good – 'we got there in the end'. Amongst the remaining 35 groups the response was invariably that co-operation had been 'easy', 'very easy' or, for example, 'we were fine'.

Pupils in ten groups volunteered that the reason for this was because they had been allowed to work with friends, and pupils in many other groups referred to the importance of friendship in response to various other questions. This issue links in to the factors considered in Chapter 5, of choice, autonomy and enjoyment:

–Hana: Yeah, plus being able to choose the groups, be with your mates and stuff, that's better.

–Shane: Working with your friends, and just sticking together to help you through the project was good, 'cause before I didn't really enjoy the old music lessons, but now it's a lot better.

–Alex: Well, we're all quite close friends, so it was easy to co-operate.

But the issue goes deeper than one of mere choice about who to work with, or the enjoyment of being with friends. Friendship plays a fundamental role within informal learning in the realm of popular music, for reasons tied up with the nature of what is being learnt. Learners nearly always begin by aurally copying music that they have selected for themselves, with which they are familiar, and with which they can identify. In groups, it is necessary to be with friends in order for such selection to take place, since it relies on being able to reach some kind of a consensus over what music to choose. This is particularly so given that there is no adult, expert or higher authority to make the selection on behalf of the learners. But most significantly, the selection of the music is no mere practical matter – on the contrary – for allegiances to particular sub-styles and/or musical tastes are major aspects of young people's identity and friendship groupings. As I mentioned in Chapter 3, there is evidence to suggest that some young people in schools may conceal part of their musical allegiances or tastes in favour of joining in with mainstream mass-mediated music. However, even within mainstream music, there are of course a number of sub-cultural, racial, ethnic, gendered, fashion and other divisions between sub-styles and their followers. Informal learning in the popular music sphere is fundamentally tied up with learning to reproduce and create music which affirms and celebrates, rather than contradicts or threatens, one's individual and group identity. Therefore, working with friends is not merely enjoyable because of any qualities of friendship itself, but it is a necessary prerequisite for the selection of the music which, in this case, enters the curriculum.

As expressed by pupils:

–Nicola: I think it's better to be like, with your friends, 'cause then, I don't know –
–Rhona: You're more likely to get on and want to do the same stuff …
–Nicola: But like, when they just put you in groups, with like people like you don't ever speak to, it's like really annoying … and you don't exactly enjoy the lessons.
–Rhona: Yeah, especially in music, 'cause loads of people have different tastes in music.
–Nicola: And plus it's practical so –
–Rhona: And so when you're with your friends you're more likely to have the same sort of taste.

–Imran: Yeah, because we got to choose our own groups.
–Charandeep: And we get along with each other so, like, it could work.
–Manpreet: Yeah, because if it was, like, other people, and we'd be like 'No, we don't want to do that, no.' But because we know what each other –
–Trishanker: But if the teachers chose the group, then –
–Imran: Because like we all agreed on one thing so like it's –
–Trishanker: Because we all like similar things.
–Harjoat: Because if she didn't like something we would change it for her, or if I didn't like something we'd change it for me.
–Manpreet: So we'd do something we all liked.

Some degree of group co-operation is needed as the foundation of group learning and peer-directed learning. If co-operation breaks down beyond a certain point, so will music-making, and with it, learning. But so long as co-operation is adequate, then simply by virtue of working together to produce a piece of music, members of a group are likely to be learning something about music.

As we saw in Chapter 2, the project teachers anxiously anticipated that group co-operation would be problematic. This was particularly due to the fact that teachers were asked to stand back and observe pupils working in friendship groups, rather than controlling group make-up, structuring tasks, setting goals and directing pupils in more customary ways. However, within the first one to three lessons, the teachers agreed that co-operation was better than normal, and they expressed some considerable surprise about this, as we will see later. Further, group co-operation improved as the project went on. One reason for this, as pupils themselves indicated and as I will illustrate in due course, may have been that they were acquiring and refining their co-operation skills at the same time as advancing their musical skills.

'Group learning' within the project

Our observations, as well as those of the teachers as expressed in interviews and meetings, contain records of pupils acting together in co-operative ways that correspond to the concept of unconscious or unintentional group learning suggested above. This happened in two main ways. One occurred during music-making itself, through listening to each other's handling of sonic materials and their relationships, watching and imitating each other, without any discussion. The other occurred in between music-making, through group discussion, exchanging ideas, planning, organizing and negotiating.

Firstly, let us take the issue of group learning through music-making. To distil from a number of observations: typically, one pupil would be playing a rhythm on a drum, which may have borne little relationship to what was in the song being copied. Meanwhile, another pupil would begin to play something that more closely resembled the beat of the song, using a different drum. No words would be exchanged. The first pupil would then start watching and listening to the second, aurally comparing what she was hearing with what she was playing, then change her playing to bring it more in line with the other's.

Basic ensemble skills themselves were also picked up in such ways. Below, for example, is a field observation, backed up with a recording transcript, of a group of boys at Westways School. Janet, the Head of Music, had identified them as 'never having done any work before', and by their own accounts, during the first one or two lessons, 'some of us didn't co-operate' and 'we didn't get our work together quickly'. However, eventually 'we knuckled down, and then we done it'. I cited an observation of them in Chapter 3 in relation to the concept of 'musicking'. We now see that such 'musicking' is also heavily related to the issue of group interaction. Here is the same observation, now viewed from the perspective of the latter issue:

> There were three vocalists, and who sang what had been well organized; one boy playing the hi-hat with his foot, and a Chinese block with his hands (which you can't hear), and another boy playing an audible cow-bell. At certain places the percussion drops out, and this was signalled by one of the vocalists, who momentarily took a leadership role, gesturing frantically at them to stop and then start again. All the boys were looking around at each other to ensure they came in and went out at the correct time.
> *(Westways School, Stage 1, lesson 3; Deepak, Jaspinder, Declan, Indulal and Sanjay's group; LG's field notes and transcript of recording)*

The description below concerns Bobby's group, who were mentioned in Chapter 5, as the most 'disaffected' and least motivated group across the seven main-study schools during Stage 1 of the project. Here they are in the third lesson of Stage 2, with each member of the band playing one or more of the simple riffs that they had learned from the broken-down versions on the supplied recording of 'Word Up':

28:25 The CD track 1 goes back on again, and the playing along continues. They have been playing non-stop now for over seven minutes. It continues. 29:58 The keyboard player is now able to swap seamlessly between two riffs; the pan player is swapping between three riffs. They are all in perfect time the whole time. Nice bit to play at induction, as they seem to be musicking. They are really grooving at around 31:50. You can hear keyboard, drums, pans (there were actually two keyboards); you can hear the other one later at c. 32:33. Track 1 on the CD stops. 32:40 Track 1 goes back on and the playing continues. You can hear that the pans and the keyboard are playing the same riffs as each other and changing riffs at the same time – this has happened without any discussion between the players concerned! It is not happening at regular intervals either, so it is a kind of uncanny interpersonal intuition. These boys have not stopped playing yet. 33:55

 (Southover School, Stage 2, lesson 2; Bobby, Drew, Liam, Austin and Danny's group
 (Bobby however, was absent); LG's field notes and transcript of recording)

It is possible to gauge, not only the fact that the boys seemed to be 'musicking' or to be 'in flow' (as discussed in Chapter 3), but also that the level of communication between them was possessed of the kinds of spontaneous inter-personal togetherness which would normally be expected of more advanced musicians. In particular, the keyboard player and the steel pans player, who were situated about two yards away from each other and could not see each other's hands, had an interesting inter-sonic communication. Bobby himself was absent on that occasion. The other four boys referred to this experience in their interview at the end of Stage 2, as having been 'excellent' and 'fun'.

In their interviews, pupils themselves identified group-learning practices, without using that expression, when they reflected on what they had been doing. Firstly, as with the examples above, some of these related to group co-operation involving ensemble skills during music-making:

–Olivia: We learned how to work in a group and also learn how to, if one person come and another person come, we learnt how to come in and how to come out, and I thought that was great because, it was quite hard, you know when other person playing and another person had to come in after a hard part, but when we get used to it we find it quite easier. I know what to do now.

Secondly, there were a number of ways in which groups organized themselves in between music-making. Pupils themselves showed their awareness of this when they were asked to reflect on how they had co-operated:

–Stacey: In partners, like, I worked with someone on the drums and then they went on the piano, and two people were on the guitars, and that was all sort of like just in partners, so like lots of little groups in one big one …
–Alyssa: And the fact that we were such a big group, [a group of 8], we'd never worked like that before, and I think we did it quite well. We didn't really muck around.

–Lindsey: And we had to listen to each other. Usually we just talk over each other, but we had to listen to what each other was saying and what notes they were playing …

–Ameera: ... like someone's trying to play an instrument and someone else is trying to play another thing, and it's all going over each other, so like what we decided to do is to do one instrument at a time and help that person. But it was quite easy to work together.

–Ian: We all really worked together, I mean there weren't really anyone bossing anyone around.

As time went by during the following stages of the project, a number of pupils became increasingly aware of the make-up of personnel in their group and of who would fit in best, but now this was not so much according to criteria of musical taste and friendship, but according to the complement of musical ability within the group. Pupils also showed concern about the different ability levels that they perceived within their groups or their classes as a whole, including estimates of both high and low ability:

–Hana: Even the poorest people who don't usually produce anything, produced something good I thought.

–Cameron: Luke is really good.
–Mantsebo: Luke is really good.
–Cameron: [To Luke:] You're not really good, you're excellent.

In interviews they were able to reflect on ability differentials, and on how they addressed them through group organization. Pupils themselves took over the role of encouraging everyone to join in, showing concern about including each other, and discernment about what tasks would be suitable for whom:

–Joshua: We know everyone else's capability, we know like what they can do, so if we picked another song, next time we did it it'd be a lot easier, 'cause we know.

–Sophie: Because we got more practice now and we know how to work as a team and we know who's good at what and what who's not good at what and all that.

–Cameron: Also the fact that like, the aftermath of the last project (that is, Stage 1) kind of contributed to this project (that is, Stage 2) because er, Jared didn't actually have a lot to do last time, but this time he had like a lot, a lot to do ...
–Luke: Well one of the things, well, after this, well if we were to go back [and do Stage 1 again] then it would be a tiny bit better because we know what everyone, because we'd be able to fit Jared in, and everyone would do something, because, because we know other instruments which Jared and stuff could play.
(End-of-Stage 2 interview)

In Stage 1, no one showed any concern for choosing group members who would be 'good' at music, and only one group showed awareness of choosing someone they would work well with as a musician, rather than a friend. We also saw in Chapter 4 that pupils began to move away from current or very recent music during Stage 3. A similar thing happened with the choice of personnel in their groups for some pupils. By Stage 4, teachers noted that some of them were breaking away from their friendship groups and choosing to work with those that they felt they could make music with more effectively. For example, the instruments they wished to play complemented each other, or one of them had a strong rhythmic sense whilst the other was a good keyboardist, and so on. This indicates to me that, as well as becoming more aware of the capacities of group members, the pupils were more aware of and concerned about the inter-sonic meanings of the music than at first. They were listening more acutely, and this in turn enabled them to plan ahead and make judgements about the demands of the music's inter-sonic meanings. They became willing to loosen their ties to some extent with delineations that expressed personal taste and identity. In these senses, their musical knowledge and skills had progressed, and their openness to a range of music had broadened.

'Peer-directed learning' and leadership in the project

As mentioned earlier, in what I have referred to as 'group learning', pupils unconsciously or semiconsciously pick up skills and knowledge through watching, imitating and listening to each other. This is distinct from 'peer-directed learning', which involves a more explicit exchange of knowledge and skills, in which one or more pupils take on something resembling a teaching role. I also suggested that a teaching-and-learning exchange between peers has qualities that are distinct from a teaching-and-learning exchange between an expert and a novice. This exchange can be understood in two main ways within the project.

The first involves a series of informally rotating roles which are haphazardly swapped between several, or all members of the group. For example firstly one pupil, then another, might take over the role by giving advice, demonstrating a riff or helping someone to hear an inner part in their chosen song. This type of peer direction operates in the form of a co-operative rather than a hierarchy. Within some groups there was a consciousness that they had worked in such a way:

> –Trevor: Well basically someone went in charge so we could actually get it done. ... I think it was actually, all of us decided we can't just mess around, so we just picked the song that we definitely wanted to do ...
> –Dylan: So, like one of us went off to work out the notes for the music and it started from there ...
> –Trevor: And then it sounded brilliant.
> –Dylan: And then we mixed it all together.

The second aspect involves a more hierarchical form, in which an individual emerges and is identified by the group members as a leader in some way. In some groups two leaders emerged, and – perhaps counter to what might be expected – worked co-operatively alongside each other:

> –Michelle: ... me and Gabrielle were sort of like helping everyone, and then it came down to what we were supposed to be doing and we were like, 'What do we have to do?' sort of thing.

However, as I will discuss later on, pupils intimated that they had quite a different response to being taught by their peers rather than by a teacher.

Teachers' views of co-operation and leadership

In interviews, the teachers strongly agreed that group co-operation had been high, and that both group learning and peer-directed learning had been far more evident and more effective than they had seen before, or had anticipated:[2]

–Sandra: ... I think their group work, and working as a team in a positive way has improved a lot. I haven't seen anybody arguing in the same way that you quite often get with kids, 'Oh, that instrument, Oh I don't want to do that.' They seem to have chosen an instrument and stuck to it and it's been accepted that that's what they're doing. And there has been a huge amount of positive encouragement between the students, so students who are naturally good at this are jumping in to help others, and they're helping others with their own parts, and they're helping others by playing to them and demonstrating what to do, and it's been, it's been really interesting to watch that come out. Whereas ordinarily I think people tend to just play their bit and then go off task and have a big fight over who's doing what, and not always work as positively in a group as they have done with this.

–Richard: [I've learnt] that actually pupils can decide their own learning, and actually if somebody is, one pupil is struggling in one particular aspect they can actually, another pupil can actually help them out. So it doesn't actually need the teacher to help them out, but another pupil can help out. So it's like peer assessment or peer teaching if you like.

On the topic of leadership, teachers expressed surprise about the extent to which leaders emerged in many of the groups. They were especially interested to see that the particular individuals involved were, in many cases, pupils who had not previously

---

2   In the anonymous end-of-project questionnaire, the 17 teachers rated the following statement: 'Pupils have benefited from being given more responsibility to direct their own learning.' The results were: 12 'strongly agree', 3 'agree' (including the two EBD schools), and 2 'neutral'. For the statement 'I have been surprised at how capable pupils are to direct their own learning', results were: 12 'strongly agree'; 2 'agree', including the two EBD schools, and 3 'neutral'. For 'I have been surprised by how trustworthy and co-operative pupils can be when given responsibility', results were: 10 'strongly agree', 4 'agree' and 3 'disagree', including one EBD school. In addition, 4 teachers ticked that group co-operation was 'well above normal expectations', 8 'above average' and 3 'average', one of which was an EBD school, and the other EBD school ticked 'below average'. For 'Group work where pupils successfully taught each other' the results were: 8 'well above normal expectations', 4 'above average' and 5 'average', including the two EBD schools. For 'group organization of own learning' the results were: 6 'well above', 7 'above', 2 'average' and 2 'below', both of which were EBD schools. For 'ability to direct their own learning', the results were: 5 'well above', 7 'above', 3 'average', and both EBD schools ticked 'below average'.

shown themselves to be either able or willing to participate enthusiastically in music lessons: [3]

—Sandra: ... we don't give ourselves time to actually watch and see them do it themselves, we just – self-directed learning, the group ethos – and the kids that help each other aren't always the kids that you expect to help each other either.

—Janet: I found it quite interesting. In one of the other boys' groups, I went into the room to see them and one boy [Deepak] was taking the leadership role, and he wouldn't usually do that sort of thing. I wouldn't imagine that he would ever be like that, and he was saying like, 'You're going to start now, you're going to start now,' and he was leading them, and I was really surprised at that. And they all followed him as well. ... Yeah. I think he must have really enjoyed what he was doing, to do that. I've never seen him do that before.

Pupils in those groups who had strong leaders recognized the fact, but no one suggested it had been a problem. Below, Abigail asked a one-off question to a group which, we had observed, had a particularly strong leader:

—Abigail: Do you think there was any particular leader, do you think anybody took control a bit to organize you?
—Ian: I reckon Stephen the drummer, 'cause like he's like really experienced at drumming, and he's like really good 'cause he does loads of different music.

Leadership and peer teaching and learning

'Often,' says Slavin (1995, p. 4), 'students can do an outstanding job of explaining difficult ideas to one another by translating the teacher's language into kid language.' He cites a body of evidence within developmental psychology, ranging from work by Piaget and Vygotsky to more recent research, which suggests that learning from a peer can be particularly effective.[4] One reason for this may be that, contrary to

---

3   In the 17 anonymous questionnaire responses, the statement 'I have been surprised to see certain individuals exhibiting musical ability' attracted 10 ticks in the category 'strongly agree' and 7 in 'agree'. The statement 'I have been surprised to see certain individuals behaving cooperatively' resulted in 9 'strongly agree', 6 'agree' and 2 'neutral'. The category 'emergence of leadership qualities in some pupils' resulted in: 8 'well above normal expectations', 7 'above average' and 2 'average', one of which was an EBD school. The category 'achievement by pupils who had not previously shown musical ability' resulted in: 7 'well above normal expectations', 8 'above average' and 2 'average'. The two EBD schools ticked 'well above' and 'above' respectively to both questions.

4   For example, Vygotsky (1978, p. 86) suggests collaborative activity among children promotes growth because children of similar ages are likely to be operating within one another's 'proximal zones of development', that is, their personal potential for learning. Similarly, 'Piaget (1926) held that social-arbitrary knowledge – language, values, rules, morality, and symbol systems (such as reading and math) – can be learned only in interactions with others' (Slavin 1995, p. 17). In addition, 'The importance of peers operating in one another's "proximal zones of development" was demonstrated by Kuhn (1972), who found that a small difference in cognitive level between a child and a social model was more

the notion that peers tend to use traditional pedagogic methods with each other, as discussed earlier, they do find different ways to teach. Within the project, many of the approaches that we observed being taken by pupils as peer teachers were quite subtle, and often involved finding idiosyncratic ways of teaching particular things to particular individuals in particular situations.

Several pupils expressed an explicit preference for being helped by a peer rather than a teacher. Notice how Madeline below indicates that she and her peers communicated *more* than they do with the teacher:

–Madeline: [We learnt] how to like communicate with each other a lot more. Because this project, we didn't have teachers to help us, we asked the rest of our group how to do it, so we communicated more.

Bennett and Dunne (1992) place emphasis on talk as the main medium through which peer learning takes place in group work, and indeed, on one hand there was much evidence of that in the project. But on the other hand, as already noted in Chapter 4, peer teaching was more often directly wrapped up with inter-sonic musical meanings than with conceptual or linguistic modes of communication. Indeed, we have only one example of a pupil *suggesting* an alternative approach to another one verbally. Rather, as a rule they found non-verbal ways to help each other, based around listening, watching and imitating. As I mentioned in Chapter 4, pupils tended to avoid using technical or non-technical musical vocabulary, in favour of gestures such as 'If I go (plays guitar); and you go (play again) …'. So, rather than using talk as the primary means of peer direction, they tended to *show* each other what to do, without using words which may have been extraneous to their goals and to their understanding. This may be particularly significant in music, whose inter-sonic meanings form invisible, non-verbal and non-conceptual means of communication. But no doubt similar issues might apply to other subjects whose currency is essentially non-verbal or non-conceptual, such as sport, art and design, drama and others, or to areas such as maths and science.

By contrast to peers' often non-linguistic approaches to teaching each other, as we saw in Chapter 5, pupils portrayed teachers as using use too much 'theory', including technical vocabulary such as 'What's a perfect fifth?' As an anecdotal observation rather than a finding of the current research, those music educators who are responsible for the education and training of teachers will know how often the beginner teacher makes the mistake of using theory to illustrate a point, when they could instead simply sing or play the point on an instrument. It seems the pupils in the project had arrived at just such an appropriate, and in some ways more advanced teaching strategy, by dint of having no other means to teach!

Not only is learning from a peer considered to be effective, but there is evidence from research on peer tutoring, that the act of teaching can enhance learning for the teacher him or herself. As Slavin explains, research in cognitive psychology has found that if information is to be retained and understood, the learner 'must engage in some sort of cognitive restructuring, or elaboration, of the material' (Slavin 1995,

---

conducive to cognitive growth than a larger difference' (p. 18). Also see Watkins (2005, pp. 122ff.) on the notion of 'reciprocal teaching', or peers teaching peers.

p. 18). One of the most effective means of doing this is by explaining the material to someone else. We have no evidence of pupils in this project explicitly stating that they had learnt from teaching each other, although the evidence from teachers' estimations of pupils' activities strongly supports such a claim. Here is one example, taken from Stage 6:

–Sandra: ... and also for the most able kids as well. People like Tanya – she's actually, I think she's got more out of this than she would ever get out of doing the traditional curriculum. Because she can help the others. But she's helping a bass guitarist instead of helping on an instrument that she plays. So she's experienced that really. ... Tanya's group were fascinating. Harry was saying 'Well we need to do Gymnopédie, because it's easier,' and Tanya was saying 'Well actually in the Penguin Café [orchestral piece] it's only me who's got to play the hard bit, we can simplify the bass part,' and they were going 'We should do the easier one,' but she actually got Harry overruled on that. She worked it out for herself in about two minutes. Although she doesn't think she does, she very quietly leads that group.

(End-of-Stage 6 interview)

As the project went on, those pupils who had taken up leadership roles during Stage 1 tended to retain and strengthen their positions. In addition, new leaders gradually emerged, so that by the end of Stage 3 it was possible to identify one or more leaders in most groups. Again, many of these leaders were individuals who, their teachers said, would not have been predicted to take up such roles. In the next chapter, I will consider how leadership roles and peer-directed learning developed during Stages 6 and 7, when classical music was introduced (as already evidenced in the quote above). For now, I wish to consider how peer-directed learning operated particularly in relation to Stage 5.

The peer workshop: Stage 5

During Stage 5 a new angle was introduced in relation to peer-directed learning, which was significantly developed by Abigail in the following year across 13 of the schools. Whilst Stage 4 involved group composition, the beginning of Stage 5 was marked by a workshop given by a visiting band or duo of pop musicians. In three of the main-study schools, the workshops involved professional community musicians, but what became most fruitful was that one school, Heath, used a band from amongst its own pupils. During the following year, this approach was adopted by all 13 schools which took part in these stages. In some cases the band members were one or two years older than the project class, and in others they were the same age. The bands, whether adult or teenage, usually played two or three songs they had written themselves, and then illustrated how the songs had been put together. This became something that we particularly recommended henceforth.[5]

---

5   In the final year of the project Abigail organized a series of events in which bands, made up of pupils from across three or four schools at a time were given the opportunity to write songs together during a day of music-making at a centre away from the schools. At the end of the day they were given guidance by musicians from the Hertfordshire Rock Project about how to introduce the songs and the composition process to their peers. They then took

Richard's school was the only one of the seven main-study schools that used a peer band during the year when our detailed research was taking place. The band was made up of pupils one year older than the project class. Richard declared a year later that this had been the aspect that 'really turned my teaching around', and that he had found it 'the most incredibly inspiring thing about the project':

–Richard: I think they really appreciated having the Year 10 band coming to perform, because they knew they were peers. I think they learn off peers better sometimes than they do off teachers. They can ask different questions, and they put things across differently in the way they think and feel, and you know the kids can grasp onto that sometimes.

The following year he introduced peer band workshops systematically for the whole year group. Teachers and pupils in the other schools who used peer bands also identified similar responses amongst their pupils.

Peer-directed learning was regarded as less threatening by pupils, because the peer teacher is only a few steps ahead of the learner. Even though the visiting musicians were older than those in the peer bands, most of them were younger than most of the teachers; and moreover they were perceived by pupils to be more like peers than like teachers. Peer teachers and visiting musicians were all regarded as kinder critics:

–Janine: And he wasn't like, and when we did it wrong he wasn't like 'No that's wrong!' He was like 'No, you've got, you've got to do it like this.' He was nice.

–Dylan: I thought we could already do that though, but they showed us a bit more.

Pupils across all the schools were also impressed with being able to see how a song can be put together by 'ordinary' people rather than stars. On one hand, this contrasted with the ways that, in pupils' eyes, teachers tend to make things appear more complicated than pupils feel they need to be. On the other hand, it contrasts with the trappings of the music industry, whose production and marketing techniques make popular music appear to be beyond the capacities of ordinary people. As I have suggested in various parts of this book, one of the potential benefits of informal learning in the music classroom is that it encourages pupils to focus aurally on their own, familiar music. Rather than locking them into what they already understand, this has the capacity to enhance their awareness of its inter-sonic meanings. Thus they are more likely to develop a greater degree of 'critical musicality' in making judgements about musical quality, and in discerning the hand of the music industry in the dubbing, engineering and marketing of musicians. Rather than being mystified by the slick gloss of the musical commodity:

---

the songs back into their schools and provided the workshops for their peers. This initiative was extremely well received by the pupils, both those who were involved in demonstrating and those who were on the receiving end of the workshops. It was a significant step which is unfortunately beyond the bounds of the present book to consider in detail. More information is available on the Musical Futures website: <www.musicalfutures.org>.

–Craig: They showed us how simple it is. Just simple things can sound good.

–Harry: It was, it was, I don't know – cool.

–Sophie: It was good as well listening to their music that they'd made up and sort of played it to us.

–Tanya: Yeah.

–Harry: Yeah, 'cause like you knew that they'd made all their songs up from scratch as well and all of that, and they don't have like a really big music you know, like pop people have, you know like big music places where they do it all on computerized, and it's all like fake. They were basically just like us but older.

A related set of issues, which were unsought but emerged from this, concerns some of the assumptions that pupils tend to make about their music teachers. Listening to the pupils talking about the workshop musicians, both those who were peers and those who were adults, one could be forgiven for imagining that the pupils' 'normal' music teachers were unable to play any instruments, or that they knew little or nothing about music! As music teachers, we hardly ever get together in bands and play songs to our pupils in styles that are familiar and celebratory for them. They rarely see us operating as musicians in any other role than as accompanists to pupil performers, filling the ranks in pupil orchestras or other ensembles, or as musical directors and conductors. Furthermore, we are nearly always playing or conducting fairly elementary or 'educational' music, because we are operating at the level of the pupils. I believe the findings from Stages 4 and 5 of the project – which are based on very exploratory work and are not presented here in detail – suggest the need for further research, in which teachers would do more live performance in front of their pupils, perhaps in bands made up of parents or teachers from other subjects or neighbouring schools, playing music that celebrates pupils, at teachers' own level. The findings also suggest that it would be worthwhile to do some further investigation into ways to involve pupils more *formally* in demonstrating to and teaching each other, as well as fostering such relationships in a more informal vein.

Group co-operation, group learning and peer-directed learning as learning outcomes

When asking pupils the question 'What, if anything, have you learnt from doing the project?', I had not anticipated that several answers would point to non-musical outcomes, and still less that several of these would centre around group co-operation. As seen in Chapter 3, the largest number of responses referred to playing instruments. A small number also concerned other *musical* issues related to group co-operation, such as 'coming in at the right time on the instruments' and 'timing'. But there were many others which were essentially not about music as such. Below is a selection taken from both Stages 1 and 2:

Stage 1

Question: What, if anything, have you learnt from doing the project?

–Ian: Working together. Like, working as a team better.

–Trevor: You need to work as a team to get things done

–Rob: Er, how to work together better, co-operation… it's probably 'cause we're doing it for something that we actually want – we want it to sound really well.

Stage 2

–Chantelle: How to work as a group.
–Makayla: And how to listen to everyone's opinion.
–Chantelle: And everyone's ideas.

–Deepak: Teamwork – how to work as a team. We should have started when we started. We shouldn't waste time.
–Sanjay: So we don't struggle at the end.

Some pupils suggested they had not worked together so well before, and others that they had not worked together *at all* before, which, as with some of their other comments about previous or 'normal' lessons, was in fact not the case:

Stage 1

–Stacey: And it was really good being able to work as a group, 'cause we've never done that before.

–Kaylee: I've also learnt how to work in a group as well, 'cause I've never normally done that before, I normally work on my own.

Stage 2

–Barjarji: Co-operating. We weren't that good before.
–Abdul: Because we had different ideas (from each other). We had different ideas what to do.

–Daniel: I think I've learnt to, like, work more as a team, like listen to each other, whereas before like I used to like, always be speaking over everyone kind of thing, but I've like got used to working as a group now better.

Pupils did not seem able to offer any reasons why they felt that co-operation was stronger than in previous lessons, or why they considered that they had not worked as a group before. We can surmise that it was – perhaps ironically – to do with the absence of direction from the teacher. For this results in an organic type of group cohesion, in which negotiation is in the interests of the members. This is quite different to the hierarchical relationship which would normally exist when a group is carrying out instructions given by a teacher. Slavin explains that the essence of co-operative learning is that it makes students want each other to succeed, whereas traditional classroom teaching makes students compete and want each other to fail. If students 'want to succeed as a team, they will encourage their team mates to excel and will help them to do so' (1995, p. 4). Therefore, co-operative group work is likely to be cohesive:

... cooperative goal structures create a situation in which the only way group members can attain their own personal goals is if the group is successful. Therefore, to meet their personal goals, group members must help their group mates to do whatever helps the group to succeed, and, perhaps more important, encourage their group mates to exert maximum effort. In other words, rewarding groups based on group performance (or the sum of individual performances) creates an interpersonal reward structure in which group members will give or withhold social reinforcers (such as praise and encouragement) in response to group mates' task-related efforts.

The critique of traditional classroom organisation made by motivational theorists is that the competitive grading and informal reward system of the classroom create peer norms that oppose academic efforts (see Coleman, 1961). Since one student's success decreases the chances that others will succeed, students are likely to express norms that high achievement is for 'nerds' or teachers' pets. (Slavin 1995, p. 16)

In the present case the team was a musical band, and the rewards available to pupils included both inter-personal rewards, and those that can arise from the enjoyment of making music that was celebratory for them.

The 'free rider'

As Slavin discusses, one important pitfall of this kind of group work is that it can encourage what he calls the 'free rider' effect, 'in which some group members do all or most of the work (and learning) while others go along for the ride' (Slavin 1995, p. 19). There were instances of this within the project, for example in the first lesson at Grange School, when Alice was heard to say to her group: 'I'm not going to do anything at all; I'm just going to sit here all year.' Overall, across the seven schools studied in detail, field notes identify six individuals in 6 of the 40 groups who were apparently doing little or nothing during Stage 1 of the project. This occurred despite the fact that, as I indicated earlier, the project 'required a performance' out of the pupils, since it is always possible to be more or less involved in producing a performance.

However, two qualifications are called for. One is that, as evidenced also in the anonymous questionnaire and discussed in Chapter 5, there was consensus among the teachers that a higher proportion of pupils than usual were motivated and involved in their work. By Stage 4 of the project Alice, for example, was integrally involved in playing the bass guitar within her group. The other qualification is that just because a pupil is sitting, apparently doing nothing while others around them are making music and organizing their tasks, this does not *necessarily* mean that they are not learning anything. Some students may need longer to adjust themselves to what is required by music-making, especially those whose previous experience has included no opportunities to make music. As I suggested earlier (Chapter 3 and elsewhere), structuring lessons into timed segments with a variety of tasks and clear goals was seen by many pupils as detrimental to their ability to 'flow', and as interruptive to their learning. In addition, some pupils, especially those who were new to the UK, may not have been familiar with the music chosen by their peers, and needed time to listen to and familiarize themselves with its inter-sonic meanings. Even those to whom these meanings were familiar, as we saw in Chapter 4, may never have listened to anything other than the lyrics before. Simply by sitting in the room while the music was being played, such pupils were becoming encultured into it through 'distracted' listening, if nothing else, and may have been engaging in 'purposive' listening.

In short, we cannot always tell whether someone is listening attentively to music by watching them; nor can we tell, by the direction of someone's gaze, exactly what they are seeing; and we never know what another person is thinking. As educators, we are perhaps too concerned that every learner should be visibly demonstrating involvement and learning at every possible point in time. In addition, according to some of the findings I presented earlier, we rarely give pupils due credit for involving each other in learning when one person appears to be left behind.

Ability, achievement and differentiation

As well as examining how pupils related to each other socially as members of a group, the research sought to investigate how they fared as individuals within the group, specifically with reference to differences in ability and achievement. We did not apply musical ability tests as part of the research, nor did we use objective measures of achievement.[6] Rather, the research drew from the considered opinions and the in-house records of the teachers on the team, taking their meanings and assumptions at face value. So when I refer to concepts of 'low' or 'high' ability or achievement here, I am placing these in the context of teachers' normal use. What matters for this particular discussion is how the teachers used these terms, and whether they perceived any differences in their own estimations of these factors as the project went on.

One Head of Music was concerned that, whereas Stage 1 stretched pupils in both the low- and high-ability ranges, it did not reach those in the middle range:

–Debbie: ... kids who are so mid-range, they will find a little pattern, and think 'Oh that's a nice pattern, I'll stick with that', and they won't actually, I've found that it was very difficult to make them do anything different other than repeat that pattern continuously. Whereas if it was in a class situation you might say 'OK, you've got that so far, what can you do with that now? And what happens next?' But because it was theirs, they felt comfortable with it and they knew it fitted so they stuck there, they didn't take it any further. I don't know if anybody else found that? ... Some of the kids could do a bit more. The low ability I was really amazed with, but some of the kids could do more.

However, by the end of the project Debbie felt more comfortable with adapting the role of the teacher, and had identified ways to help pupils of differing abilities to progress without necessarily insisting on their strict adherence to instructions.

---

6   In order to measure ability and scientifically assess whether achievement was enhanced or not by the project, we would have had to introduce a number of controls within and across all the schools, and compare the results with other schools whose variables were also controlled, and who did not undertake the project. All this would not only have required resources beyond our disposal, but would have called for a different kind of project as well as, or instead of, the present one.

Another Head of Music felt from the outset that the project reached all ability levels:

–Sandra: I think regardless of their ability this is something that everybody can succeed in at their own level because they're, they're making their own choices, they're making their own decisions about what they play, and with a bit of help from us and a bit of input from us to help them find a more simple drum beat or, you know, a more simplified chord pattern or something like that, it is possible for them all to access this at their own level.

The other main-study teachers were initially concerned that the project would not be accessible to pupils with low ability, and it was agreed that those groups who had most trouble accessing the project did tend to be designated as having low ability within the school generally. However, as time went by a majority consensus emerged that the project could help a significant proportion of low-ability pupils to shine, and many teachers were surprised to see such pupils taking part and achieving in ways they had not witnessed before.[7]

Teachers also noticed that pupils with a range of ability displayed their musicality in new ways:

–Hugh: I think I've seen and heard that kids can produce slightly different outcomes, because, you know, what we plan to do, we also kind of plan an expected outcome from what they're going to achieve. Whereas because the project was a bit more open and you know it's, the kids achieved different things on different instruments that we might, you know because they chose their own, suddenly I'm, I'm slightly more aware of who can play what and what they can do on different instruments, rather than saying 'Today we're doing this on these particular instruments.' ... Yeah, it did reveal it, definitely revealed some hidden musicality. Mantsebo, for instance, I didn't know he was quite so good on the drum kit. Because the drum kit's not ordinarily in the classroom. Now I know he can play that well.

I have already mentioned that, as well as revealing 'hidden musicality', to adopt Hugh's term, the strategies seemed to have revealed 'hidden leadership qualities'. For several individuals who took up leadership roles were ones who were not expected to do so by their teachers. It is now pertinent to add that many of those individuals were, in addition, pupils who had previously been designated as having low ability:

–Debbie: Well it's really weird, because one of the boys I was thinking of who was singing, he gave up on guitar because he thought 'Oh I'm not going to do it, what can I do instead?' ... And actually today ... he was one of the best guitarists there; and he's really low ability, he's statemented [given additional support and on the Special Needs register], he can hardly write his name. And this is what's really opened my eyes to this project. ... Kids who I wouldn't have expected have come out with things which –

---

7   In the 17 anonymous questionnaire, the results for the statement: 'Inclusion of pupils with low ability' were: 2 'well above normal expectations', 11 'above average', including the two EBD schools, 3 'average' and 1 'below average'. Also see note 3.

–Richard: They [the 'lowest ability' group in the class] were the ones who made my eyebrows raise, and think 'Yes, and I've reached and touched them.' And they, they stuck on that, they sat in that room all on their own and … they just kept at it, and at it, and at it, and at it. And initially I was concerned because I thought, 'There's no way they're going to produce the work' in the first week. You know, in the end I think personally they've probably come out the top group, and that's great.

–Yasmin: I've seen an increase in knowledge, even in the weakest children. Even in the weakest, in that they are able to pick out riffs, even if we have shown them the riffs, they will then continue on, once they've been helped they will continue on over that and try and improve that.

Regarding pupils designated as most able, there was general agreement that they were also stretched:[8]

–Yasmin: And the stronger, more musically able children, I've noticed a huge improvement just in their manner and attitude towards the subject, that they just want to get on with it, they just want to be able to produce more and more music. … No, I don't think I've noticed any deterioration, absolutely none.

Pupils who take additional instrumental lessons are likely to have greater skills and knowledge than the majority of pupils, who do not have such training. However, that is of course a different thing from having more ability, and it is important to distinguish between the two areas, one of which relates to achievement, the other to a propensity to achieve. Around 15 per cent of the pupils across the four main-study Hertfordshire schools, and less than 10 per cent of pupils across the three London schools, were taking extra-curricular specialist instrumental lessons at the time of the project. Most of these were in the realms of classical music, although a few took electric guitar or drum lessons in the popular sphere, and in Westways School some pupils had taken Indian classical and traditional music lessons in the past.[9] The extra tuition that had been available to such pupils of course meant that, regardless of ability, they tended to have more skills and knowledge than their peers. These related to general musical practices such as keeping time, and theoretical aspects of music including technical vocabulary. It was interesting to see whether the teachers would consider that such pupils benefited from the informal learning practices within the project. The majority opinion was that they did indeed benefit, and that the project represented a complement to their instrumental lessons.[10] For the project stretched them, not only in relation to the areas addressed by their instrumental tuition, but

---

8   In the 17 anonymous questionnaires, the teachers rated the statement 'inclusion of pupils with high ability'. The results were: 8 'well above normal expectations' and 9 'above average'.

9   Nationally, the proportion of pupils of this age (13–14) who take instrumental lessons is probably less than 15 per cent. However, this does vary enormously from school to school. See Lamont et al. (2003) for a helpful overview.

10   In the 17 anonymous questionnaires, the teachers rated the statement: 'inclusion of pupils who have instrumental lessons outside the classroom'. The results were: 7 'well above normal expectations', 6 'above average' and 4 'average'.

also through introducing them to other skills, as well as other instruments, that were not covered by the tuition.

For the classically trained pupils in the early stages of the project, these skills mainly centred around playing by ear. Normally they approached this using keyboards, regardless of what orchestral instruments they might be able to play. Indeed, they were reluctant – as was the case with these pupils in the 'normal curriculum' – to bring their orchestral instruments into class. One such pupil who was proficient on the saxophone did not bring in her instrument until Stage 6 of the project, but instead chose a saxophone sound on the electric keyboard during Stage 1. Therefore, to begin with, the new skills they were developing involved ear-playing, and for those who did not otherwise play keyboards, the use of the keyboard:

> –Sandra: The students who are classically trained have tended to start on keyboards, and haven't really wanted to take the risk of picking up a guitar or picking up a drum set, and have had to be encouraged into doing that, but have come up with absolutely fantastic results, none the less.

As time went by these pupils began to try out a range of instruments including electric guitars, bass guitars and drum kits. During the classical stages, as we will see in the next chapter, they began to bring in their orchestral instruments.

It was interesting that the classically trained pupils, if working in a group with other pupils who did not have such backgrounds, did not seem to put their greater knowledge and skills forward during the early stages of the project, but rather held back while other pupils, often those who had been considered low-ability, came to the fore. Many of the classically trained pupils then 'came to their own' in the classical stages of the project, when others in their groups recognized and called upon their skills. They then established their roles as leaders. The teachers felt these pupils had particularly benefited from taking on peer teaching roles, and gaining the respect of their peers, which may have been absent before. I quoted Sandra earlier on this, saying:

> –Sandra: People like Tanya – she's actually, I think she's got more out of this than she would ever get out of doing the traditional curriculum. Because she can help the others. … Although she doesn't think she does, she very quietly leads that group.

Pupils with popular music instrumental training tended to take on leadership roles and arrange music for their groups at quite early stages, and their skills were also highly valued by peers.

Overall, there was agreement amongst the majority of teachers that the task across all stages involved what has become known as 'differentiation by outcome'. This means that all pupils were set the same task, but they were expected to produce outcomes at different levels according to their various abilities. In other words, the task was adaptable to the differing abilities of individual pupils, not by virtue of being divided up into different, progressive levels of difficulty within itself, but according to what each individual produced as the outcome. Most teachers agreed that pupils differentiated the task for themselves, by selecting parts to play which matched their abilities.[11] It is worth quoting Richard on this subject at length:

> –Richard: And also because they're different skills like, you know, it's totally differentiated. But, it is differentiated by outcome rather than task, which is another sort of thing I've had to struggle with. But at the end of the day, each pupil has actually made significant progress. And I have been convinced, you know, even when the groups performed. There are one or two individuals, well several individuals, who I thought 'No I don't, I would never give them the credit to be able to do that' you know, sort of bass lines on bass guitars you know, there's a girl in one of the extracts, and I just thought there's no way she would ever have been able to do, have the option to do that, in my standard music curriculum. And so that's been really good as well …
>
> The musical abilities of the pupils in our class are very, very mixed. You've got some there who are possibly Grade 5 or 6 sort of standard musicians [music-performance grades recognized in the UK as quite advanced for 13- to 14-year-old pupils]. And you got some pupils in there who've actually got very little musical experience other than the standard music curriculum. I think they've all achieved. A lot of the pupils on bass guitars, for example, don't have guitar lessons. They picked out the notes, worked them out, and with a little bit of help managed to perform them very accurately. So I think they can walk away thinking, you know: 'I can play an instrument!' You know, so, I've been quite staggered actually, the lower end of the musical experience if you like, they've made significant progress and certainly the [last] boys' group, for example they were very, very successful in what they produced, and actually, possibly the best group, compared to groups who actually had the more musically able pupils in.

Overall, during the project, teachers came to question how they had previously judged low and high musical ability. In the past, I and others have argued that music education tends to quite narrowly proscribe what counts as musical ability, by adopting criteria that relate more to questions of pupils' musical taste and previous access to music, rather than to any specifically musical criteria of their potential.[12] The identification and reward of musical ability has, in this sense, been a reflection of educators' ideas about music and musical value, rather than a reflection of children's potential or even in some cases, their achievement. Musical ability has been measured without apparent awareness of the unintentional but systematic exclusion and alienation of many pupils, who have been negated by either or both the inter-sonic and the delineated meanings of the music that has been in the curriculum. Within the project it has been possible to trace how, by an alternative approach, definitions of musical ability can change, and how we can expand our capacity to recognize and reward musical ability in a greater range of areas. This arises partly because the approach begins by allowing pupils to select music whose inter-sonic and delineated meanings are positive for them, partly because it is a holistic approach, and partly because it is based on informal learning practices that are drawn from the 'real world' of music learning outside the school.

---

11   In the 17 anonymous questionnaires, the results for the statement 'Differentiation of tasks so pupils of different abilities could achieve' were : 3 'well above normal expectations', 11 'above average', including the two EBD schools, 1 'average' and 2 'below average'.

12   See, for example, Gammon (1999), Green (1988, 1999a, 1999b, 2003a, 2003b), Shepherd and Vulliamy (1994) and Martin (1995).

Disaffected pupils

As with the concepts of low and high ability, the notion of the 'disaffected' pupil was drawn from the project teachers' everyday assumptions and meanings. They did not tend to use the word 'disaffected' to describe pupils, but I put this term to them in a meeting, and it was agreed that it could stand for a range of traits which were variously described, at different points in the project, in relation to pupils whose behaviour or attitudes were found challenging. As with pupils of low ability, many of those who were identified as 'disaffected' rose to turn around these labels in their teachers' eyes. This occurred in three main ways. One was that they became leaders in their groups; another was that they often showed musical ability where it had not been apparent before, and the third was that they often transformed into enthusiastic, willing and co-operative pupils. I will illustrate some of the ways in which such transformations occurred by focusing mainly on one pupil, Connor from Courthill School.

Connor

Connor was described by his Head of Music, Debbie, as 'really tough' and an example of a 'problem kid' from a 'nightmare class'. In the first lesson her view of his group's work was negative:

> –Debbie: We had the strong personality group who were the 'cool' group, who got the least amount done. … they've got nothing to show at the end. Not that they haven't anything to show – they haven't even decided on a song, and that was the worrying thing.

She believed that Connor was largely responsible for this, and after the second lesson he was excluded from class. However, his group members said they could not work properly without his leadership, and begged for him to be allowed back in. After one lesson of exclusion this wish was granted on condition of good behaviour. Here is a field note taken by Abigail in the lesson following that:

> Spent about 15 minutes with Connor's group. They were on task the whole time. Connor is very much leading this group. Initially they were all practising their riffs separately (but along to the CD so sort-of together), and there was a slightly chaotic feel … After about eight minutes Connor stopped them all and said they needed to work out how to fit it all together. They switched off the CD and Connor got them to each play their parts in turn. I suggested to them that they should think about how to start and end their performance, but gave them no other help, and Connor immediately grasped onto this idea and worked out a sequence for how they should all come in and how they should fade out at the end.
>
> *(Courthill School, Stage 1, lesson 4, AD's field notes)*

At the end of the lesson, Debbie asked him how well his group had been getting along:

> –Connor: Well, we didn't have nothing last week, so to have that was really good, the tune was quite good.

–Debbie: I have to say Connor, that I totally agree with you. Last week I didn't think you were going to produce anything, but today all three of you really pulled yourself together and sorted it out. Well done.

–Connor: I thought I done quite well on the guitar 'cause I thought it would be hard to play the tune.

She also asked how he got on with the drum beat:

–Connor: Well I asked Mr X [the assistant teacher who was helping in the lesson] to do it, and he showed me. He just went (plays beat), but I thought 'Nah that don't sound like the beat', so I thought (plays beat, actually more accurate than the one Mr X had shown him).

–Debbie: Superb, and it really works doesn't it? Absolutely brilliant. Did you all listen to the keyboard as well?

–Connor: It sounds like 'Postman Pat' a bit (plays keyboard notes).

–Debbie: It does actually. But – brilliant – but OK, it does work doesn't it with the beat? Absolutely fantastic.

(Courthill School, Stage 1, lesson 5, AD's field notes and transcript)

I wish to notice four factors here, and without attempting to psychologize, to suggest some possible reasons for Connor's change of attitude, which are related to issues of group learning, peer-directed learning and musical meaning.

One factor concerns a theme which I have been developing throughout this book and elsewhere. It is that pupils' engagement with inter-sonic musical meanings enables them to recognize that delineations are not fixed components of music, but cultural constructs that are to a large degree arbitrarily related to the inter-sonic meanings. In turn, they can also recognize that inter-sonic meanings are themselves open to interpretation, according to the knowledge and skill of the listener. We have here a similar issue to pupils' willingness to use a xylophone, as discussed in Chapters 3 and 4. When they are constructively and purposively engaged with music's inter-sonic meanings, pupils are less concerned about whether its delineations might or might not affirm their identities.

'Postman Pat' refers to a theme tune for a TV programme which had long since been taken off air, and which was aimed at children aged around 3 to 6. It carries a well-known connotation, or musical delineation, of an endearing cartoon character for children, which Connor – a cool, street-wise, deep-voiced 14-year-old standing taller than his teacher – would normally, it is fair to suggest, have responded to with great negativity if the teacher had asked him to play it. One reason why this is a fair suggestion is that Connor himself was vocal on how meaningless and generally unpleasant he had found the curriculum in the year before the project: 'I used to hate, dreading coming to music …'. His apparently positive and willing invocation of this delineation is possible, it could be suggested, because his direct engagement with the inter-sonic meanings of the music he had been making, had overridden what he would otherwise have considered to be 'naff' and babyish in the realm of delineation. This overriding of negative delineations through concentration on inter-sonic meanings is one of the factors that, I would suggest, allows pupils who might otherwise present themselves as disaffected in school life, to respond positively.

(The way one type of musical meaning can override and influence another is more fully theorized in Green 1999b, 2005a or 2005b.)

Secondly, Connor wanted to change the drum beat that he had been shown by the teacher. We saw in Chapter 3 how pupils often followed what the teacher had shown them, but then played it in their own way; and how the role of the teacher in the project was to avoid correcting them on such occasions. I suggested that the open-endedness of the learning strategies, and the presence of a CD recording as the musical model to be aimed for, were less threatening to pupils than the authority of a teacher. Also, as we saw in Chapter 5, many pupils believed that 'when you teach yourself you learn more', and along with this they expressed relief that if there is not a teacher telling you what to do, 'You can't do nothing wrong.' This, as so many pupils observed, takes the threat out of the learning situation. In turn, it is likely to temper the negative feelings of pupils who present themselves as disaffected. Connor was deeply encultured in the music he was attempting to play, more so than the teacher who showed him the drum rhythm. He knew what an appropriate drum beat should sound like. This gave him some expertise which, we can postulate, acted as a motivational factor. It also allowed him that much valued 'freedom' to be the judge of not only how he learnt, but what the required outcome should be, and that affirmation of his cultural identity which he felt had been denied in previous lessons.

Thirdly, as evidenced above, Connor was recognized as a leader in his group, the members of which specifically requested the teacher to allow him back in because they 'needed' him. Such recognition will enhance the sense of belonging and purpose of most individuals. In addition, as I mentioned earlier, when a group learning task involves a shared project in which every member plays an integral part, this in itself can lead to group cohesiveness. Such cohesiveness is also likely to enhance the sense of security of all group members, and make those who would normally cause disruption more motivated towards the task, and more able to show themselves to their peers and to their teachers as being co-operative. According to Slavin:

> In a cooperative classroom, a student who tries hard, attends class regularly, and helps others to learn is praised and encouraged by group mates, much in contrast with the situation in a traditional class. ... Students in cooperative learning classes felt that their classmates wanted them to learn. In cooperative groups, learning becomes an activity that gets students ahead in their peer group. (Slavin 1995, pp. 16–17)

Thus the need for a 'disaffected' pupil to maintain his identity as such, and to keep up his reputation amongst peers, is diluted.

Fourthly, by his own account, Connor enjoyed making music in the project, perhaps experiencing some of that flow and playful engagement that I discussed in Chapter 3.

All these factors had allowed both his musical ability and his leadership qualities to emerge. At the end of Stage 1 of the project, Debbie said:

> –Debbie: I mean, they've been co-operating brilliantly. We've just had, I mean, we haven't had any instances of – we've had one haven't we, with Connor [when he was excluded] – and he's fitted in perfectly now. He's absolutely perfect. And he knows where the line

is now so he won't cross it. So that's the only – but I mean, it's amazing that he's *in* music because he's basically out of every [other] lesson, so that's good in itself.

In every interview throughout the year, Connor himself described his responses to the project in consistently positive terms. He particularly noted the benefits of having choice, 'being trusted to go into a room by yourself', being allowed to try out different instruments, and being able to 'do it yourself'. He considered the tasks more realistic – 'You're becoming a musician, I suppose' – and 'funner' than previous lessons.

Tyler, Hana and Justin

Connor was by no means an isolated case of a pupil previously considered disaffected who changed. In order to give a broader picture I will very briefly illustrate a similar transformation in the case of three other pupils, one selected from each of the other three main-study Hertfordshire schools. The reasons for selecting these is that we were able to work with these classes for a whole year. In the London schools there were similar stories, with probably only Bobby at Southover School standing out as a 'non-convert'. However, even then it must be said that Bobby was absent for a great deal of the project, and there were other circumstances which contributed to his disillusion.

Tyler   Tyler was on a school initiative to focus on under-achieving boys. Sandra, his Head of Music, put a report into my hands one day which she had dug out from the records relating to Tyler during the preceding school year. It read:

> Tyler has failed to do any work in music for the past two weeks. In today's lesson, he did not have any equipment and was constantly out of his seat. There were a number of silly instances including hiding behind the door, playing with the projector screen, etc. He was frequently talking, calling out and interrupting, despite warnings, and at the end he was asked to stay behind so that I could enter a detention in his diary. He did not have his diary and continued arguing about the punishment. He claimed that it was not his fault … and that it was my problem. He finally walked off saying that he was not coming to the detention, that he hated me and that I was ugly!
>
> *(Grange School, behaviour report for Tyler during the previous year)*

Unsurprisingly, Tyler gained nothing but D and E grades – that is, the lowest – for both effort and achievement throughout that year. During the project year, however, up to the point for which I have records, which is the end of Stage 5, he gained nothing but A grades all round. He turned up early for class to help set up instruments, he was co-operative and focused at all times, polite to staff, and helpful to other students:

> –Sandra: Well there's one group in particular that were causing me concern because they'd grouped themselves together. And they were three boys (Tyler, Bob and Chris) who had had quite serious behavioural problems in music last year and were on the verge of being removed from the class and not able to take part anymore. And within that group they've actually been almost the most positive group that there is. One student (Tyler) comes early to every lesson to set up the equipment. They just work together

so positively. There's been no problems with any of the behaviour we saw last year, so in terms of that particular group it's been fantastic. And they're keen and enthusiastic, and they smile when they come to a music lesson which is brilliant. Other groups [pause] similarly really, there's been no, absolutely no problems with behaviour.

As with Connor, Tyler was an enthusiastic leader within his group, which can be ascertained from this recording of the group (now with Ian added to it), in Stage 2 of the project:

–Tyler: Stop a minute. I've had a phat idea, yeah. I should come in first, yeah, I'll be on the drums, and I should go (plays a rhythm with a cymbal).
–Ian: Yeah and you could have a steady beat. (Tyler plays the Dizzee Rascal drum rhythm)
–Chris: Oh, I wonder where you got that from!
–Ian: Yeah, but you could have Bob come in, and then we could come in on the guitars.
–Tyler: What do you mean, like walking in on the guitar?
–Ian: Yeah.
–Tyler: I could just be going (plays a rhythm).
–Ian: Yeah, Tyler will start doing that and then Bob can –
–Bob: No!
–Tyler: No, I'm not on about that. When we start the performance –
–Ian: Yeah, that's what I mean. You can start, and then Bob can come in and then I'll walk in.
–Tyler: I could go (starts playing drum rhythm, Bob starts playing piano part).
–Tyler: And then I'll press play, and we can all go (starts playing fast rhythm drums). Did you hear that?! Shush listen! (plays fast rhythm again).
–Ian: That's wicked!
–Tyler: It kills your arms. I've had a phat idea. I could be going like that (plays rhythm) and then Bob just walks in, sits down at the piano, and when Bob sits down I could go (plays rhythm), and then you come in, skid on your knees and go 'BOOOWWWWWEEEE!' And then I'll be going (plays rhythm).
       (Grange School; Stage 2, lesson 2, AD's field notes and transcript of recording)

Notice again the role of the music's delineations and of imaginative play for Tyler – the way he conceives of the group entering the room, the skidding on the knees, and so on. I mentioned in Chapter 5 a group of girls, also considered by their teacher to be the most disaffected and least musically able in the class, who had spent time cutting out paper men and looking for an umbrella to use as props for their rendition of their chosen song, 'It's Raining Men'. I suggested that such delineations and the way they connect with the imagination are fundamental aspects of musical meaning and of musical play, and that as such they should not be ousted. This may be particularly the case for pupils who have difficulty with academic work, or come across as disaffected in school.

Hana Immediately before the project started, Hana was described by her Head of Music as a 'madam', with 'an attitude', and someone who would be likely to cause trouble. 'Watch her,' he said. She also described herself in interviews as having been a troublemaker in music last year:

–Hana: I thought 'Oh I've got Mr. X this year, what a load of rubbish, what, what is this lesson going to be like?' And then we got in and he was like, we got really excited, we was like 'woo!' not him for three weeks! [Laughter] ... The reason I remember about worksheets is because I was always in isolation in music because I hated it that bad, I always got kicked out of it [laughter]. Until this year ...

By contrast, here we see her taking a strong leadership role in a Stage 1 lesson. Note how her leadership is not disputed by others in the group, and how Hana and another girl who also displays leadership, Kimberley, work constructively alongside, rather than against, each other:

> (General noise is going on. Hana tries to quieten everybody down:)
> –Hana: One, two, three, BEEEEEP!
> (General noise from talk, CD recording and instruments.)
> –Hana: Everyone! Ssshhh! Ssshhh! Ssshhh, ssshhh, ssshhh, ssshhh, ssshhh! (Noise quietens.) Right Jade, Jade, to start opening, to start the music once, Jade, what I think you should do, is go 'one, two, three, four', and then start, and then it goes, two counts in, and then –
> –Jade: Yeah, but we need somebody to come in at the beginning.
> –Jenny: Have you got a battery in your bag? ...
> –Hana: all you lot just be quiet, until it gets to look (inaudible). I'll count, I'll count (inaudible, various voices and music.)
> –Kimberley: (Into the microphone) I'll just go, (Hana is still giving instructions in background.) 'one, two, three, four, five, six, seven, eight' – everyone. Yeah? So you do (inaudible) at the beginning, and then it can go, it can go, yeah, with the help of (inaudible). And then I'll go 'one, two, three, four, five, six, seven, eight' and everyone comes in.
> Music begins then stops.
> –Hana: Right, everyone ready? So you lot sshh, just be quiet for this first bit and then I'll count you in, yeah? Yeah, is everyone ready?
> –Jenny: Shall I go?
> –Hana: OK, sshh.
> –Jade: Are we gonna need this?
> –Hana: No, no, that's fine. Right, one, two, three, go.
> CD starts and Kimberly sings.
> *(Heath School; Stage 1, lesson 3, LG/AD's field notes and transcript of recording)*

Justin Justin came into Stage 1 of the project in the second lesson, having been excluded from a previous school. We were, unusually, not present for that lesson, but were told he had attempted to disrupt it badly. However, during the following lesson he transformed into a musically highly able pupil who offered patient help to his peers. Over the next couple of weeks, and throughout the project, his help was increasingly sought by pupils in his own and other groups, and he was consistently co-operative. At the end of the year he contributed to a teacher induction meeting for the extension schools, where he spoke in a mature and thoughtful manner about pupils' perspectives on the project. At the end of Stage 1, Abigail asked if he enjoyed being able to help others:

–Justin: Yeah.

–Abigail: … Why do you think you enjoyed that?

–Justin: Um, just to show someone else how much that, they could enjoy music.

–Abigail: Right. OK.

–Justin: Just to start, 'cause if they think music's not good, 'cause like, they can't play, they got to learn to play and learn to like it …

–Abigail: Yeah. OK. This is something that, we threw you in a little bit at the deep end with this, it was quite a difficult thing to ask people to do. What do you think about that? …

–Justin: Well it's um, it [pause] sort of you, it's good in a way. Like so people can learn on their own what to do, so build up self-confidence …

–Abigail: OK. Great. Do you feel that you've learnt anything from doing this?

–Justin: Um, [pause] sort of yeah. Um.

–Abigail: What do you think you might have learnt?

–Justin: How, about working in a team to help others, in trouble.

Justin will return in the following chapter, so I will leave this scenario there for now.

In the anonymous questionnaires to all the main-study and extension schools, 10 of the 17 teachers indicated that 'inclusion of "disaffected" pupils' was 'well above normal expectations'; with 4 ticking 'above average' and 3 'average'. The two EBD schools ticked 'well above' and 'above' average respectively. Many pupils who were initially identified as disaffected, seemed to find new ways to respond to music classes during the project. Some of the reasons for this are simply connected with the same reasons why many of the other pupils responded positively to the project: having freedom of choice, working with friends, and having the circumstantial autonomy to direct their own learning. Also, many pupils responded well to the fun, the flow, the playfulness associated with informal music learning practices. But it is not only these issues that may have caused any turn-around amongst disaffected pupils. For, as Moore (1999) discusses, bringing popular culture into the curriculum is de-mystifying at a wider social and cultural level: it shows pupils, by paradox, that the curriculum is indeed a *selection* of culture made by groups of people, not a universal set of values from which some pupils are by virtue of their cultural values, eternally to be excluded. Also, as Seifried found in his guitar class, through the adaptation of informal learning practices disaffected pupils were possibly able to 'act out' their oppositional personae.

As I indicated in Chapter 1, the project was designed for use in mainstream schools. However, three of the 13 extension schools were for pupils with Special Educational Needs (SEN), involving moderate learning difficulties, and emotional and behavioural difficulties. Although I have been unable to give consideration to these settings in this book, it is perhaps worth mentioning here that, at the time of writing, in her role as National Co-ordinator for the roll-out phase of Musical Futures, Abigail has been seeking the views of the teachers in those schools, and has made the following note of a meeting:

It was very moving to hear the teachers talk about how this approach has not only moved their students forward musically but has also given the students training in how to work together, and in how to actually be friends with one another. They noted that it is common in SEN settings for the students to lack 'real' friendships. One of the teachers said that the approach 'lends itself to peaceable learning'. We also went through each of the principles to try to establish if any of them couldn't be followed in SEN, and the only one really that they felt needed to be adjusted was that of 'haphazard learning', as students in these situations generally need structure and an idea of progression indicated to them by the teacher; otherwise they can feel vulnerable, nervous of failure and it can risk damaging their self esteem. So this is where the teachers feel that their roles have to be slightly different from mainstream project schools. But at the same time, they all had really interesting things to say about how they had tried hard to leave the ownership in the hands of the pupils, and still operate in as informal way as possible.

(AD's note of January 2007 meeting with SEN teachers during the 'roll-out' phase of the project – see <www.musicalfutures.org>)

Overall, the levels of group co-operation and the emergence of leadership and musicianship qualities were higher, and were evident across a greater range of pupil ability, experiences and attitudes than teachers had anticipated.

Chapter 7

Informal learning with classical music

This chapter concerns what happened when informal learning practices were adapted for Western classical music, broadly defined, during Stages 6 and 7 of the project. The use of classical music involved two immediate differences from the previous stages. Firstly, the music was neither chosen by the pupils nor, in most cases, familiar to them. Secondly, such music is not normally passed on, at least in the present day and age, through informal learning practices.[1] In other respects, most of the main issues that have already been discussed in preceding chapters were pertinent to the classical music stages as well, in general terms. These include how pupils approached the listening-and-copying task as music-makers, how they developed as music listeners, how they responded to being given some autonomy to direct their own learning, and how they co-operated in groups. I will avoid repeating findings relating to such themes, although they will be implicit in the discussion, since they provide its context. But my main aim is to focus on those aspects of the findings that were specific and unique to the use of classical music within the project. Although we were not able to investigate other musical styles, the findings also contain implications for further research going beyond classical music, to touch upon the use of 'world musics', or any music, in the classroom.

The chapter begins with a brief explanation of the pedagogy and curriculum content for Stages 6 and 7. It then investigates how pupils described their views and feelings about classical music before they knew that it was about to be introduced. In discussing these issues, I attempt to build up an understanding of how pupils in this age group tend to think about and respond to classical music in general. The chapter then considers how the pupils approached listening to and copying classical music as music-makers and music listeners in the light of their expressed views, and how those views began to change as the pupils continued working through the strategies. The views of teachers and how they developed are also examined. Through considering these issues, the chapter offers some thoughts on the processes that shape young teenagers' responses to classical music, and how music education might play a constructive part in those processes.

---

1   There are some notable exceptions to this amongst classical musicians, such as Julian Bream, who at the earliest stages of development adopted informal music learning practices in ways that are startlingly similar to those of popular musicians. See Julian Bream, *My Life in Music*, Music on Earth DVD 002. In the past musicians tended to learn much more through immersion and enculturation within the family than is often the case today.

The rationale, pedagogy and curriculum content of Stages 6 and 7

The rationale of Stages 6 and 7 was to continue to adapt informal music learning practices, but drawing pupils away from what they already know and into the wider world of music. Some school pupils do of course take classical instrumental lessons, and enjoy playing classical music.[2] But even amongst those pupils, as we found in this study, the vast majority rarely *listen* to classical music through a recording, broadcast or concert. Indeed, the reason why classical music was chosen for these stages of the project was partly because, as we will see, it is the most prominent category of music about which secondary school pupils of this age-group are collectively and self-declaredly most negative and ignorant. I did not anticipate that teachers, either, would want to try out the strategies using classical music, and as we will see, they did have grave doubts about doing so. But by testing the extreme case we are likely to learn more than if we had only used music that was familiar and well liked, or what I have termed 'celebratory', for pupils. The implications of the study are that if pupils can achieve certain results with a style of music from which they are so alienated, then they can do so with any style of music.

The materials used in the project can be replicated in any musical style by any teacher wishing to adopt a similar approach. If more time had been available we would have developed this area as a contribution to research in inter-cultural music education. For example, the approach could be adopted using music from styles as diverse as African, Javanese, Cuban, Chinese and Indian music, to name a few. This issue relates to a large and growing area of music education in which a great deal of research is being carried out, some of which does indeed involve various approaches to informal learning practices in classrooms using a range of music. Unfortunately, there is no space to enter further into such issues here.[3]

As well as the advantages of testing an extreme case, there are other reasons why classical music was chosen. On one hand, it is the category of music that has for many years been used as the central measurement of ability within formal music education, and it is music which, despite its relatively small listenership, has a very high profile within society, flying the flag of cultural superiority and high attainment. School pupils are culturally disadvantaged if they cannot be brought to understand that markers of high culture within music, literature, art and other realms are selected partly according to relationships of power and control in the society, rather than any *necessarily* intrinsic superiority over other cultural objects. On the other hand, I cannot accept any crude version of the relativist position that such a selection is completely arbitrary. Some music is indeed 'better' and more worthwhile than other music – but this cuts across styles, rather than involving the entirety of one style over and above another. Many adults come to love and enjoy classical music later

---

2   The proportion of pupils who were taking classical instrumental lessons in the schools under study here was around 15 per cent. This is a smaller figure than those who took instrumental lessons overall, since the latter included lessons on drum kit, electric guitar and other instruments primarily involving popular music.

3   For discussions of multi-cultural and inter-cultural music education practices and issues, see, for example, Campbell (1991), Campbell et al. (2006), Lundquist and Szego (1998) and Volk (1998).

on in life. Yet young people today are in many ways, as we will see, intimidated by and alienated from this music, which, if their ears were more open to it, they could enjoy and welcome.

Ideally, we would have run these stages earlier in the year, but due to a number of considerations they were placed in the final term, in some cases very much towards the end of the year. This perhaps gave an unintentional impression to both pupils and teachers that they were less important within the project. It also meant that fewer schools were able to try them out fully, and those schools which did try them were involved in exams, day trips, shows and other events, which often interrupted timetabling. Thus the work discussed in this chapter is more akin to a pilot study than the other stages discussed in the book. Like them, but even more so, it calls for further research.[4]

Stage 6: into the deep end with classical music

The pupils were told to get into their small groups as before. They were given a CD containing five tracks. The task was to listen to the tracks, choose one, and copy it by ear, as a group, using instruments of their choice and directing their own learning strategies. Thus in all senses, apart from the provision of the pre-selected tracks, Stage 6 was similar to Stage 1. The CD contained four pieces in the classical idiom, and one in a classical/folk/process-music style played on an electric keyboard and an ensemble of orchestral instruments. The pieces were by Handel, Puccini, Satie, Richard Strauss and the Penguin Café Orchestra.[5] Following much discussion amongst the teaching team, all the pieces were taken from television advertisements. This was because teachers felt that introducing completely unfamiliar classical music to pupils could result in a negative reaction that might be hard to overcome. In addition, as I mentioned earlier, copying music aurally is bound to be more accessible and possible if the music is already familiar to the learner, since it can more readily be repeated in the 'mind's ear' without requiring so many repetitions of the recording. The teachers, Abigail and myself together selected the pieces on the basis of the following two main criteria: that they were being, or had been, broadcast in a current or recent television advertisement, and that the melodies were not too fast, long-breathed or far-flung to make it impossible for pupils to even attempt copying them. This latter judgement was arrived at on the basis of experience. Overall, the playing standard required was above what we considered would normally be given to a

---

4   Overall, observations of Stage 6 were undertaken with 30 groups in six classes across five schools (one of which was an extension school), and Stage 7 with 20 of those groups in four classes across three of the main-study schools. Interviews took place at the end of Stage 7 with 25 groups in five classes across three of the main-study schools and one extension school. Two other extension schools did Stage 6, one of which was an EBD school; one other did Stage 6 in an adapted form. Most of the schools ran each stage for only two or three lessons, and there were sometimes gaps of two or more weeks between lessons.

5   They were: Handel, 'Sarabande' from *Harpsichord Suite in D minor* (arranged for orchestra); Puccini, 'Nessun Dorma' from *Turandot*; Satie, 'Gymnopédie' No. 1 (piano version); R. Strauss, 'Sunrise' From *Also Sprach Zarathustra*, and Penguin Café Orchestra, 'Perpetuum Mobile'.

beginner using notation, and would be more likely to be expected of a player after one, two or three years of lessons, depending of course on the player, the instrument and the interpretation.

Stage 7: modelling aural learning with classical music

Stage 7 introduced aural learning using music that was taken from the core of the classical canon, and that was mostly not familiar to the pupils, and not associated with advertisements. The pedagogic strategies were similar to those in Stage 2 of the project, in that the CD given to the pupils included the original piece, followed by separate, simplified, repeated sections of the melody and bass parts individually. This meant that pupils could hear the parts more easily, and copy them independently by playing along with the CD before putting them together as a group. The pieces included one that was likely to be familiar to many of the pupils, Beethoven's 'Für Elise'. I chose this because there are pupils in many schools within the UK as well as other countries who have already learnt to play its first few notes by ear and rote, or in other words, through informal learning practices; and many are familiar with it also because its opening has been sampled several times in popular music.[6] Normally, we tell them to leave their one-finger renditions of 'Für Elise' behind and stop 'messing around' on the piano so that the 'proper' lesson can begin. But by bringing their versions of such music into the classroom and recognizing their approach to learning these as legitimate, we are affirming pupils' natural inclinations towards music-learning, and their existing approaches towards classical music, making them count for something within music education.

The other pieces on the CD were by Bach, Clara Schumann, Brahms and Borodin, and were not known by any of the pupils.[7] These were chosen by me without discussion, on the basis of the following criteria: that pupils were unlikely to know any of them; that the melodies were, again, not too fast, long-breathed or far-flung, and that the required playing standard was commensurate with what experience told me the pupils would be likely to find challenging but accessible.

The roles and expectations of the teachers

As with previous stages, the role of the teachers was to stand back, observe, diagnose, guide, suggest and model, attempt to take on pupils' perspectives, and help pupils to achieve the objectives that they had set for themselves. Generally, the teachers had become accustomed to this way of working by that time; but they were nervous

---

6   See Yang (2006), who analyses the adoption of 'Für Elise', amongst other musical emblems connected with Beethoven, in contemporary popular culture.

7   They were: Brahms, Symphony No. 1, fourth movement theme; Clara Schumann, Piano Trio, second movement opening; Bach, Minuet in G minor from Anna Magdalena Notebook No. 3; Borodin, 'Polovatsian Dance No. 4' from *Prince Igor*. The recordings used in the study were not in all cases exactly the same as the ones in the final teachers' materials available on the website (<www.musicalfutures.org/PractionersResources.html>). Also, the excerpt from Clara Schumann's String Trio was substituted on the final CD for a flute and guitar duet by Elizabeth Claude Jacquet de la Guerre.

about it in relation to these particular stages, for different reasons than before. For one thing, they expected pupil achievement to flounder, and we all anticipated that pupils would need more help earlier. The reasons for this were partly because the music was relatively unfamiliar, the melodies were longer, and in most cases they ranged over a greater intervallic span than in the popular music of the previous stages. But the main issue was that teachers expected motivation to plummet, and with the loss of both achievement and motivation, they foresaw reductions also in application and co-operation. This was because pupils were no longer allowed to select or to compose their own music, nor even to work with a pre-selected song in a familiar vernacular idiom as in Stage 2. All of this, in different ways, had previously been a major boost to motivation, as we saw in Chapter 5. Now, both choice and familiarity were taken away. But most importantly, the teachers were by experience well acquainted with the generally negative views that pupils have of classical music.[8] I played the Stage 7 CD with its broken-down parts to the teachers during a meeting at the end of Stage 2, and explained the strategies. Some of the teachers later declared that they had thought these stages would be a 'disaster'. Sandra said she had been 'horrified' on hearing the CD, and had thought the approach was a 'completely inappropriate thing to do'.

It is worth bearing in mind that as well as the above challenges offered by Stages 6 and 7, the pupils had been working with popular music throughout the year, nearly all of which was of their own choosing or their own composition. No doubt they expected to carry on doing so, particularly since no one mentioned to them, that any change of curriculum content was on its way. In addition, the role of classical music within the National Curriculum in England, as in many other countries, has been by no means prominent in recent years. Classical music, if anything, takes second place to a variety of popular musics, and vies for curriculum time also with folk and traditional musics, jazz and other musics from around the world. The pupils in the project schools were, like pupils in many countries, not well accustomed to studying it in class.[9]

One possible manifestation of the teachers' nervousness was in the ways they introduced the strategies to the class. They had decided in a meeting immediately preceding Stage 6 that it would not be a good idea to mention to pupils that they were going to be working with classical music. Thus the task was introduced to each class

---

8   For discussions of adolescents' musical tastes and identities, see later in this chapter, and for literature, see, for example, Jackson (2005), Lamont et al. (2003), Stålhammar (2003, 2006a, 2006b) and Tarrant et al. (2002).

9   The position of classical music in the curriculum in England has been a highly contested area, particularly when the National Curriculum was first developed in the early 1990s. For the current National Curriculum, see <http://www.qca.org.uk/>. For a historical overview, see, for example, DES (1992), DFE (1995), Cox (2002), Pitts (2000), Shepherd and Vulliamy (1994), Swanwick (1992) and Rainbow with Cox (1989/2006). Today, classical music is given equal weighting with other musics in the documentation, although there would be a case for suggesting that it is still implicitly valued more highly by the exam system as a whole. In a survey of secondary music teachers in England in 1998 (Green 2002b), classical music was given less prominence than popular music, and almost the same as 'world music', with jazz, twentieth-century classical and folk musics close behind.

with minimal explanation, and pupils were left to discover the CD's contents for themselves in their small groups. Two teachers told their classes that the music was from adverts, but in the event it became clear that pupils none the less expected it to be in some kind of vernacular idiom. In addition, the teachers avoided any whole-class listening activities at the outset, even though such activities would have been commensurate with the project, as in Stage 2, and would have represented one way to familiarize pupils with the music that was to be copied.

Teachers in one main-study school and one extension school, which was not included in the observation or interview data collection, attempted Stage 6 in a more formal way, more akin to the 'normal' curriculum. One told pupils to ignore three of the tracks and choose between only Satie's 'Gymnopédie' or the Penguin Café piece, and the other only allowed 'Gymnopédie'. The former also told pupils not to attempt to copy the music, but to improvise over it; the latter went in the opposite direction and wrote the names of the notes on the blackboard. These approaches therefore did away with many of the central characteristics of informal learning on which the strategies drew, including: the small amount of choice and autonomy that were involved in selecting one out of five pieces; the requisite group discussion and co-operation; the strategy of learning by aural imitation prior to creating one's own music; and the corresponding necessity to listen purposively to the music. As we will see, these things were implicitly and explicitly identified as crucial by pupils when they evaluated their responses to the classical stages.

Pupils' views of classical music

At the end of the term before Stage 6 of the project began, we asked around 200 pupils in 41 groups across eight schools (the four main-study schools plus four extension schools) the question: 'What kinds of music do you like, and what kinds do you dislike?' Whether their responses referred to popular, classical or any other style, the reasons they gave for *not* liking music were more graphic than their reasons for liking it. These negative reasons related to both aspects of musical meaning that I have been discussing, and were common across many interviews. In relation to inter-sonic meanings, pupils particularly mentioned negative responses to the texture and the sound itself, especially when these involved vocalizations such as 'screaming', 'snorting', 'shouting' or going 'woo woo'. Such expressions were used in relation to heavy metal, 'greebo' and opera, amongst others. In relation to delineation, negative responses were sometimes associated with lyrics, as in: 'Gothic I hate, and I can't stand listening to people screaming about eating guts'; and sometimes they were associated with general extra-musical references or connotations, as in: 'I don't like country because it reminds me of like, donkeys – yeah, grass and flowers.'

Most pupils did not mention classical music at all in response to our question. Typical answers, for example, were: 'I like hip hop and I don't like pop', or 'I only used to like R'n'B but now I like hip hop and rock, and everything really.' However, it became clear that 'everything' for many pupils did not include classical music, which, by that token, therefore did not really count as music for them:

–Harry: I like loads of music … I like pop, I like hip hop, I like basically everything, I even like some like soft rock, like Stereophonics and all that. I mean like I'll listen to anything, as long as it's good.
–Brianna: No I hate rap, I seriously hate rap, R'n'B and rap.
–Harry: You don't like R'n'B?
–Abigail: What about outside pop and rock – for example the sort of stuff we were playing in –
–Harry: Oh, classical! [Laughter]
–Abigail: Not necessarily classical, just other music.
–Harry: I'm not exactly going to go home and like read my book and listen to classical music!
[Laughter]
–Michael: I like all music.
–Stephen: Yeah, I like all music.
–Aaron: Everything apart from classical.

If pupils did not mention classical music of their own accord, we asked them specifically what they thought of it. Overall, the response was very negative indeed. Only eight individuals across the 41 small groups had even faintly positive things to say about it; and only one group had a consensus that classical music was acceptable. However, even that view was hardly presented in glowing terms:

–Abigail: OK. What about classical music? Do you have any opinions on whether you like or don't like?
–Jasmine: It's alright.
–Nick: It's alright I suppose, 'cause it can calm you down.
–Marcus: Yeah, it's sort of neutral.
–Nick: Makes you go to sleep.
–Sammy: Yeah.
–Nick: Not in a bad way.
–Marcus: I can listen to it.
–Jasmine: Yeah.
–Abigail: So you do listen to it?
–Nick: Yeah. If you're like feeling ill or something, 'cause it really like calms you down.

In the other groups that contained one or more pupils who were willing to say something less than negative about classical music, such an opinion was expressed somewhat against the grain of the group consensus, and by someone who was willing to stand out from their peers:

–Abigail: OK. So, you said that you didn't like classical music. What do the rest of you feel about that? Like, dislike?
–Georgina: I like some classical music, I don't like some.
–Vicky: I don't like it.
–Ameera: I really, really, really don't like classical music. It's really boring and depressing.

–Amy: I don't really like it.
–Lucy:: Yeah?
–Amy: I just think it's boring.

–Lucy: Mmm. Anybody else?
–Nicola: I think some of it is alright.
–Rhona: Yeah, some of it is alright.
–Nicola: But not the ones with like the singing in it.

Even some of those individuals who made faintly positive statements at some point in the interview also made negative statements at other points, such as Lindsey below:

–Ava: I hate classical.
–Vicky: Oh yeah.
–Abigail: Why do you dislike classical?
–Lindsey: 'Cause it's so boring and it's just a bit pointless.
–Jacob: It just goes over and over again.
–Vicky: It's like [inaudible].
–Lindsey: Some bits are good.

I mentioned in Chapter 3 that some pupils keep secret about their *popular* music tastes for various reasons, one of which is likely to include peer pressure to conform to mainstream definitions of socio-musical belonging. Although the pupils in the groups above did not exert any evident peer pressure on each other, there are grounds to suppose that some of the general negativity in those and other groups, was indeed the result of a huge groundswell of implicit, assumed and unspoken pressure both from peers and from the media. To stand out against that involved taking a risk. For example, Gabrielle made it an admission of a 'secret' that she liked G4, a vocal group with a slightly classical edge, no doubt anticipating the shocked response of her peers:

–Gabrielle: Well my secret is that I like G4.
–Madeline: Oh God!
–Abigail: OK.
–Gabrielle: That's my secret.
–Abigail: So that's kind of a bit opera/classically.
–Gabrielle: Yeah, I think it's good.

Many adults might be tempted to dismiss pupils' negativity about classical music on the grounds that the negativity is not a 'real' indication of their responses, but is rather a result of social pressure to conform. If so, the argument would run, there might be many pupils who do 'really' like classical music 'in secret', but they just 'pretend' that they do not like it. This would be the case, particularly with those pupils who take classical instrumental lessons, and therefore have more familiarity with the inter-sonic meanings of classical music and presumably gain some enjoyment from playing it themselves (a presumption which is implicitly borne out by evidence later in this chapter). If such pressure does affect pupils' willingness to express certain musical allegiances – whether in the classical or any other sphere – however, then that is clearly a cause for concern amongst music educators. Music is fundamentally a social practice, and we form our allegiances to it in relation to our social and personal identity. Furthermore, the pressure on pupils to dislike classical music does not stop at social relationships amongst themselves, but is fundamentally wrapped up with the very delineations of the music itself. For as we will see shortly, the idea that classical music is not suitable for their age group is probably one of the music's strongest and most unquestioned delineations for them. If pupils have negative relationships to delineated meanings for whatever reason, as I have argued earlier and elsewhere, the likelihood is that this will spill over to also negatively affect their responses to inter-sonic meanings (Green 1988, 1997, 1999b, 2005a, 2005b, 2006).

Of the remaining pupils, negative views were expressed in vociferous and colourful terms. Often they said they 'don't like' or they 'hate' classical music, especially mentioning opera; and they gave reasons including, in more than one case and often many cases, that it is: 'boring', 'old', 'slow', 'depressing', 'shit', 'crap', 'rubbish', 'pretty bad', 'long', 'gay', 'weird', 'cheesy' and other epithets. Many said they found it repetitive, in accusations such as 'it just goes over and over again', 'it goes on for ever' and 'it drags on and on'. They did not like the fact that either there were no words or they could not understand the words – 'It's all in Italian or Latin or some language that you can't even understand – what's the point of that?' Many associated it with negative images of performers – 'It's just a load of fat people shouting.' Large numbers considered it to be suitable only for 'old people', and associated it mainly with elderly relatives, including parents, grandparents or in one case, a great-grandparent: 'It's something my Nan would listen to, or my Dad's Nan.' For many pupils, it was something that they were forced to hear in circumstances from which they could not escape, notably the car. Otherwise, they declared that they mostly heard it 'only if it comes on the radio, and I switch it over to the other channel'.

Why do so many pupils so forcefully express antipathy towards classical music, and how do their opinions relate to their personal experiences as music listeners and music-makers? I wish to suggest that it is helpful to understand pupils' responses in relation to both inter-sonic and delineated meanings. From the project data we can observe that they tend to be highly unfamiliar with the inter-sonic meanings of classical music. This is partly a result, and partly a cause, of the fact that they very rarely listen to it, or even hear it in the background. As I have suggested, unfamiliarity with inter-sonic meanings is likely to lead to a dulled response, since the listener will be unable to detect patterning, similarity, difference or other relationships between the musical sounds, both within one piece of music and between pieces. Further, such a negative experience of inter-sonic meaning is likely to spill over so as to negatively influence listeners' responses to delineations as well. On top of that, the delineations of classical music, as we have seen, are already overwhelmingly negative for this age group, regardless of any personal experiences of its inter-sonic meanings.

I hope to show that young teenage pupils are not in any simple way 'prejudiced' against either the inter-sonic or the delineated meanings of classical music. Perhaps as adults we have forgotten what it was like, musically, to be a teenager; perhaps most of us who went into music teaching, not being musically typical within our teenage peer group, are in any case poorly placed to understand the perspectives of the majority; perhaps we do not really know much about what it is that teenagers like and dislike in music, or why they respond to it as they do. Perhaps, on their part, teenagers are more self-aware and able to articulate thought-out reasons to justify their tastes, and are more open-minded, able and willing to comprehend unfamiliar styles than their talk and behaviour would initially seem to suggest. In the remainder of this chapter I hope to cast some light on those possibilities, and to connect them with some of the overarching issues currently facing classroom music education.

Observations and interviews in Stages 6 and 7

Given the pupils' negative views of classical music, we were interested to observe how they responded when they first listened to the CD provided in their small groups at the beginning of Stage 6. As already mentioned, they had not been prepared for what was on the CD, which comprised five tracks of music by Handel, the Penguin Café Orchestra, Satie, Puccini and Strauss (see note 5 for details). I will illustrate some of the more violent responses that we witnessed or audio-recorded shortly, but first of all I will give an indication of the more mild type of response that in fact occurred in the majority of the groups. For despite all their misgivings, the teachers agreed that in most cases pupils applied themselves to the task, certainly with less enthusiasm than in previous stages of the project, but without the level of antipathy and the corresponding lack of application and co-operation that had been feared. There were some initial expressions of bemusement and anxiety, with politely put questions such as: 'Miss, can I ask why they're all peaceful songs?', 'Miss, why are all the songs slow?' and 'Miss, can we have another CD - ours is all classical music?' But overall, pupils relatively uncomplainingly 'took it on board', as Head of Music Debbie put it.

Although the music was familiar to some pupils through television adverts, this proved to be the case only for some of the pieces for some of the pupils. Even if they recognized the music, they were often unsure of the exact context in which they had heard it before:

> Madeline's group are playing the Handel [on the CD].
> –Gabrielle: Where have I heard that?
> –Madeline: I recognize this, it's like –
> –Michelle: I recognize this but I don't know where from.
> –Gabrielle: I don't know where I recognize this from.
> They play the Penguin Café Orchestra piece and don't comment. Then they play the Puccini.
> –Michelle: This is um –
> –Gabrielle: It's 'Nessun Dorma'!
> –Michelle: This is in 'Bend it Like Beckham'!
> –Gabrielle: This is 'Nessun Dorma'!
> Laughter when Pavarotti starts singing.
> –Michelle: I don't want to sing this!
> –Madeline: I'm not singing this!
> Laughter.

> *(Courthill School; Stage 6, lesson 1, field recording, no*
> *teacher/researcher present, AD's transcript)*

Overall, the pupils' initial responses to hearing the music seemed to include far more attention to delineations than had been the case when they engaged with their own music, or with the 'Word Up' track in previous stages. In some cases their first discussions concerned what product the music promoted on television, and in others a wide a range of other delineations in the form of explicit extra-musical references:

–Jacob: Ballet! Rob, this is ballet!
–Rob: What?
–Jacob: Ballet!

The conversation below throws up a veritable salad of delineations crossing a span of time and a disparate array of cultural forms. There is also a reference to the content of lyrics (which were in Russian), and the – no doubt sarcastic – possibility of changing them to bring them into line with teenage culture:

> 'Für Elise' comes on and Harry momentarily starts singing it. The radio is put on, and Harry seems to be juggling with a maraca.

–Sophie: I like this one.
–Tanya: Yeah, I like this one.
–Harry: This one sounds too medieval, you know like, we could all like – it reminds me of Peter Pan, when like they all wear those funny little outfits.
–Daisy: It reminds me of castles.
–Harry: Yeah, and like –
–Sophie: You know like Mario Brothers, those game things, they always get like 'doo doo doo'.

> Borodin comes on.

–Harry: I like this one! I could sing! [Starts singing in a high voice]. Maybe we could do that but we could change the words – 'Yo, yo, what's up?'

(Grange School; Stage 7, lesson 1, field recording, no teacher/researcher present, AD's transcript)

One way to interpret the pupils' apparently increased attention to delineations at the beginning of these stages is that because the inter-sonic meanings were largely unfamiliar and the pupils' responses were therefore negative, the pupils were 'thrown' into delineation, almost as the only way of gaining access to the music at all. As time went by, and they began to manipulate the inter-sonic meanings as music-makers and to hear more inter-sonic detail as music listeners, this tendency to focus on delineation waned. For example, although their initial talk was sometimes about the adverts associated with the music or other cultural associations, when they started listening purposively and choosing a piece they ignored such delineated meanings, and made their choices according to the music's inter-sonic properties and relationships instead. Thus pieces which advertised products that were associated with teenagers, such as Handel in the Levi jeans advert, were by no means favoured over and above pieces that advertised more mundane things such as eating cornflakes or buying electrical goods. From this I would tentatively suggest that it is not fundamentally delineation that throws teenagers off classical music, or off any music, but that delineation may be the main handle with which they open the door to music that is otherwise unfamiliar in the first instance. This may indeed be the case for most music listeners, including adults.

Later on, when they described their responses on first hearing the music, the pupils indicated that they had felt shock and disbelief. The largest category of response, from pupils in 21 out of the 25 groups interviewed, was that they thought the task was going to be much too hard: 'How the hell are we going to make this work?'; 'All of them are well hard!' and 'Oh my God, what are we going to do?'

We have field notes suggesting that although pupils did 'mess around' more than in previous stages, this was not enough to bring group co-operation and application to a halt. Overall, the groups began to approach the task in ways that were similar to the previous stages: listening, discussing features of the music, focusing firstly on delineations then inter-sonic meanings, choosing a piece, then beginning to select instruments, playing along with rhythms and starting to search for pitches.

The fact that they had already undertaken the previous stages was considered by all the teachers to be crucial. I asked them all the (rhetorical) question:

–Lucy: Do you think they could have done this without having done the previous stages?
–Sandra: [Laughs.] No! No chance. I think we would have had a lot more non-participants, just not being able to access it at all, not having the listening skills to be able to pick things out on the CD, not even understanding the task ... I think if you gave that to Year 9s at the beginning of Year 9 there is just no way. You would have behavioural difficulties probably, you know wandering about rooms, not staying on task ... They wouldn't understand the task, and you know they wouldn't have the established group ethos that this lot have got which has developed so well, and they know exactly how to work together and exactly what they'll play, who will do what, and you know, that's really important to establish that first really.

–Richard: They may well have rejected it completely. Because ... they may have been more educated than they realize at this point, that could be a possibility. They are now used to the skills of sitting down, listening and working out.

–Debbie: [The previous stages are] just underpinning it and holding the thing together. If this had have happened in the first stage they wouldn't have had a clue. But because of what they've done, although it's very difficult, the whole concept is different, the culture is different, but they're not letting go of it.

In some groups occasional, rather grudging, indications emerged as time went by that their initial negativity could be transmuted into something different:

I spent some time with Craig's group who initially were being very negative about the task, especially Josh and Trevor, saying things like 'classical music sucks' and 'this task is crap – why can't we do our own music again?'. I encouraged Dylan to work out the notes for the Strauss on the guitar, and him and Tom (on drums) immediately started playing together and being a little more enthused. I showed Craig and Ian the basic notes on the keyboard, and Trevor where C was on the bass guitar, and then left them. When we came back to hear them perform, in the space of ten minutes they had put together their own 'rocked-up' version of the Strauss, and their enthusiasm had completely shifted to 'this is cool'. ... After the lesson Tom said 'That was the most amount of work we have done in a lesson so far, and we did it all by ourselves.'

(Grange School; Craig, Ian, Josh, Trevor, Adam and Tom's
group; Stage 6, lesson 3; AD's field notes)

As already mentioned, the pupils were encouraged to arrange the music for their own choice of instruments. For many of them this was a relief and a positive aspect of the task. One reason for that relates, as in previous stages, to their appreciation of being granted choice and some autonomy to direct their own learning. But not only that, for it also enabled them to select instruments which, on one hand, carried more affirmative delineations than those on the recordings, and on the other hand, produced more affirmative sonic qualities. However, interestingly, pupils did not grasp onto the idea of using alternative instruments easily. They had to be reminded about this option as we went around the groups at the start. One example is Tyler, who was featured in Chapter 6 as 'disaffected', and was on a school initiative to focus on under-achieving boys. He had been playing the drums enthusiastically all year, and was dismayed on listening to the CD that 'None of these have got like, drums in them!' He had to be guided to the idea that the music could be arranged for different instruments, and shown how to put a drum beat to the different tracks. It proved almost impossible for him to play in triple time. However, once he had understood the possibility of arrangement in principle, his motivation and ability to carry out the task returned, at least enough to enable him to continue attempting the task and co-operating.

One reason for pupils' hesitation to arrange the music for different instruments was probably because, as in Stages 1 to 3, they were keen to try to replicate the inter-sonic meanings of the music by choosing instruments whose sound was as close as possible to the original. This I find particularly interesting, given that the music, including the sounds made by many of its instruments, was of a sort that they were so negative about. One result of this desire to be faithful to the original, which has a different slant to the approach we encouraged for Tyler described in the paragraph above, was that there was an expansion in the types of instruments they selected. For pupils such as Tanya and Kristen in the group below, who took or had taken lessons on orchestral instruments, the task engendered a new motivation to use their instruments inside the classroom. As I will discuss below, this new motivation partly resulted from the fact that other pupils now valued, rather than disdained, the skills involved in playing those instruments. Sandra, their Head of Music, said they had never brought their orchestral instruments into a class lesson during the preceding two years at the school. Notice also Linda's allusion to the violin:

> As soon as the Satie comes on they start discussing what instruments they could play it on. This doesn't happen with any of the other pieces. They have a vote on what to do. They think that the Satie is the easiest so want to do it.
>
> –Kristen: If we had the music [notation] we could play flute and clarinet.
> –Sofia: Yeah but what's the song called?
> –Stacey: I know it, but I don't know it.
> –Linda: But that's a violin playing it.
> Go back to listening to the Satie.
> –Sofia: It's pretty!
> *(Grange School, Stage 6, lesson 1, no teacher/researcher present, AD's transcript)*

Other instruments that were brought to class for the first time by pupils who took lessons on them included the trumpet, saxophone, clarinet and flute.

Not only those pupils who took instrumental lessons, but also those who did not, began to experiment with a greater variety of classical instruments, or a greater range of instrumental sounds on their electronic keyboards. For example, Jenny chose a violin and started playing it with wide bow strokes on the open strings, never having held the instrument before. One group used a different voice on the keyboard for each part of the Brahms, and changed voices at the end of each phrase. Another group (containing 'disaffected' boys) found a harpsichord sound for the Bach, and combined it with a glockenspiel. Teachers agreed that pupils normally do not experiment in class with different voices on the keyboards, but simply use the default setting. Although we did not discuss this, I am sure they would also agree that, by contrast, if given a keyboard to *play* with, the first thing that children (and adults?) of any age will do, is experiment with the different sounds it can make. This tendency again suggests a disjunction between the notions of musical 'work' and musical 'play', such that 'work' involves a decrease in free, goal-less experimentation as well as enjoyment. Whereas such a decrease is educationally necessary at times, if introduced right from the start, and if it is the only approach to learning, it would seem to miss out on a range of opportunity to motivate pupils and engage them directly in the perception and production of inter-sonic musical meanings.

The teachers agreed that in general, pupils with relatively lower musical ability struggled more in the classical stages of the project, and required more help than before. However, they also confirmed that overall, differentiation by outcome none the less continued to occur, so that all pupils could access the task and achieve at their own level. Generally, pupils with high ability were seen to be stretched more in these stages: 'especially the kids who are gifted and talented; it gives them a little bit more to do' (Debbie).

The teachers also agreed that those who took classical instrumental lessons and could read notation, as well as having other musical skills and knowledge, were in demand from their peers and were stretched in these stages. As I have mentioned before, the project was intended, not as an alternative, but as a complementary approach to such pupils' classical training. It rewarded them for playing by ear, and made aural playing a more central and legitimate part of their education. It also combined with their existing skills to encourage them to take on leadership roles, arranging and directing music for their groups. This was the case in earlier stages, particularly the composing stage of the project. But during the classical stages a new development was that, as distinct from their previous shyness about bringing their orchestral instruments to class, as I have already mentioned, some of them tentatively began to do so. It is likely that their previous reluctance was the result of peer pressure. Pupils who do not play instruments often feel that those who do are 'show-offs' (as stated by some in interviews). Such feelings and the pressure to which they lead are, in turn, likely to result from a sense of inferiority on the part of the majority of pupils, who do not have the same skills or perhaps the privilege of instrumental lessons. Yet those receiving classical training had gradually begun to use their skills more within the group, and found these to be appreciated and respected by their peers. In Chapter 6 I referred to the arguments of Slavin (1995) and others that traditional classroom teaching makes pupils compete and want each other to fail, whereas co-operative group learning causes pupils to want to succeed as a team, and thus to encourage and help each other to excel. This perspective can throw light on why the able pupils were more prepared to display their skills in the project setting than in the 'normal' curriculum.

However, although many of the classically-trained pupils now brought in their instruments, they none the less displayed attitudes connected with those instruments, which *contrasted* with their own earlier informal approaches within the project. These attitudes also contrasted with the more informal approaches that the rest of the group continued to adopt. As with many young musicians who experience both formal education and informal learning, they did not seem to make a connection between the two approaches (see Green 2002a). For example:

> Michelle got out her clarinet for this lesson (trying to learn 'Für Elise'). She seemed nervous about trying to learn it by ear and wanted to go and find the notation on the Internet. She seemed worried about playing the wrong notes. Interesting, as she hasn't been inhibited before on other instruments, and has tried various instruments including singing, but seemed very shy when trying to play the clarinet, which is *her* instrument. Seemed more important to her to get it right.
>
> *(Courthill School, Stage 7, lesson 1, AD's field notes)*

Also observe that in an earlier quote, Kristen looked around for the notation – 'If we had the music [notation] we could play flute and clarinet' – as if it would not be possible to play them without it! It took a while for these pupils to bridge the connection between formal and informal approaches, and realize that they could aurally copy music from a recording on their orchestral instruments by ear.

The pupils' 'classical' musical products

What did the pupils' 'classical' products sound like? As already indicated, some of the lower-ability groups did have trouble keeping in time together, and some individuals found the melodies difficult to sustain for longer than two or three bars. However, overall the teachers agreed that the musical products were of a higher standard and quality than they had expected. Furthermore, even in the weakest group the tendencies which I am about to describe were none the less present.

One of the most interesting aspects was that pupils played their arrangements at precisely the same speed as the original.[10] Also, where mistakes were made, these were rectified as the music flowed on, without interrupting the pace. This arises from the tendency, identified in Chapter 3, that even if one person was playing out of time with everyone else, the group would simply keep going and eventually, perhaps even in the next lesson, would come into time. These tendencies are very different from

---

10   Some of the performances, especially the Beethoven, were at a different tempo from the recordings that are now available on the website. This was purely to do with the availability of recordings. Therefore, any reader who wishes to compare the tempi of the pupils' performances on the website with those on the provided recordings will find that they do not match as precisely as they matched the original. Recordings of pupils' products can be heard during and after the documentary film of these stages, on <www.musicalfutures/ Practitioners Resources.html>, Section 2.

learning by notation, in which the performance is nearly always slowed down during the first stages of learning, and for many players continues to go along haltingly right through the latter stages as well. If a mistake is made, the novice classical player who is reading will nearly always stop and interrupt the pace in order to correct or recover from it.

The pupils' tendency to play at speed had been less surprising when they were playing popular music in the previous stages of the project, since the riffs they chose to copy, or those which had been provided for them, were in most cases less demanding to play; and when they were improvising or composing, they naturally played within or close to the limit of their abilities. In Chapter 3 and elsewhere in this book I have suggested that they experienced something akin to Csikszentmihalyi's concept of 'flow' in their approaches to learning, and also that they found the CD a less threatening authority than a teacher. It enabled them to play along with the original at the same speed, make mistakes and pick up again without the usual pauses that are associated with notation-based sight-reading and learning. Now I would suggest that this tendency towards 'flow' extended into the classical stages of the project, producing performances that had more 'feel' than would normally be the case in classroom work or in music learnt from notation by most novices.

As well as the above tendencies, there were many instances across all project stages, of pupils interpreting the music in ways that were different to the recordings. This partly came about because they arranged the music for their own selection of instruments, but it also concerned the actual notes played. It was more noticeable in Stages 6 and 7 than when pupils had been working on popular music or on their own compositions, partly because, as I mentioned earlier, the melodies as well as some of the bass lines were more long-breathed and far-flung, thereby being a little more demanding to play. For example, pupils altered the music either by inserting or omitting a few notes, slightly changing a melodic contour, playing a note that was different to the original, playing in a different mode to the original, or consciously adding an introductory section. Whether such alterations could be considered as improvisations, arrangements or mistakes is something I will discuss in due course.

Further research would benefit from playing recordings of the pupils' performances to a panel of experienced music teachers and other experts, and asking them to judge quality systematically in relation to accuracy, 'feel', grade level and other aspects. This was not possible in the present study at a systematic level, but I have played examples to a number of experienced music teachers, lecturers and other educational experts at conferences and in seminars. Comments are often made to the effect that the performances have more 'flow' or 'feel', without necessarily using those words, than normal. One written response in an email from a colleague illustrates this:

> The music that the young people produced in the final classical music task was very moving for me. To my ears, which are very tuned into the music found in schools, the usual dreary, drab efforts had been transformed into sparkling, creative gems, even though most of the instruments were the same as usual. The performances we heard were musically convincing, and probably would develop further with more opportunity to do so. Very exciting musical experiences to hear!
>
> *(Dr Marion Long, email communication, 2005)*

Overall, by the end of Stage 7 the few teachers who were involved all considered that the pupils' achievement and products were of a higher standard than expected, and were different to pupils' normal products in ways such as those suggested above.[11]

Justin and Chris: disaffection, musical taste and the construction of musical ability

I will now consider a particularly strong negative response from Justin. He was introduced at the very end of the previous chapter, as a pupil who had originally been identified as 'disaffected', but who had subsequently shown considerable musical ability, as well as co-operation and patience in helping his peers. At the beginning of Stage 6 we caught his response to the classical CD in a field recording which he possibly did not realize was being made:

> Justin's group. Listening through to the pieces.
> –Justin: Why the bloody hell do we get all this shitty crappy classical music?
> –Billy: The second one's better.
>   They play the Satie.
> –Justin: Next!
> –Rob: Oh, I know that one.
> –Anthony: This one's funny.
> –Michael: It's all piano.
>   Someone starts momentarily playing a drum rhythm to the Satie. Put on the Strauss. Rob starts picking out notes on the guitar immediately.
> –Anthony: I can do that!
>   Someone starts playing a drum.
> –Rob: I've got that note – that's the last note.
> –Justin: 'Star Wars'!
> –Billy: We need like a drum beat and stuff.
> –Justin: [Shouts] I'm never going to be able to play that shitty, classical fucked-up music.
>   Discussion about which one to do. Alex says the last one is best.
> –Justin: I'm going to go and ask if we can have more music, 'cause this is all shit.
>   Goes out of room. The others carry on listening through and discussing which ones they like. They then lock Justin out of the room.
> > *(Broadacres School, Stage 6, lesson 1, field recording,*
> > *no teacher/researcher present; AD's transcript)*

Field notes contain a record that must have been taken from outside the room just at this point:

> Justin came out of his room after having listening through to the CD and said to Yasmin, 'Miss can we have another CD - ours is all classical music?' He looked a little disgruntled when she explained that that was what everybody had.
> > *(Broadacres School, Stage 6, lesson 1, AD's field notes)*

---

11   Of the five who responded to the relevant part of the questionnaire, 2 ticked 'strongly agree', 1 'agree' and 2 'neutral' in response to the statement: 'Pupils' skills and knowledge progressed well through Stages 6 and/or 7.'

After re-entering the room he gradually began to co-operate. By the first lesson of Stage 7 his attitude seemed to have changed. We have a field note and a corresponding recording of him playing 'Für Elise' on the piano. He knew how to play the melody of the first sub-section before the lesson, but had worked out the rest of the ritornello section during it. He was playing fluently with both hands, not sticking to the simplified version provided by the broken-down tracks on the CD, but using the full version and playing most of the notes in the original parts:

> Justin already knew the melody of the A theme from 'Für Elise' before the lesson. During the lesson he learnt the bass, and the whole B theme with two hands. His ear is fantastic; he did it without hardly listening to the CD. He played it over and over and over again, as it can go around in circles. But he can cadence correctly on the tonic when he wants to (unlike many kids). At the end of the lesson I said 'That's really good Justin! You've done so well this lesson. I shall look forward to hearing that again next week.' He replied 'I shall look forward to playing it again next week – it's a cool song.'
>
> *(Broadacres School, Stage 7, lesson 1, LG's field notes)*

How can we reconcile the apparently radical shift in Justin's responses, from the ejaculation 'I'm never going to be able to play that shitty, classical fucked-up music!' to 'I shall look forward to playing it next week – it's a cool song'? In the interview at the end of Stage 7, I asked him for his views of classical music:

> –Justin: Well my views of classical music, I don't really prefer it myself. I like more like, music with a good beat and a good rhythm, like. Classical music isn't really my style.
> –Lucy: No. So what did you think when you got the CDs and you found they were all full of classical music? What was your response?
> –Justin: Um, I wasn't too happy, but it wouldn't, I was with my group so it made it a bit easier. It would have been better if there was some better music in there.
> –Lucy: Mmhm. The work you did, you chose 'Für Elise', and you produced very good stuff. What is your feeling about what you did on that?
> –Justin: Well, I chose 'Für Elise' 'cause my, my grandpa used to play the piano and he taught me how to play that song before he died. So I recognized the song and I just felt like playing that one. … Well, my grandpa, he taught me the first part and I figured out all the bass, and then it just got better from there really, 'cause I got help off other teachers and other people and put it all together, and it sounded pretty cool. … Well I enjoyed playing it 'cause it makes me feel, it makes me feel good when I'm playing it, it's quite hard to explain.
>
> *(End-of-Stage 7 interview)*

I think one of the explanations is that it was *possible* for him to play the music. At first, like many of the pupils who told us they expected the task to be too difficult, he had railed against it because, in his own words, he felt that he would 'never be able to play' it. Threat of failure and corresponding embarrassment are of course de-motivating for any learner, and especially so in a performance art which is as public as music. Making the music more accessible by making the learning practices more accessible to some extent may have reduced the threat that it might otherwise have carried. In addition, the satisfaction of achievement will dispose a learner more positively towards the content of what is being achieved. We also saw that Justin associated this music with his grandfather, now deceased, and no doubt he had some fond memories of learning to play it with him. The association of the music with an old person once again picks up a theme that was expressed by many pupils, but in a form that was touching and very personal. In a completely different way to the popular music in the previous stages of the project, this music none the less connected with Justin's life outside school. (Finally, it is possible that he did not 'count' Für Elise as being classical music at all. Classical music may, in the definitions of many pupils, be 'music I don't like'. I will return to this topic later.)

There is one further point I would like to suggest in connection with the above, although I did not investigate this systematically. I noticed that amongst the pupils who responded most violently *against* the classical music stages were those – such as Justin, as well as Amy, Chris, Harry, Madeline and Alex – who were 'untrained' but who had been identified as having a high level of innate musical ability. This was demonstrated in their quickness to pick up music by ear and to find pitches on a range of instruments, their ability to play in time, their facility and dexterity on instruments, their attentiveness to musical detail as listeners, and/or their improvisational and compositional creativity. Another area for further research would be to investigate the extent to which pupils' level of antipathy to classical music is matched by their musical ability. Possibly, those children who find it more difficult than average to respond positively to classical (or any other) music are in fact those who are *most* musically sensitive, and whose musical responses are stronger than average. As music educators, we must be so careful to remain open to all possibilities, and avoid preventing such pupils from showing their abilities.

When pupils show that they are antipathetic to classical (or any other) music, it is tempting to assume that this is because their knowledge and skills are inferior. We may see them as not being mature, sensible, cultured, able or 'musical' enough to appreciate classical music. We might, as I have already discussed, also consider that their responses are in some way not 'real' *musical* responses to inter-sonic meanings, but merely a kow-towing to social pressure and delineations. Yet they may have well thought-out reasons.

For example, Chris was another pupil who was particularly negative about classical music:

–Abigail: OK, so what was your response when you first heard the music on the CD?
–Chris: Why the hell are we doing this?
–Abigail: OK. Can you explain a bit more about why you thought that?
–Chris: I thought that because it's classical. And I know classical is very important to music, and it's a good one to learn, but at the end of the day I don't like classical, and something that I'm not involved in, or that I don't like, normally isn't – I can't play to it – it's quite different.
–Abigail: OK. Did your views change at all during the course of doing this?
–Chris: Honestly? No.
–Abigail: So, you've got to the end of this and you feel exactly the same?
–Chris: I think classical might be good to go and watch, like in a theatre maybe, but to perform it doesn't do anything for me. ... The reason why I don't like it is because it's made to sound very complex, and yet it's very simple, and the tone just gets annoying because it can get sometimes very repetitive, [but] the ones that change all the time don't sound right. That's what I'd say. Because sometimes you get the violins and you

think 'Oh, it's a violin song' and then in comes another instrument. And, I know lots of songs have lots of different instruments, but [in classical music] they're so completely different, to me.

Whether Chris would have listened to classical music in such ways before the project, or whether he did so as a result of it, I cannot guess. But it is of no relevance to the point I wish to make. For either way, he had clearly listened carefully to classical music in relation to a variety of parameters, including complexity and simplicity, repetition and change, tone, instrumentation and others. He had thought about what he likes and does not like in it, and why. I believe his view should be respected, whether or not it is agreed with, precisely because it is a view that *can* be argued with. It cannot be put down as mindless dismissiveness or kow-towing. Unless we listen to pupils' voices, as I argued in Chapter 1, we may never find out many aspects of what they know, think and feel. Therefore, we may introduce them to music – or other cultural forms and knowledge – and assume that either this will elicit a positive response in them or there is something deficient about them. Such assumptions circumscribe and delimit not only how musical ability is constructed in our society, but actually how it is *produced*. Pupils like Chris, as well as Connor, Hana, Tyler, Justin, Lauren, Amy and many others in this project, have so often come out of school believing themselves to be unmusical. The school, by that token, has produced and circumscribed the difference between musicality and non-musicality at the same time as delimiting the former to a minority of pupils who conform to existing definitions.

Did pupils' views of classical music change?

At the end of Stage 7 we asked pupils whether their views of classical music had changed since they had been doing the task. Out of over 100 pupils interviewed in 25 small groups, nine individuals were confident that no change had occurred: 'Honestly? No.' (Chris); 'No, not really. Just, not into it.' (Amy); and 'No, I still think it's a bit crappy.' (Harry). However, a large number said that although they had hated classical music before, their views had changed to some extent as Stages 6 and 7 went on.

Firstly, there were indications that the task had either turned out to be less difficult than expected, or had become easier as time went by:

–Stephanie: 'Cause at first it was really different from what we had been doing, but once you get used to it, and get the hang of what you're doing it's OK.
–Andrea: At first I thought it would be really hard for like, Josie to find something to play on the piano, and for us to fit vocals to it, and Stephanie to play guitar, but then as the weeks went by and as we were like working together, we were all like helping each other to fit everything in, so it ended up OK.

–Tim: My views definitely changed.
–Abigail: OK. For the better, for the worse?
–Tim: For the better.
–Ethan: Yeah, probably the same here.

–Abigail: Yeah? Can you explain why?

–Ethan: I dunno, I just sort of got used to the music and it started to flow a bit better, and it sort of like got better really as time went on.

A critic might say that the pupils quoted below were deluded about how easy or difficult classical music is. However, music education has always tried to make music easy enough for beginners to play and understand. In so doing, we have tended to take specially composed pieces, break them down into the simplest possible components, and teach them bit by bit. Contrastingly, these pupils were discovering that music can be made easy if approached holistically through aural, informal learning practices, and only afterwards, if at all, broken down into its component parts and simplified. The notion that the music was possible for them came across as a revelation, through which they overcame some of the barriers that had previously been present:

–Madeline: 'Cause like when we first listened to Beethoven, you're like 'Oh my God, you'll have to do it so fast you won't be able to get it' but [now I realize that] classical music is just as easy as other music –

–Kaylee: Other music.

–Madeline: 'Cause all you need to do is listen to the beats and stay with it really, and then you find it as easy as anything else. ... All the other music things that we've been doing, like it's the same really, sticking with the beats.

–Kaylee: That's why, I thought it was really hard, but now I can just do it. ... Yeah, when we learn the notes like it's easy to learn. When we don't know the notes it's not really easy.

Earlier I mentioned that pupils sometimes consider classical instrumentalists to be 'show-offs'. For some that view was now challenged – and interestingly, this was not because they were now perceived to be lacking in skill and therefore not showing off, but the opposite:

–Shelley: Yeah, it's like, like originally we personally would have thought that the people playing the music are like, no offence, but a bunch of show-offs really, 'cause like they were playing all the really complicated bits. But as it goes on, and as you're trying to play it yourself, you're like 'Oh you must have talent to be able to play something like that.'

As Kaylee indicated above, it was the fact of being able to play the notes themselves that provided the greatest spur. Others had similar experiences:

–Jacob: Well, 'cause we didn't really know about it, we didn't really know what it was about, and it was pretty boring. But now, I've progressed and know how to play it a bit, which is pretty cool.

–Abigail: So, you don't think it's so boring now, is that what you're saying?

–Jacob: Not at the moment.

–Rob: It's boring when you don't know how to play the tunes, but once you know how to play the tunes it's like –

–Daniel: It's good.

–Jacob: It's cool.

–Rob: 'Cause you can actually get on.

–Daniel: I wouldn't say it's as cool as like normal music.

–Jacob: Nah, it ain't as street as like rap or hip hop.

–Ian: Yeah, it got a bit more interesting I think, 'cause like, 'cause you're playing it I guess.

–Madeline: Um, I, before we did this project I didn't really like classical music. I'd still listen to it, but not for a long time. And like, as, I think my views have changed because like, I can have a little bit of joy in playing it now that I know like how to do stuff and like, I can listen to it. I've sort of got a bit more joy in it …

As indicated earlier, pupils responded positively to being allowed to arrange the music for their own choice of instruments. In the absence of notation, such arrangement could only take place through performance. It became apparent that what was important to them was that through their performances they were able to 'make the music their own', by 'changing it a bit' or adding 'our own sort of new bits in it'. As indicated by the groups below, this seems to have been a turning point:

–Ameera: Nah, it's better when you do it yourself.

–Lindsey: When you play it.

–Lucy: Why is that?

–Ameera: Um, 'cause it's not like it's boring …

–Lindsey: Yeah, 'cause when you're like playing it yourself it's different.

–Lauren: And you can change it a bit.

–Jacob: Well, 'cause you don't, when, before this bit started I didn't know nothing about classical music, and I thought 'Oh, this' –

–Rob: I knew a bit about it 'cause of my Nan! [Laughs.]

–Daniel: Yeah, they always listen to it in the car!

–Jacob: It's something that my Nan would listen to, or my Dad's Nan or something like that! …

–Rob: Before I thought it was rubbish because our grandparents listen to it.

–Abigail: So what's changed?

–Daniel: Well we've learnt to play it kind of thing.

–Rob: We've added our own sort of new bits in it.

–Swami: And you get used to it.

–Daniel: And made it better.

'Making it your own': improvising, or making mistakes?

On listening to the pupils' 'classical' products and observing them playing, we could in many cases say that they were improvising, but mostly without realizing that they were doing so. Alternatively, we could say that they were not improvising, but making mistakes – again, possibly without realizing it, and certainly without seeming to care. For, to them, they were 'getting it right' and 'making it better'. This again brings us full circle to the notion that the pupils were 'at play' rather than 'at work', symbolized by their lack of concern with being 'correct' in relation to what was on the CD, as in previous stages. (See Chapter 3.) In this sense it is of no importance whether what they were doing was improvisatory or whether it was wrong. It is an irrelevant issue to the learner in such a context.

Most music in human history, including classical music, involves elements of improvisation.[12] In some cases improvisation is prime, in others it is restricted to ornamentation. It was only in some twentieth-century Western classical music that composers began to take control over every nuance of a performance, stripping the performer of as much decision-making power as possible. The way that young classical learners are taught often unintentionally leads them to suppose that there is only one 'correct' way – and several 'incorrect' ways – to do things. (For full discussions of this at HE level see Kingsbury (1988) or Nettl (1995).) Indeed, this is so even when it comes to ornamentation, correct knowledge of which is often assessed through notated tests. Yet it seems somewhat 'anti-musical', and it seems to fly in the face of why humans make music in the first place, to insist too much upon correctness, particularly for learners at the earliest stages. I am sure many critics will feel it is wrong to encourage pupils to play classical music on electric guitars and drum kits, putting in their own notes and their own ideas at their own level to 'make it better'. But I believe that if through doing this they can become less alienated from the music's inter-sonic properties and its delineated associations, and can 'get some joy' out of it, that serves as its own justification. Further, it is through such direct engagement in the 'flow' of music-making that accuracy will develop later on, as has been demonstrated in countless ways through the efficacy of informal learning practices in popular music and many other musics around the world.

Below, although Josh was one of the pupils whose views on classical music did not change during the project, he was none the less willing to say that his own group's version of their piece was 'cool'. A large number of other groups expressed satisfaction or even pride in their product:

–Abigail: OK, so how did your views change then, what did you do to make it –
–Josh: They didn't. I hated classical music before I started, and I hated it afterwards.
–Abigail: Yeah, but you said, when you did that one thing, you did say that was cool, I remember, it's on tape.
–Josh: Yeah, because we made it cool.
–Abigail: Yeah, so what did you do?
–Trevor: It still wasn't very good.
–Abigail: But what did you do? How did you get to that point?
–Josh: We made it our own.
–Trevor: We brought Ian in and he changed it ...
–Josh: ... the music [that we had to copy] was just not that brilliant.
–Tom: We jazzed ours up so it sounded cool.
–Josh: Yeah, we made it work in the end.

---

12 Lines (2005b) offers a philosophical argument about improvisation as 'cultural work' in music and music education; T. Wiggins (2006) discusses where to draw the line between improvisation and composition; also see Burnard (2000) for work on how children integrate improvisation and composition, and J. Wiggins (2006) for a review of issues and literature relating to this area.

–Jake: Well Justin did a solo and the bass was quite good, and Angelo's drums were cool, so, Declan was good too on the keyboard, so it got quite good in the end.

–Madeline: Maybe we don't like listening to it, but as you do it yourself you're like really proud of yourself, saying 'Yeah, I can do classical music' …

Surprisingly, given the antipathy to classical music, there were even a few expressions of having had fun in Stages 6 and 7, although only a handful compared to Stage 1. This was also usually associated with the sense of achievement arrived at by the end:

–Aston: Well it was a bit boring when we started, but it was fun when we got there, it was fun.

Listening and appreciation with classical music

I suggested in Chapter 4 that listening to and copying their own music had opened the ears of many pupils during Stage 1, and made them more critically aware as listeners. In the classical stages of the project, listening, copying and developing the ability to play basic parts within classical music also, for many pupils, led to an increased ability to respond positively to the music's inter-sonic meanings. For those below, this seems to have been restricted to the music they were copying in class:

–Vicky: Yeah, 'cause I never really like listened to any like, classical music or anything before, so it was sort of the first time I really listened to it properly.

–Lauren: And you listen to the song [piece] more.
–Ameera: And you hear the notes and everything isn't it? …
–Lindsey: Yeah, 'cause when you're like, playing it yourself, it's different.

Others were able to listen with more awareness to the inter-sonic meanings of different classical music, *beyond* what they were listening to in the classroom:

–Rebecca: It helped you like, know what to listen for in the music. So like if I listen to another piece of classical music I know what to like maybe pick out if I were going to do it myself.

–Jane: [If we heard classical music now] we'd be able to tell the parts, but like, tell it apart from the melodies and the chords, and we'd be able to notice them 'cause now we've studied them more.

For many pupils, this ability to listen with more awareness and to understand more of the inter-sonic meanings in classical music reduced the general negativity they had previously felt in connection with the musical style:

–Maria: I used to really hate classical before I did this project. Then I started to like see the real, I just started to like it, it sounds nice now.
–Abigail: Can you explain why you started to like it? Is there any –
–Maria: I think it's because I can tell the notes, some of them …

–Abigail: … How would you describe your views of classical music before this term?

–Sofia: I thought it was a lot more boring than it actually was.
–Stacey: It's not like boring, but it's like not really my thing.
–Linda: After you've heard it loads of times it's like –
–Sofia: Yeah, I thought it was worser than it was.
–Abigail: OK.
–Stacey: It's got more to it.
–Sofia: If that makes sense … once we started playing them we found out all the different
   parts to it.
–Others: Yeah.
–Stacey: Yeah, there were loads of different parts.

Not only were pupils able to hear and understand more of the music's inter-sonic relationships, but, mirroring the ways in which their appreciation of popular music had increased in Stage 1, this new awareness in turn had a positive effect on their classical music appreciation in other ways. Further, this was not only related to inter-sonic meanings, but also to delineations. For example, it affected pupils' views about classical music's cultural associations with certain kinds of people, instruments or genres:

–Michelle: Well, before I kind of thought 'Oh classical, that's really boring', um, it's not
   really my sort of music. But now, not all classical music is boring, some of it is quite
   good.
–Lucy: And why do you say that now?
–Michelle: Um, because now I've listened to a bit more I see that it takes a lot more work
   to try and do classical music than it does like the pop music. 'Cause most of the pop
   music, they've all got like the same drum beat and things like that, where classical
   music is totally different …
–Gabrielle: I think before that, before we started the classical project we didn't think it
   was as appealing to listen to classical music, but as we, as we went on with the project
   we saw that people must have had a lot of talent, a lot of practice to be able to play
   the pieces. So it's been a lot more appealing than it was before. And it's all a matter of
   being creative as well, because as Michelle said, most of the like, pop stuff is the same
   drum beats and all. But like classical music, you have to be a lot more creative, there's
   more variation of styles. … I think I'm more aware of it now.
–Lucy: And why is that?
–Gabrielle: Um, because like before, whenever a piece of classical music came on it
   would be like 'Oh it's classical music, that's going to be really boring', being quite
   stereotypical about it. But now, like, we've pretty much rounded off the classical
   project, yeah, it's been a lot more of a 'Oh, I wonder how they created this piece?'

–Lucy: … Has doing that exercise changed your view of classical music at all?
–Peter: Yeah. It's more interesting than before …
–Ed: If we had to pick, I wouldn't listen to it, I still think it's quite boring, but I thought it
   was more interesting than I first thought …
–Arlene: There's more to it than just like pianos and like opera singers and stuff like that.

Earlier in this chapter I indicated that pupils had initially been daunted by the task, fearing that classical music was 'too difficult' for them, but that this had gradually given way to a realization that it was 'easy'. A third phase then seems to have come into operation, in which they realized anew how 'difficult' it is, both to play and to compose. Often the same person would put forward both the view that it is easy and the view that it is difficult at different points in the interview. This reminds me of an old Chinese saying: 'First I saw mountains, then I saw no mountains, then I saw mountains.' Possibly we can theorize the process like this: the first reaction was that it would be too difficult for them to play, because they were unfamiliar with the style and had negative responses to both the inter-sonic and the delineated meanings. Then they began to listen purposively, which made the textures more transparent and the inter-sonic relationships more meaningful. Then they began to play the music and realized that its inter-sonic properties and relationships were possible to play if they 'made it their own'. In so doing their ears opened further, enabling the realization that to play it 'properly', or to compose it, must be extremely hard:

–Alyssa: You sort of like appreciate how hard it is for people to make it up and stuff.

–Abigail: So did your views change at all about how good or how bad the songs [pieces] were?
–Sofia: Yeah.
–Abigail: Yeah.
–Sofia: We thought they were better, at the end.
–Abigail: OK, why did you think they were better?
–Sofia: Dunno.
–Stacey: It's really hard to make them, to like play them. So the person that sort of wrote it-
–Alice: You had to like listen to it in a different way.
–Sofia: Yeah.
–Stacey: Yeah, the person that wrote it was obviously really like talented at it so you kind of-
–Sofia: Yeah.

–Matt: [If I heard classical music on the radio now] I'd appreciate it more, 'cause I know how hard it is to play it now.

–Ryan: It might make you respect it a bit more, 'cause you can see how hard the people do work to get it right.
–Geoff: How long it takes.

Once again, as with the popular music stages, pupils' attention to delineations when they talked about the music gradually waned, and they attended more to the inter-sonic meanings. Connected with the discovery that classical music is not, on one hand, so difficult for them or quite so boring, and that, on the other hand, it 'had more to it' than they realized, there was also for a few pupils a further realization: that its delineated association with 'old people' was not immutable:

–Ava: You've like been able to find that classical music is actually OK to listen to, 'cause like it's sort of, I don't know, like you're always told like everyone, they're teenagers, 'You shouldn't be listening to classical music, that's for older people.' Once you've like listened to it in lessons and stuff and sort of enjoyed it then like –

As with the popular music stages, by the end of Stage 7 the teachers were again in agreement that pupils' skills as music listeners had improved, and that their appreciation of classical music was enhanced. They expressed some surprise at the sight of pupil groups listening quite intently – whether with positive or negative reactions – to Brahms, Bach and other classical composers:

–Debbie: And the fact that they've been listening to classical music in a different way, and also classical music, from what they are saying, is a little bit more complicated and a little bit more complex and a little bit more interesting, from what we've looked at, to actually work out as a group to perform. All groups have listened to a piece of classical music and looked at the different layers of a piece of classical music. And they've all, we have all noticed that once they start performing and practising the pieces and it becomes familiar, that they actually start to enjoy and like the pieces of music. And I think it's, they've enjoyed that aspect of it, it's a little bit more challenging. ... I think it's made it accessible to them, and the fact that they can break it down and it's not this complicated nightmare that only very clever people can do it. And I think it's broken down that barrier, that actually these melodies, even though they are a little bit more complicated, they are, they can play them ...

The 'normal curriculum', classical music and 'other' music

Overwhelmingly, the groups told us that they preferred Stages 1, 4 and 5 most, particularly being able to compose their 'own' music. But despite that, and despite the negative feelings which we have seen them express about classical music, they none the less felt that they learnt more and got more enjoyment through the *pedagogic* approach of the project in Stages 6 and 7, compared to the 'normal' curriculum. Out of the blue, in the midst of some very negative statements about classical music, Nicola assured me that:

–Nicola: We don't *mind* doing classical.
–Rhona: It's alright to do, but it's just that we prefer doing songs that we're familiar with and know better and stuff.

–Daisy: I didn't really mind doing this, but I would prefer something different.

–Kaylee: I think the other music [previous stages] that we done before was better than this one ... 'cause you know more of the tune, but these ones you don't really know. But it's interesting to learn them as well.

In Chapter 5, mainly in relation to Stage 1 of the project, I discussed pupils' positive responses to being given some autonomy to direct their own learning. By the end of Stage 7 these views had, if anything, become stronger and were expressed more forcefully; 19 out of the 25 groups interviewed indicated without any prompt whatsoever, and despite the fact that they could only choose between five pieces of disliked classical music in each stage, that this way of learning was both more effective and more enjoyable than the 'normal curriculum'. The reasons overlap with issues discussed in Chapter 5 and other parts of the book. They were that the approach involved more choice generally, and choice of instruments specifically; it was more practical, and included making music rather than writing about music; it afforded more independence to the learner, causing them to make their own decisions, and it involved working co-operatively in groups. I will not present any of the data itself here as it does not add anything substantially to the discussion in Chapter 5. But the point that I wish to note is that these views were now put forward in relation to classical music, a music about which pupils had been so overtly negative. This suggests, therefore, that those aspects of the 'normal curriculum' which pupils found unhelpful were not so much to do with curriculum *content* as with *pedagogy*. Once again, this is particularly interesting, given the fact that the 'normal' curriculum is, in teachers' eyes and in the documentation, a much more practical and less theoretical affair than it seems to be in the eyes of the pupils.

One other aspect of the pupils' spontaneous comparison of the classical stages to the 'normal curriculum' is worth picking out here. It relates to the possible expansion of informal learning practices to other musics within the classroom context. Earlier I discussed Chris's views of Stages 6 and 7, in which he made it clear that the task had not altered his negative opinions of, and responses to, classical music. Yet he was equally clear that although he personally disliked classical music, it should have a place in the curriculum. Furthermore, despite his dislike of it, be evidently found playing classical music within the project far more meaningful than what he had been doing in the previous year. As in Chapter 5, one of the connections here was with the instruments he had used, as well as the nature of the tasks that he had been given:

–Chris: … it's just I hated the xylophone.
–Abigail: You hated doing xylophone, last year?
–Ricky: Yeah, that was awful.
–Chris: Yeah, it's the worst thing ever, I'm serious. We would hear a song and it wouldn't matter, because at the end of the day you were playing 'A, B' wait five seconds 'A, B', and it's repetitive. … [This year] I've actually learnt more about music, and I've actually, my grade has gone up in music, my attitude has gone up in music, everything has gone up in music, and I enjoy music more, whereas before I was dreading music lessons, 'cause I was listening to South Africans playing instruments that really wasn't the group playing them, and then you had to play it on the xylophone, and that was boring as hell.

My hypothesis would be that if there had been more time in the project, and we had asked the pupils to listen to and copy African music through classroom informal learning practices, or gamelan music, or any music, however unfamiliar its inter-sonic meanings might sound to their ears and however distant its cultural delineations might be, they would, as with classical music, have found it more approachable, meaningful and enjoyable as time went by. In other words, their responses to both inter-sonic and delineated meanings would, at least in some cases, have become more comprehending and more positive. As was echoed again and again in countless interviews, it was the *approach to learning* that made the tasks more meaningful and the musical experiences more positive. I think possibly the most important aspects of the approach are, as I have mentioned many times before in this book, that it is based on the real-life learning practices of musicians drawn from the world outside school;

it is fundamentally developed by learners through learning; it is therefore accessible; it affords autonomy to the learner; it involves group work; and it is holistic. Now it is possible to add another: that it uses not merely music selected by pupils themselves, or music in styles with which they can identify, but any music, so long as it is 'real'. Abigail made the following note during the first lesson of Stage 7:

> When asked what she thought of the music, Gabrielle said 'It's good because in the last one we did all advert music, like music that was written for adverts, whereas in this one the music is by real composers.' I told her that the advert music was actually all written by real composers as well and she seemed surprised.
>
> *(Courthill School, Stage 7, lesson 1; AD's field notes)*

Pupils' views of the place of 'other' music in the curriculum

We asked pupils whether they thought classical music ought to have a place in the curriculum. Their responses were generally broad-minded and altruistic, even among pupils such as Chris, who had said they had found the classical music stages boring, and whose views of classical music had not changed for the better as a result of the project. Out of the 25 groups interviewed, only two gave a unanimous 'no' to the question. Amongst the other groups, there were four individuals who said 'no'. The main reasons concerned classical music's unpopularity with their age group:

> –Justin: I don't really think it should be in the curriculum 'cause it's not our generation's music really.

This was not only an issue of taste, however, as a couple of students observed:

> –Billy: It's harder to play it if you don't like it, I find.

Otherwise, all the other individuals in those four groups, and all the other groups unanimously, said 'yes' to the question. Reasons included, in two cases, that 'it was fun', and in others, issues such as: 'it's different', ''cause they're famous in history', 'it's how music started' (!) and 'it's important, like to know about it … you need like a range'. Several said classical music should be included in moderation: 'a little bit, not too much', and 'I think it should be balanced, so like you listen to a bit of classical but then we could decide to have other music.'

Reasons for this included a concern that pupils should be informed about the wider world around them:

> –Ava: So, it's like if you only ever hear pop music then you're automatically not going to, well if someone said 'Do you want to listen to classical?' you'd be like 'Oh no, I don't really like it', even though you've never really listened to it before.

Pupils also expressed a wish to be fair to all interest groups, and to show respect for other people's interests:

> –Abigail: Do you think that music in schools ought to include some classical music –
> –Chris: Yes.

–Abigail: – or not? You do?

–Chris: Yes. As long as it's not on the xylophone.

–Abigail: OK. But if you don't like it, and if you don't like learning it, why do you think it should be in schools?

–Chris: It helped.

–Abigail: This helped you?

–Chris: Well, no because at the end of the day, it's music, and classical helps because we've been doing like rock music, rap music and then doing classical. It just, because for some people classical ticks. I know a group that really enjoyed doing the classical work because they could jazz up classical. It's just, you know, I don't like classical, I don't appreciate it, some people do, and then you should give someone the option. You can't say 'Well because one group didn't like rap we're not going to do rap anymore', 'cause rap could be really good for another group. I still think you should have classical 'cause it works for other groups. … All music should be in Year 7, and Year 8 is to open you up to music, and then you should do something fun in Year 9. This is really fun.

–Amy: Some people might think that what *we* like is rubbish, and they like classical. So it should be like a variety.

–Ryan: 'Cause some people have got different interests isn't it? And you've got to, you've got to teach them. It's like in maths, if you only taught them to add and subtract they wouldn't know how to times or anything, so you've got to give a range in it, so they can see if they like it or not.

For others, including classical music involved a sense of duty, regardless of whether you liked it or not, rather like eating your greens:

–Stephen: Not my favourite music but –

–Michael: I suppose you've got to learn it.

–Stephen: You've got to do it, yeah.

–Patrick: Just a little bit because all that, like classical, you have to have some, because like, it is a part of music.

–Siobhan: So you're more open to different types of music for when you get older.

The same pupils also affirmed that other 'world musics' and jazz should have a place in the curriculum, for similar reasons.

Teachers' views of the classical stages

Richard offered an unsolicited view of the project's approach to classical music, compared with his 'normal' approach to it. In this he touched on the topic of 'real' music:

–Richard: I was thinking while I was teaching other Year 9s, in fact I'm playing other classical music for them … when I compare what I'm asking the majority of my Year 9s to do, compared to this experimental group, I know, actually it's making me wince now when I'm asking them to do what's on my normal curriculum. I'm thinking I really would like to switch over to the Musical Futures idea with them for the rest of the term. Because I think they might just get that little bit of inspiration from it.

–Lucy: So what is it that makes you wince?

–Richard: I think [pause] twee-ishness. It's sometimes a bit twee, and I think, Oh, it's so terribly predictable, music teachers' type approach, and I hate doing predictable things, and [pause] it just makes me cringe, because I know it's going to work, because it's going to be controlled, it's a nice piece of music, and I'm enthusiastic about it, but they're going to listen to it in silence, and then off they're going to go and work in their groups and … they actually come out with terribly sensible stuff … all the kind of stuff you expect to get at Key Stage 3, sort of programme music … Ofsted [government inspectors] come and it's fine, great, no problem. But it's not real music, and the kids know it's not real music. And I just feel, I know that what the Year 9s [in the project] are doing, if they can get it right, it's just so much sharper, the work.

Sandra declared that her prediction that Stage 7 would be a 'completely inappropriate thing to do' turned out to be 'completely wrong'. There was agreement that although pupils' motivation had dropped, it did not plummet as far as expected:

–Sandra: … there was nobody refusing to do it. That was a slight surprise to me I have to say, 'cause I did think there would be people saying 'I'm not doing this, I don't want to do it.' There were a few kind of grumbles, but it was no more than that, and everybody did the task and everybody achieved something at the end of it, so I think their motivation has pretty much stayed the same.

–Richard: I didn't get a moan. I was expecting 'ugh' and all that stuff, I was thinking 'Right, here it goes, I'm going to give them two weeks, and then I'll pull the plug.' But no, actually.

–Yasmin: … I was quite impressed that they just took it on board and just got on with it. … I think sometimes they think 'Oh we can never do this, it's going to be too difficult', but having it broken down on the tracks [Stage 7] and they realized … actually that it could be done very simply, and still be quite effective.

Teachers also felt that the pupils' responses to the music were on one hand more open-minded than expected, and on the other hand capable of shifting away from reacting to the cultural delineations of the music, and towards its inter-sonic meanings:[13]

–Debbie: What I was actually interested in was in their reaction in playing the pieces, whether it would instantly turn them off. And from the experience within my school, it didn't turn them off, it actually made them, you know, they didn't take it as 'classical music', they took it as music, a task … They've actually just taken it on board and said 'Right let's get on with it.' They haven't, which is not the case of 'Oh I don't like this any more.' It's a case of, and I think they have a good feeling of what it feels like to have a group piece which they've created, and they like that feeling of having some

---

13 Five teachers responded to the statement 'Pupils' appreciation of classical music was enhanced during Stages 6 and/or 7' thus: 2 'strongly agree', 2 'agree' and 1 'neutral'.

work which sounds good and sounds like the original. And now it's not a case of what are they copying, it's a case of 'Let's get this music-making happening' really ...

–Lucy: Have you learnt anything about children by doing this project as a whole, not just this?

–Debbie: They are, you can influence, you think that they come in with these pre-judged like, you know judgments about music, and that they've got their own little culture of music and you can't touch that, but actually you have quite a big influence on the way that they think about certain styles, and like I didn't realize that you could break that, or influence them in that way, change their minds on things like classical. 'Cause music is very, well, it's very personal isn't it? OK, and I didn't realize, I mean that you could produce a piece of classical to them and they wouldn't be instantly turned off by it. They are open, yeah? And they don't instantly pre-judge it as boring.

Why did pupils' views of classical music change?

As mentioned at the beginning of this chapter, a number of pupils said the only time they heard classical music was 'in the car', and this experience was without variance referred to in the most negative terms. In the car there is no choice but to listen to whatever music the 'old people' are playing (unless the young ones have remembered to bring a personal sound source and headphones with them!). For young teenagers, the car is a place where adults are in control. It is also a place from which teenagers, once going along, cannot escape. In these respects, we can compare the car with the classroom. Normally, pupils have little or no choice but to listen to the music the teacher gives them; the classroom is a place where an adult is in control, and a place from which pupils cannot easily or legally escape. If classical music is played in classrooms, it is perhaps, from their point of view, a bit like being forced to listen to it in the car. From that perspective, the classroom could contribute to making pupils strongly dislike, rather than appreciate, classical music.

When asked to listen purposively to classical music's inter-sonic meanings, and copy them on an instrument by ear, as a member of a group, I would suggest that pupils got past the barrier that is normally erected by their unfamiliarity with the music's inter-sonic meanings, and by their negative associations with its delineations. Purposive listening and copying provided a doorway into the music's inter-sonic meanings; and once inside them, the cultural arbitrariness of the delineations became more apparent. Through such approaches, music-makers and music listeners can realize that music can mean all kinds of things to all kinds of people, both inter-sonically and in relation to delineation. In short, what I am suggesting is this: when pupils' listening experiences are meaningfully connected to some amount of social action, which is both autonomous and co-operative, and when these experiences also involve the direct production of musical inter-sonic meanings in a way which can 'flow' and which can be playful, and when pupils are stimulated by whole pieces of 'real' music, then their musical awareness and response, or 'critical musicality', seem to open up.

Chapter 8

Afterword

The project discussed in this book has left many questions unanswered, and many avenues unexplored.[1] All the teachers who took part went on to develop and incorporate the project's underlying principles in their curricula. The six teachers in London, who had been involved in the early stages only, said afterwards that the project's pedagogy had seeped into and positively affected their approaches to teaching generally. Amongst other things, they particularly found themselves standing back and allowing pupils more autonomy to direct their own learning. At the time of writing, two of the Heads of Music, including Ken from the pilot school, have started to run the project in its final form; the other two are planning to do so. All the teachers in the Hertfordshire schools who were still in post at the end of the project also went on to include some or all of its stages, either in the same or an adapted form, in their official curricula. In addition, those teachers who had moved to other schools – and we were able to remain in touch with all but one of them – took the project with them. The final statement of the anonymous questionnaire in Hertfordshire was: 'Using informal learning practices in the classroom has generally changed my approach to teaching for the better.' Twelve teachers ticked 'Strongly agree' and the remaining five ticked 'Agree'.

However, if school pupils were to follow the project and nothing else, they would be likely to miss out on what most people would agree are some essential aspects of the music curriculum. These would include theoretical knowledge of harmony, scales and other pitch relations, rhythm, metre, technical vocabulary, and skills in reading and writing notation. It is important to stress that there is no *necessary* disjunction between informal music learning and the acquisition of such theoretical knowledge. Rather, informal music learning practices as they occur in the world outside school, are likely to involve a long period – in many cases a period of years – during which learners engage with music primarily as music-makers and music listeners. Later on, and in most cases only later on, many such musicians go on to develop theoretical knowledge, to a greater or lesser degree depending on individual

---

1   As mentioned in Chapter 1, after the research phase of the project had ended, the project strategies (Green with Walmsley 2006) were made publicly available to any school which wishes to adopt them. They can be accessed in the final teachers' materials available on <www.musicalfutures.org/PractionersResources.html>, Section 2. Although the Musical Futures research phase is over, the Paul Hamlyn Foundation is continuing to provide follow-up co-ordination and support for teachers who take up any of the ideas developed by its pathfinders. At the time of writing, around 1000 schools in the UK have downloaded the materials, and the feedback has been positive. But it remains to be seen to what extent the majority of schools who take them on board will have similar experiences to those considered in this book.

circumstances. This theoretical knowledge comes about through a variety of means, and may involve formal education, personal study, or simply continued contact with other musicians and with music itself. Such knowledge is more readily assimilated, and more meaningful, because as it is acquired, it can be put to immediate use within music-making or music listening activities, rather than remaining an abstraction.[2]

Within the project it is possible to discern the seeds of such knowledge and understanding. As one teacher, Katerin, said in Chapter 4, pupils began to acquire knowledge of technical terms through *using* them, in the same way that language is picked up by young children. It was also through use that they began to work out relationships between sounds for themselves, such as when a group of girls discovered triadic harmony, also quoted in Chapter 4, or a group of boys realized that the music was organized in 16- or 32-beat groups, quoted in Chapter 2. In formal music education we perhaps run the risk of attempting to introduce technical terms and to bring about theoretical understanding at too early a stage, possibly before pupils have enough grasp of music itself – how to make it and how to listen to it – to be able to apply the terms and internalize the understanding meaningfully.

Thus an ideal situation could involve an integration of informal learning with more formal approaches, which is exactly what the teachers in the project went on to develop. Yasmin described the way her school approached this:

> –Yasmin: … it would never be: 'This is a Musical Futures lesson, this is going to be a formal lesson.' We would want to incorporate all of this sort of thing into every lesson, but also bring back some of the more formal basic theory skills. Just so that it works alongside.

Her school developed what is known in the UK as a Scheme of Work, in which the first five project stages were complemented by more formal approaches in half-term blocks across the academic year. In Richard's school, the project stages were alternated with blocks of lessons in the ICT music room. In Sandra's school, aspects and stages of the project were infused into the curriculum for all year groups, including the use of informal learning practices with classical music, Latin American music, film music and others. Debbie took some leave and is planning to implement the strategies on her return to work.

During the final year of the project some teachers in the extension schools made up their own materials using music from various styles across the world, along the lines of the project's funk and classical stages (Stages 2, 6 and 7). One school developed a helpful integration of a formal and an informal approach for part of a term. This involved putting pupils into 'sectional' rehearsal groups, so that, for example, all the bass guitarists would be in one room, all the drummers in another, and so on. They learnt their instrumental parts aurally from CD tracks (as in Stage 2)

---

2   See, for example, Bayton (1997), Bennett (1980), Berkaak (1999), Björnberg (1993), Campbell (1995), Clawson (1999a), Cohen (1991), Davis (2005), Finnegan (1989), Green (2002a), Horn (1984), Kirshner (1998), Lilliestam (1996), Negus (1999) and other references in Chapter 1, note 3.

in their separate 'sections', then dispersed to form bands (which could, if desired, be made up of friendship groups).[3]

These, and many other aspects of the project remain as yet unanalysed. Amongst others, for example, we have data relating to the notion of creativity and its manifestation, which I have been unable to consider in this book. (For literature, see Chapter 5.) In the anonymous questionnaire, as I mentioned in Chapter 5, 11 of the 16 teachers who did Stages 4 and 5, agreed that pupils' compositions were 'more musically interesting and sophisticated than usual'. However, two teachers indicated that they 'strongly *dis*agreed' with a different statement related to composition, which was: 'In Stages 4 and 5 (composition) pupils built creatively on what they had learnt from copying during Stages 1, 2 and 3.' In addition, one teacher 'disagreed' to that statement, and one was 'neutral'. Even though the majority (10 out of 16) did agree, this disparity in the teachers' views interests me. One reason is that this was the only statement in the entire questionnaire that attracted a 'strongly disagree' response. Another reason is that this was the only area of the project in which the evaluations of teachers appeared to conflict at all significantly with my own. For I had considered that pupils *did* build creatively on what they had learnt in the previous stages. Part of the problem may be the difficulties of defining 'creativity' and the likelihood that, more so than the other terms used in the questionnaire, each respondent, as well as the researcher, had a different thing in mind. I hope to write an article in due course investigating the reasons behind the teachers' disparate opinions, reviewing how pupils talked about this issue, and analysing the notion of creativity and its manifestation in relation to informal music learning practices in the classroom.

Another area that we did not investigate concerned the benefits or otherwise of pupils performing their musical products in front of the class or in a concert situation to peers, parents or other audiences. After Stage 1 of the project, pupils in 7 of the 40 interview groups expressed nervousness about performing in front of peers, or compared themselves unfavourably with others: 'Nah, it's crap, compared to everyone else's man,' and 'I was scared to sing in front of people.' Yet teachers felt that the sense of competition and comparison engendered by performance increased both focus and motivation; and some pupils were positive about the experience: 'I wasn't scared. I like performing in front of people,' and 'It was scary, but it was good.' At the very end of each of the two years in Hertfordshire, Abigail organized a mass 'Big Jam' event, as it came to be known. It was attended by hundreds of pupils from different schools, who played their music to each other on a main stage, and took part in a variety of workshops over the course of a whole day. The levels of enjoyment and motivation appeared to be extremely high, and the pupils' responsible behaviour was impressive. But again, the topic of pupils performing to peers or others, their own and their teachers' views of this, and its relation to motivation, as

---

3   The Nottingham pathway of the 'Musical Futures' project contains materials using similar principles. They can be accessed in Burton et al. (2006), which can be downloaded from <www.musicalfutures.org/PractitionersResources/html>, Section 3.

well as the question of how to organize such events imaginatively and effectively across groups of schools, all call for more investigation.[4]

The role of the musicians' workshops in Stage 5 of the project, and particularly peer teaching by bands of older or same-age pupils from within the school, raise a number of issues that would be fascinating to explore. Also, in Chapter 5 I suggested that pupils would benefit from seeing their teachers performing in bands, playing music that pupils were familiar with and liked. A small project is waiting to be undertaken there. The issue of 'disaffected' pupils and the benefits that informal music-making, both inside and outside schools, can offer them is a huge field demanding exploration, as is that of the different ways in which musical ability manifests itself in different educational contexts.

As well as areas for which we have unexplored data, there are of course many aspects and implications of the project's strategies that were not investigated at all. One major area concerns how pupils in different social groups approached informal learning practices, and how they responded to the different project stages. We already know that, in many respects, girls and boys collectively approach music-reception, music-making and music-learning practices differently from each other.[5] How that applies and what shapes it may take in the case of informal music learning in the classroom is wide open for further work, and was left completely unexplored in the present study. At the time of going to press one main study school has indicated that many more boys than girls are beginning to engage with music. It is possible that if such learning practices become embedded in a school, there is a risk they may become dominated by boys. Similarly, ethnic differences were only touched upon, and issues of class, age, location and many others call for further investigation.

Another central educational issue that was left untouched, at least from a research point of view, concerns assessment. As I mentioned in Chapter 2, teachers found that they could apply their usual assessment methods to the project. It would be fascinating to investigate exactly how they did this, and to develop approaches that combine best practice, or that offer alternative methods. How the project relates, for example, to the theory of 'multiple intelligences' of Howard Gardner (1993), and particularly to the assessment strategies developed by him and his colleagues, would be a fascinating area to study. This could include considering approaches to assessment based on apprenticeship models of learning, as well as how to give more weight to pupil self-assessment and peer assessment.

Further work on ability groupings would be helpful. It could shed light on the extent to which pupils do or do not gravitate towards others whom they consider to have similar ability levels, the extent to which mixed ability groupings are or are not beneficial, and more. A study measuring and comparing outcomes between an

---

4   See DfES (2006) for information on community music provision in the UK, and recommendations about the setting up of 'music hubs' and other ways to enhance provision through consortia.

5   For literature on girls' and boys' musical practices within schools, see, for example, Armstrong (2001), Bruce and Kemp (1993), Caputo (1994), Charles (2004), Colley et al. (1993), Delzell and Leppla (1992), Delzell (1994), Green (1997), Harrison and O'Neill (2002), Koza (1994), O'Neill (1997) and Zervoudakes and Tanur (1994).

informal and a formal music classroom, focusing on the quality of pupils' products, as well as the knowledge, skills, motivation and co-operation that went along with them, would no doubt be fascinating. In connection with this, as I mentioned in Chapter 7, more work could be done to systematically assess the pupils' products that come about as a result of informal learning, and also to compare the technical and expressive aspects of those performances with performances that were learnt by notation or through teacher-instruction. Very importantly, more work is needed to ascertain the extent to which the incorporation of informal learning practices in the curriculum does, or does not, prepare pupils for further study in and beyond the school, particularly within Higher Education, and the extent to which it does or does not prepare them for professional roles in the music industry.[6]

As a final thought, I wonder to what extent educationalists in other curriculum subjects will recognize and support the issues considered in this book. The main one, to my mind, concerns the extent to which pupils can and should, or cannot and should not, be given more autonomy to decide on curriculum content and to direct their own learning strategies. Within Sandra's school at the time of writing, Departmental Heads of other curriculum subjects have visited the Music Department in order to observe the project in action, and Sandra has provided induction sessions and materials to introduce them to the underlying principles of informal learning as they are set out in the project. Both the ICT and the Modern Foreign Languages departments are currently embarking on their own adaptations of informal learning in the classroom. One Head of Music in an extension school wrote in a final report: 'Musical Futures has changed the whole atmosphere of learning, not just in music but in many other areas of the school.'

I do not wish to claim that the project I have considered in this book brings with it no problems or challenges, nor that it could provide a complete musical education. But to me, the issues at its heart are worth considering. They centre around the importance of listening to young people's voices and taking their values and their culture seriously. This in turn involves observing how they learn, not necessarily in educational institutions, but particularly when they are *enjoying* learning and when they are learning voluntarily. From that base, we can perhaps bring some of the flavour of that enjoyment, and the learning that goes along with it, into the school. Without pandering or dumbing down, it is possible to provide challenging curriculum content that authentically reflects the world outside the school, and effective pedagogic strategies based on observation and analysis of how learners learn best.

---

6   See Youth Music (2002) for a helpful report on a number of issues in this area within the UK.

Appendix A

Information about schools

This Appendix gives a general description of the main schools that are considered in this book (anonymized), and the main data collection methods used in them. They are listed in chronological order of their involvement in the project, followed by the pilot school. The Appendix also gives basic information about which parts of the project were run by each of the main-study, pilot and extension schools.

Main-study schools

Southover School

Role in the project: Stages 1 and 2, 2003–2004
Location: outer London
Type of school: mixed comprehensive
Make-up of student population: ethnically diverse; mainly working-class
Data collection methods: participant observation; audio and video recordings; pupil interviews; teacher interviews; teacher induction and feedback meetings
Teachers involved: Head of Music, Denise; newly qualified class music teacher, Barbara
Number of classes in project: 1
Number of classes considered in detail: 1

Deansgrove School

Role in the project: Stages 1 and 2, 2003–2004
Location: inner London
Type of school: mixed comprehensive
Make-up of student population: ethnically diverse, including a high proportion of recent immigrants, refugee children and children speaking English as a second or third language; mainly working-class
Data collection methods: participant observation; audio and video recordings; pupil interviews; teacher interviews; teacher induction and feedback meetings
Teachers involved: Head of Music, Brian; newly qualified class music teacher, Hugh
Number of classes in project: 1
Number of classes considered in detail: 1

Westways School

Role in the project: Stages 1 and 2, 2003–2004
Location: outer London
Type of school: mixed comprehensive
Make-up of student population: 75% from the Indian sub-continent, 15% Black (African and Caribbean-origin), the remainder mixed
Data collection methods: participant observation; audio and video recordings; pupil interviews; teacher interviews; teacher induction and feedback meetings
Teachers involved: Head of Music, Janet
Number of classes in project: 1
Number of classes considered in detail: 1

Courthill School

Role in the project: Stages 1–7, 2004–2005; repeated in 2005–2006
Location: town in Hertfordshire, a county just north of London
Type of school: mixed comprehensive
Make-up of student population: mainly white working- and middle-class
Data collection methods: participant observation; audio and video recordings; pupil interviews and questionnaires; teacher interviews; teacher induction and feedback meetings
Teachers involved: Head of Music, Debbie. (Also, two class teachers whose classes were not observed and who were not interviewed as part of the research. Before 2005–2006 the Head of Music and one of the class teachers left; the project was repeated by the other class teacher, who became Acting Head of Department; Also one peripatetic teacher was involved, but not interviewed as part of the research)
Number of classes in project: 2 in 2004–2005; 2 in 2005–2006
Number of classes considered in detail: 1 (Stages 1–5); 2 (Stages 6 and 7)

Grange School

Role in the project: Stages 1–7, 2004–2005; repeated in 2005–2006
Location: town in Hertfordshire, a county just north of London
Type of school: mixed comprehensive
Make-up of student population: white working- and middle-class
Data collection methods: participant observation; audio and video recordings; pupil interviews and questionnaires; teacher interviews; teacher induction and feedback meetings
Teachers involved: Head of Music, Sandra. (Also, one other class teacher who took some project stages, which were not observed, and who was not interviewed as part of the research; one peripatetic teacher who was involved for some of the time)
Number of classes in project: 2 in 2004–2005; 8 in 2005–2006
Number of classes considered in detail: 1 (Stages 1–7)

Heath School

Role in the project: Stages 1–6, 2004-2005; repeated in 2005–2006
Location: town in Hertfordshire, a county just north of London
Type of school: mixed comprehensive
Make-up of student population: mainly white working- and middle-class
Data collection methods: participant observation; audio and video recordings; pupil interviews and questionnaires; teacher interviews; teacher induction and feedback meetings
Teachers involved: Head of Music, Richard. (Also, one peripatetic teacher in some classes, who was not interviewed as part of the research)
Number of classes in project: 1 in 2004–2005; 4 in 2005–2006
Number of classes considered in detail: 1 (Stages 1–6)

Broadacres School

Role in the project: Stages 1–7, 2004–2005; Stages 1–5 repeated in 2005–2006
Location: town in Hertfordshire, a county just north of London
Type of school: mixed comprehensive
Make-up of student population: mainly white working- and middle-class
Data collection methods: participant observation; audio and video recordings; pupil interviews and questionnaires; teacher interviews; teacher induction and feedback meetings
Teachers involved: Head of Music, Yasmin; experienced class teacher, Katerin; one experienced peripatetic teacher, Carol, who was training to be a class teacher; also, two peripatetic teachers, who were not interviewed as part of the research
Number of classes in project: 2 in 2004–2005; 2 in 2005–2006
Number of classes considered in detail: 1 (Stages 1–7)

Pilot school

Parkways Girls' School

Role in the project: pilot school, Stage 1 only, 2001–2002
Location: inner London
Make-up of student population: ethnically diverse, mix of social classes
Type of school: girls' comprehensive
Data collection methods: participant observation; audio and video recordings; teacher's views given informally and in meeting with other London schools, 2003–2004
Teachers involved: Head of Music, Ken
Number of classes in project: 1
Number of classes considered in detail: 1

Teachers quoted in the text (anonymized)

Note: In some of the schools below, one or two other teachers were also involved in the project as indicated above. However, due to time constraints we were not able to observe all the classes or interview all the teachers who took part. They are not included in this list, which is restricted to those teachers who took part in the research itself as interviewees and participants in group discussions, and/or whose classes were observed.

Heads of Music who were interviewed and attended meetings across the seven main-study schools

Brian, London
Denise, London
Janet, London
Debbie, Hertfordshire
Richard, Hertfordshire
Sandra, Hertfordshire
Yasmin, Hertfordshire

Other teachers in the main-study schools and the pilot school who were either interviewed at the end of Stages 1 and 2, and/or who contributed through discussions at one or more teacher meetings

Ken, Head of Music, London (pilot school)
Barbara, Class Music Teacher, London
Hugh, Class Music Teacher, London
Carol, Trainee Class Music Teacher; experienced instrumental teacher, Hertfordshire
Katerin, Class Music Teacher, Hertfordshire

Extension schools and teachers

The 13 extension schools contained 9 mixed comprehensives catering for all ability levels and 3 special schools, one of which was for pupils with moderate learning difficulties (MLD) and two for pupils with emotional and behavioural difficulties (EBD). Some of the extension schools contained ethnic diversity; some were mainly white. Some were located in large towns, others in small towns. Across these schools, 20 classroom teachers were involved in the project, 13 as Heads of Music, and the remainder as assistant class teachers.

Table A.1   All schools: involvement for each school

School	Stage 1	Stage 2	Stage 3	Stage 4	Stage 5	Stage 6	Stage 7
Pilot school							
Parkways	X	—	—	—	—	—	—
Main-study schools							
Southover	X	X	—	—	—	—	—
Deansgrove	X	X	—	—	—	—	—
Westways	X	X	—	—	—	—	—
Courthill	X	X	X	X	X	X	X
Grange	X	X	X	X	X	X	X
Heath	X	X	X	X	X	X	—
Broadacres	X	X	X	X	X	X	X
Extension schools							
1 EBD	X	X	X	X	X	X	—
2 EBD	X	X	—	X	X	—	—
3 MLD	X	X	—	X	X	—	—
4	X	X	—	X	X	X	—
5	X	X	—	X	X	X	—
6	X	X	X	X	X	—	—
7	X	X	—	X	X	—	—
8	X	X	X	X	X	—	—
9	X	X	X	X	X	—	—
10	X	X	—	X	X	—	—
11	X	X	—	X	X	—	—
12	X	X	—	—	—	—	—
13	X	X	—	X	X	—	—

Appendix B

The project stages in brief

Each stage lasts from three to six lessons of around one hour, once a week, in normal curriculum time. They are all illustrated in the documentary films available from <www.musicalfutures/PractionersResources.html> Section 2; and the teachng materials can be downloaded from that site.

Stage 1

Pupils bring in the own choice of music. In small friendship groups they listen to it, and choose one song. They then select instruments and attempt to copy the song by ear, directing their own learning.

Stage 2

Pupils are provided with recordings of a funk track plus 15 of its riffs played separately and in combination. Still in friendship groups, they listen, discuss, and attempt to play the riffs through aural learning. If desired, they can also use worksheets giving note names, but not pitch contour or rhythm. As a group, they create their own version of the song.

Stage 3

This is a repetition of Stage 1, whose aim is to build on skills acquired during Stages 1 and 2.

Stage 4

Pupils compose, rehearse and perform their own music, directing their own learning in friendship groups.

Stage 5

Pupils are introduced to a 'musical model' of songwriting by a band of peer musicians or community musicians. They then continue to work on their own music, directing their own learning in friendship groups.

Stage 6

Pupils are provided with recordings of five pieces of classical music drawn from TV advertisements. In friendship groups, they listen, discuss, select, copy, arrange, rehearse and perform the music as an ensemble.

Stage 7

Pupils are provided with recordings of five pieces of classical music which is mostly unfamiliar. They also have recordings of individual melody and bass lines of the pieces, some of which are simplified. There are no worksheets. In friendship groups, they listen, discuss, select, copy, arrange, rehearse and perform the music as an ensemble.

Bibliography

Abrahams, F. (2005a) 'The application of critical pedagogy to music teaching and learning: a literature review'. *Applications of Research in Music Education*, **23** 2, 12–22.

Abrahams, F. (2005b) 'Transforming classroom music instruction with ideas from critical pedagogy'. *Music Educators Journal*, **92** 1, 62–8

Alderson, P. (2003) *Institutional Rites and Rights: A Century of Childhood*, London: Institute of Education, University of London.

Alderson, P. (2004) 'Democracy in schools: myths, mirages and making it happen'. In Linsley, E. and Rayment, B. (eds), *Beyond the Classroom: Exploring Active Citizenship in 11–16 Education*, pp. 31–8. London: New Politics Network.

Allsup, R.E. (2004) 'Of concert bands and garage bands: creating democracy through popular music'. In Rodriguez, C. (ed.), *Bridging the Gap: Popular Music and Education*, pp. 204–23. Reston, VA: National Association for Music Education (USA).

Armstrong, V. (2001) 'Theorizing gender and musical composition in the computerized classroom'. *Women: A Cultural Review*, **12**, 1, 35–43.

Barrett, M. (1996) 'Music education and the natural learning model'. In Spruce, G. (ed.), *Teaching Music*, London and New York: Routledge in association with the Open University.

Bayton, M. (1997) *Frock Rock: Women Performing Popular Music*, Oxford: Oxford University Press.

Bennett, A. (2000) *Popular Music and Youth Culture: Music, Identity and Place*, London and New York: Macmillan.

Bennett, H.S. (1980) *On Becoming a Rock Musician*, Amherst, MA: University of Massachusetts Press.

Bennett, N. and Dunne, E. (1992) *Managing Classroom Groups*, Hemel Hempstead: Simon and Schuster.

Bentley, T. (1998) *Learning Beyond the Classroom: Education for a Changing World*, London: Routledge.

Berkaak, O.A. (1999) 'Entangled dreams and twisted memories: order and disruption in local music making'. *Young: Nordic Journal of Youth Research*, **7**, 2, 25–42.

Berliner, P. (1994) *Thinking in Jazz: The Infinite Art of Improvisation*, Chicago, IL: Chicago University Press.

Bielaczyc, K. and Collins, A. (2000) 'Learning communities in classrooms: a reconceptualisation of educational practice'. In Reigeluth, M. (ed.), *Instructional-design Theories and Models*, vol. 2, Mahway, NJ: Lawrence Erlbaum.

Björnberg, A. (1993) '"Teach you to rock?" Popular music in the university music department'. *Popular Music*, **12**, 1.

Blacking, J. (1976) *How Musical is Man?* London: Faber.

Boespflug, G. (2004) 'The pop music ensemble in music education'. In Rodriguez, C. (ed.), *Bridging the Gap: Popular Music and Education*, pp. 190–203. Reston, VA: National Association for Music Education (USA).

Bowers, J. and Tick, J. (eds) (1986) *Women Making Music: The Western Art Tradition, 1150–1950*, Urbana, IL: University of Illinois Press.

Bowman, W. (2005) 'Music education in nihilistic times'. In Lines, D. (ed.), *Music Education for the New Millennium: Theory and Practices Futures for Music Teaching and Learning*, pp. 29–46. Oxford: Blackwell Publishing.

Boyce-Tillman, J. (2000) *Constructing Musical Healing: The Wounds that Sing*, London: Jessica Kingsley.

Bruce, R. and Kemp, A. (1993) 'Sex-stereotyping in children's preference for musical instruments'. *British Journal of Music Education*, **10**, 3.

Bruner, J.S. (1979) 'Play as a mode of construing the real'. In Katz, S.L. (ed.), *Proceedings of the Yale Conference on the International Year of the Child*, New Haven, CT: Yale University Press; reproduced in J.S. Bruner (2006), *In Search of Pedagogy, Volume II: The Selected Works of Jerome S. Bruner*, Abingdon and New York: Routledge, pp. 57–64.

Bruner, J.S. (1983) 'Play, thought, and language'. *Peabody Journal of Education*, **60**; reproduced in J.S. Bruner (2006), *In Search of Pedagogy, Volume II: The Selected Works of Jerome S. Bruner*, Abingdon and New York: Routledge, pp. 91–8.

Bruner, J.S. (1996) *The Culture of Education*, Cambridge, MA: Harvard University Press.

Buckingham, D. (2005) *Schooling the Digital Generation: Popular Culture, the New Media and the Future of Education*, London: Institute of Education, University of London.

Burnard, P. (2000) 'Examining experiential differences between improvisation and composition in children's music-making'. *British Journal of Music Education*, **17**, 3.

Burton, I. with Power, S.J., Davis, C. and Maltby. H (2006) *The Whole Curriculum Approach: Inclusive Music Practice at Year 8*; available for download from <www.musicalfutures.org/PractionersResources.html>, Section 2.

Byrne, C. (2005) 'Pedagogical communication in the music classroom'. In Miell, D., MacDonald, Raymond and Hargreaves, David (eds), *Musical Communication*, Oxford: Oxford University Press.

Byrne, C. and Sheridan, M. (2000) 'The long and winding road: the story of rock music in Scottish schools'. *International Journal of Music Education*, **36**, 46–58.

Byrne, C., MacDonald, R. and Carlton, L. (2003), 'Assessing creativity in musical compositions: flow as an assessment tool', *British Journal of Music Education*, **20**, 3, 277–90.

Campbell, P.S. (1991) *Lessons from the World: A Cross-cultural Guide to Music Teaching and Learning*, New York: Schirmer Books.

Campbell, P.S. (1995) 'Of garage bands and song-getting: the musical development of young rock musicians'. *Research Studies in Music Education*, **4**.

Campbell, P.S. (1998) *Songs in their Heads: Music and its Meaning in Children's Lives*, New York: Oxford University Press.

Campbell, P.S. (2001) 'Unsafe suppositions? Cutting across cultures on questions of music's transmission'. *Music Education Research*, **3**, 2, 215–26.

Campbell, P.S., Drummond, J., Dunbar-Hall, P., Meith, H., Schippers, H. and Wiggins, T. (eds) (2006) *Cultural Diversity in Music Education: Directions and Challenges for the 21st Century*, Brisbane: Australian Academic Press.

Caputo, V. (1994) 'Add technology and stir: music, gender and technology in today's music classrooms'. *Quarterly Journal of Music Teaching and Learning*, **4**, 4 and **5**, 1.

Charles, B. (2004) 'Boys and girls' constructions of gender through musical composition in the primary school'. *British Journal of Music Education*, **21**, 3, 265–77.

Clawson, M.A. (1999a). 'Masculinity and skill acquisition in the adolescent rock band'. *Popular Music*, **18**, 1, 99–115.

Clawson, M.A. (1999b) 'When women play the bass: instrumental specialisation and gender interpretation in alternative rock music'. *Gender and Society*, **13**, 2, 193–210.

Cohen, S. (1991). *Rock Culture in Liverpool*. Oxford: Oxford University Press.

Coleman, J. (1961) *The Adolescent Society*, New York: Free Press

Colley, A., C. Comber et al. (1993) 'Girls, boys and technology in music education'. *British Journal of Music Education*, **10**, 2.

Cope, P. (1998) 'Knowledge, meaning and ability in musical instrument playing'. *British Journal of Music Education*, **15**, 3, 263–70.

Cope, P. (1999) 'Community-based traditional fiddling as a basis for increasing participation in instrumental playing'. *Music Education Research*, **1**, 1, 61–73.

Cope, P. and Smith, H. (1997) 'Cultural context in musical instrumental learning'. *British Journal of Music Education*, **14**, 3, 283–9.

Cox, G. (2002) *Living Music in Schools 1923–1999: Studies in the History of Music Education in England*, Aldershot: Ashgate Publishing.

Craft, A. (2001) '"Little c" creativity'. In Craft, A. Jeffrey, B. and Leibling, M. (ed.), *Creativity in Education*, pp. 45–61. London: Continuum.

Craft, A. (2005) *Creativity in Schools: Tensions and Dilemmas*, London: Routledge.

Craft, A., Jeffrey, B. and Leibling, M. (eds) (2001) *Creativity in Education*, London: Continuum.

Csikszentmihalyi, M. (1990) *Flow: The Psychology of Optimal Experience*, New York: Harper and Row.

Csikszentmihalyi, M. (1996) *Creativity: Flow and the Psychology of Discovery and Invention*, New York: Harper Perennial.

Cutietta, R.A. (2004) 'When we question popular music in education, what is the question?'. In Rodriguez, C. (ed.), *Bridging the Gap: Popular Music and Education*, pp. 242–7. Reston, VA: National Association for Music Education (USA).

Dahl, K.L. (1995) 'Challenges in Understanding the Learner's Perspective'. *Theory into Practice*, **34**, 2, 124–30.

Dahl, L. (1984) *Stormy Weather: The Music and Lives of a Century of Jazz Women*, London and New York: Quartet Books.

Davis, S.G. (2005) '"That thing you do!" Compositional processes of a rock band'. *International Journal of Education and the Arts*, **6**, 16.

Delzell, J.K. (1994) 'Variables affecting the gender-role stereotyping of high school band teaching positions'. *Quarterly Journal of Music Teaching and Learning*, **4**, 4 and **5**, 1.

Delzell, J.K. and Leppla, D.A. (1992) 'Gender association of musical instruments and preferences of fourth-grade students for selected instruments'. *Journal of Research in Music Education*, **40**, 2.

Dennis, B. (1970) *Experimental Music in Schools*, Oxford: Oxford University Press.

Department of Education and Science (DES) (1992) *Music in the National Curriculum (England)*, London: HMSO.

Department for Education (DfE) (1995) *Music in the National Curriculum (England)*, London: DfE.

Department for Education and Skills, and Department for Culture Media and Sport (DfES and DCMS) (2004) *The Music Manifesto*, London: DfES.

Department for Education and Skills (DfES) (2006) *Making Every Child's Music Matter: Music Manifesto Report No. 2: A Consultation for Action*, London: DfES.

Dewey, J. (1916) *Democracy and Education*, New York: The Free Press.

Dimitriadis, G. (2001) *Performing Identity/Performing Culture: Hip Hop as Text, Pedagogy, and Lived Practice*, New York: Peter Lang.

Dunbar-Hall, P. (1996). 'Designing a Teaching Model for Popular Music'. In Spruce, G. (ed.), *Teaching Music*. London and New York: Routledge in association with the Open University.

Dunbar-Hall, P. (2000) 'Concept or context? Teaching and learning Balinese Gamelan and the universalist–pluralist debate'. *Music Education Research*, **2**, 2, 127–39.

Dunbar-Hall, P. (2006) 'Training, community and systemic music education: the aesthetics of Balinese music in different pedagogic settings'. In Campbell, P.S., Drummond, J., Dunbar-Hall, P., Meith, H., Schippers, H. and Wiggins, T. (eds), *Cultural Diversity in Music Education: Directions and Challenges for the 21st Century*, pp. 125–32. Brisbane: Australian Academic Press.

Dunbar-Hall, P. and Wemyss, K. (2000) 'The effects of the study of popular music on music education'. *International Journal of Music Education*, **36**, 23–35.

Edwards, D. and Mercer, N. (eds) (1987) *Common Knowledge: The Development of Understanding in the Classroom*, London: Routledge.

Edwards, G. and Kelly, A.V. (eds) (1998) *Experience and Education: Towards an Alternative National Curriculum*, London: Routledge.

Eisner, E. (2004a) *The Arts and the Creation of Mind*, New Haven, CT and London: Yale University Press.

Eisner, E. (2004b) 'What can education learn from the arts about the practice of education?'. *International Journal of Education and the Arts*, **5**, 4, 1–12.

Elliott, D. (1995) *Music Matters: A New Philosophy of Music Education*, Oxford: Oxford University Press.

Emmons, S.E. (2004) 'Preparing teachers for popular music processes and practices'. In Rodriguez, C. (ed.), *Bridging the Gap: Popular Music and Education,* pp. 158–73. Reston, VA: National Association for Music Education (USA).

Endo, Y. (2004) 'Japanese Identity Formation through Japanese Traditional Instrumental Music'. MA dissertation. London: Institute of Education, University of London.

Evelein, F. (2006) 'Pop and world music in Dutch music education: two cases of authentic learning in music teacher education and secondary music education'. *International Journal of Music Education,* **24**, 2, 178–87.

Faulkner, R. (2003) 'Group composing: pupil perceptions from a social psychological study'. *Music Education Research,* **5**, 2.

Faultley, M. (2004) 'O Fortuna: creativity in English music education considered from a post-modernist perspective'. *Music Education Research,* **6**, 3, 343–8.

Fielding, M. (2004) 'Transformative approaches to student voice: theoretical underpinnings, recalcitrant realities'. *British Educational Research Journal,* **30**, 2, 295–312.

Finnegan, R. (1989) *The Hidden Musicians: Music-making in an English Town,* Cambridge: Cambridge University Press.

Folkestad, G. (2005) 'Here, there and everywhere: music education research in a globalised world'. *Music Education Research,* **7**, 3, 279-87.

Folkestad, G. (2006) 'Formal and informal learning situations or practices versus formal and informal ways of hearing'. *British Journal of Music Education,* **23**, 2, 135–45

Freire, P. (1972) *Pedagogy of the Oppressed,* Harmondsworth: Penguin.

Freire, P. (1974) *Education for Critical Consciousness,* London: Sheed and Ward.

Gaar, G.G. (1993) *She's a Rebel: The History of Women in Rock and Roll,* London: Blandford.

Gammon, V. (1999) 'Cultural politics of the English National Curriculum for Music, 1991–1992'. *Journal of Educational Administration and History,* **31**, 2, 130–47.

Gardner, H. (1983) *Frames of Mind: The Theory of Multiple Intelligences,* New York: Basic Books.

Gardner, H. (1999) *The Disciplined Mind: Beyond Facts and Standardized Tests, The K-12 Education that Every Child Deserves,* New York: Simon and Schuster.

Ginocchio, J. (2001) 'Popular music performance class'. *Teaching Music,* **8**, 4, 40–44.

Glover, J. (2001) *Children Composing, 4–14,* Sussex: Falmer Press.

Goehr, L. (1992) *The Imaginary Museum of Musical Works: An Essay in the Philosophy of Music,* Oxford: Clarendon Press.

Goodson, I. (1998) 'Towards an alternative pedagogy'. In Kincheloe, J. and Steinberg, S. (eds), *Unauthorized Methods,* pp. 27–42. London: Routledge.

Green, L. (1988) *Music on Deaf Ears: Musical Meaning, Ideology and Education,* Manchester and New York: Manchester University Press.

Green, L. (1997) *Music, Gender, Education,* Cambridge: Cambridge University Press.

Green, L. (1999a) 'Ideology'. In Horner, B. and Swiss, T. (eds), *Key Terms for Popular Music and Culture,* Oxford: Blackwell.

Green, L. (1999b) 'Research in the sociology of music education: some fundamental concepts'. *Music Education Research*, **1**, 2, 159–69.

Green, L. (2000) 'On the evaluation and assessment of music as a media art'. In Sinker, R. and Sefton-Green, U. (eds), *Evaluation Issues in Media Arts Production*, pp. 89–106. London: Routledge.

Green, L. (2002a) *How Popular Musicians Learn*, Aldershot: Ashgate Publishing (first published 2001).

Green, L. (2002b) 'From the Western classics to the world: secondary music teachers' changing attitudes in England, 1982 and 1998'. *British Journal of Music Education*, **19**, 2.

Green, L. (2003a) 'Music education, cultural capital and social group identity'. In Herbert, T., Clayton, Martin and Middleton, Richard (eds), *The Cultural Study of Music: A Critical Introduction*, pp. 263–74. London and New York: Routledge.

Green, L. (2003b) 'Why "ideology" is still relevant to music education theory'. *Action, Criticism and Theory for Music Education*, **2**, 2, 3–21.

Green, L. (2004) 'What can teachers learn from popular musicians?'. In Rodriguez, C. (ed.), *Bridging the Gap: Popular Music and Education*, pp. 225–41. Reston, VA:, Music Educators' National Conference, National Association for Music Education.

Green, L. (2005a) *Meaning, Autonomy and Authenticity in the Music Classroom*, London: Institute of Education.

Green, L. (2005b) 'Musical meaning and social reproduction: a case for retrieving autonomy'. *Educational Philosophy and Theory*, **37**, 1, 77–92.

Green, L. (2006) 'Popular music education in and for itself, and for "other" music: current research in the classroom'. *International Journal of Music Education*, **24**, 2, 101–18.

Green, L. with Walmsley, A. (2006) *Classroom Resources for Informal Music Learning*, available for download from <www.musicalfutures.org/PractionersResources. html>, Section 2.

Hand, M. (2006) 'Against autonomy as an educational aim'. *Oxford Review of Education*, **32**, 4, 535–50.

Harland, J., Kinder, K., Lord, P., Stott, A., Schagen, I., Haynes, J. and Cusworth, L. (2000) 'Arts education in secondary schools: effects and effectiveness'. Slough: National Foundation for Educational Research.

Harrison, A.C. and O'Neill, S. (2002) 'Children's gender-typed preferences for musical instruments: an intervention study'. *Psychology of Music*, **28**, 1, 81–97.

Hartley, D. (2006) 'The instrumentalization of the expressive in education'. In Moore, A. (ed.), *Schooling, Society and Curriculum*, pp. 60–70. London and New York: Routledge.

Harwood, E. (1998a) '"Go on girl!" Improvisation in African-American girls' singing games'. In Nettl, B. and Russell, M. (eds), *In the Course of Performance: Studies in the World of Musical Improvisation*, pp. 113–26. Chicago, IL: University of Chicago Press.

Harwood, E. (1998b) 'Learning in context: a playground tale'. *Research Studies in Music Education*, **11**, 52–61.

Her Majesty's Inspectorate (HMI) (2003) *Expecting the Unexpected: Developing Creativity in Primary and Secondary Schools* (August). Document reference no. HMI 1612. London: HMI.

Herbert, D.G. and Campbell, P.S. (2000) 'Rock music in American schools: positions and practices since the 1960s'. *International Journal of Music Education*, **36**, 14–23.

Ho, W.C. (1999) 'The sociopolitical transformation and Hong Kong secondary music education: politicisation, culturalisation, and marketisation'. *Bulletin of the Council for Research in Music Education*, **140**, 41–56.

Horn, K. (1984) 'Rock music-making as a work model in community music workshops'. *British Journal of Music Education*, **1**, 2, 111–35.

Houssart, J. (2002) 'Simplification and repetition of mathematical tasks: a recipe for success or failure?'. *Journal of Mathematical Behavior*, **21**, 191–202.

Humphreys, J.T. (2004) 'Popular music in the American schools: what history tells us about the present and the future'. In Rodriguez, C. (ed.), *Bridging the Gap: Popular Music and Music Education,* pp. 91–106. Reston, VA: National Association for Music Education (USA).

Jackson, P. (2005) 'Secondary School Pupils' Conceptions of Music in and out of School: In Search of Musical Meaning'. PhD thesis, London: Institute of Education, University of London.

Jaffurs, S.E. (2004) 'The impact of informal music learning practices in the classroom, or how I learned how to teach from a garage band'. *International Journal of Music Education*, **22**, 3 (December), 189–200.

Jeffrey, B. and Craft, A. (2001) 'Introduction: the universalization of creativity'. In Craft, A.J.B. and Leibling, M. (eds), *Creativity in Education*, pp. 1–13. London: Continuum.

Jensen, E. (1995) *Brain Based Teaching and Learning*, San Diego, CA: Turning Point.

Johnston, P.H. and Nicholls, J.G. (1995) 'Voices we want to hear and voices we don't'. *Theory Into Practice*, **34**, 2, 94–100.

Jorgensen, E. (1997) *In Search Of Music Education*, Urbana and Chicago, IL: University of Illinois Press.

Jorgensen, E. (2003) 'Transforming Music Education'. Bloomington, IN: Indiana University Press.

Kincheloe, J.L. and Steinberg, S.R. (eds) (1998) *Unauthorised Methods: Strategies for Critical Teaching*, London: Routledge.

Kingsbury, H. (1988) *Music, Talent and Performance: A Conservatory Cultural System*, Philadelphia: Temple University Press.

Kirshner, T. (1998) 'Studying rock: towards a materialist ethnography'. In Swiss, T., Sloop, J. and Herman, A. (eds), *Mapping the Beat: Popular Music and Contemporary Theory*, Oxford: Basil Blackwell.

Kohut, D.L. (1985) *Musical Performance: Learning Theory and Pedagogy*, Englewood Cliffs, NJ: Prentice-Hall.

Koizumi, K. (2002) 'Popular Music, Gender and High School Pupils in Japan: Personal Music in School and Leisure Sites'. *Popular Music*, **21**, 1, 107–27.

Koopman, C. (2005) 'Music education, performativity and aestheticisation'. *Educational Philosophy and Theory* **37**, 1, 117–30.

Koskoff, E. (1987) *Women and Music in Cross-cultural Perspective*, New York and London: Greenwood Press.

Koza, J.E. (1994) 'Big boys don't cry (or sing): gender, misogyny, and homophobia in college choral methods texts'. *Quarterly Journal of Music Teaching and Learning*, **4**, 4/**5**, 1.

Kress, G. (2006) 'Learning and curriculum: agency, ethics and aesthetics in an era of instability'. In Moore, A. (ed.), *Schooling, Society and Curriculum,* pp. 158–78. London and New York: Routledge.

Kuhn, D. (1972) 'Mechanism of change in the development of cognitive structures'. *Child Development*, **43**, 833–44

Kwami, R. (1989) 'African Music, Education and the School Curriculum'. Unpublished PhD thesis, London University, Institute of Education.

Lamont, A. (2002) 'Musical identities and the school environment'. In MacDonald, R., Hargreaves, D. and Miell, D. (eds), *Musical Identities*, Oxford: Oxford University Press.

Lamont, A., Hargreaves, D., Marshall, N.A. and Tarrant, M. (2003) 'Young people's music in and out of school'. *British Journal of Music Education*, **20**, 3, 229–41.

Lave, J. and Wenger, E. (1991) *Situated Learning: Legitimate Peripheral Participation*, Cambridge: Cambridge University Press.

Lilliestam, L. (1996) 'On playing by ear. *Popular Music*, **15**, 2, 195–216.

Lincoln, Y.S. (1995) 'In search of students' voices'. *Theory Into Practice*, **34**, 2, 88–93.

Lines, D. (ed.) (2005a) *Educational Philosophy and Theory Special Issue. The Philosophy of Music Education: Contemporary Perspectives*, Oxford: Blackwell Publishing.

Lines, D. (2005b) 'Improvisation and cultural work in music and music education'. In *Educational Philosophy and Theory Special Issue. The Philosophy of Music Education: Contemporary Perspectives*, Oxford: Blackwell Publishing.

Lipman, M. (1991) *Thinking in Education*. Cambridge: Cambridge University Press.

Lundquist, B. and Szego, C.K. (1998) *Music of the World's Cultures: A Source Book for Music Educators*, Perth, Australia: International Society for Music Education.

MacDonald, R. and Miell, D. (2000) 'Creativity and music education: the impact of social variables'. *International Journal of Music Education*, **36**, 58–68.

MacDonald, R., Hargreaves, D. and Miell, D. (2002) *Musical Identities*, Oxford: Oxford University Press.

Marsh, K. (1995) 'Children's singing games: composition in the playground?'. *Research Studies in Music Education*, **4**, 2–11.

Marsh, K. (1999) 'Mediated orality: the role of popular music in the changing traditions of children's musical play'. *Research Studies in Music Education*, **13** (December).

Martin, P. (1995) *Sounds and Society: Themes in the Sociology of Music*, Manchester and New York: Manchester University Press.

Maryprasith, P. (1999) 'The effects of globalisation and localisation on the status of music in Thailand'. PhD thesis, London: London University, Institute of Education.

McCarthy, C., Hudak, G., Miklaucic, S. and Saukko, P. (1999) *Sound Identities, Popular Music and the Cultural Politics of Education*, New York: Peter Lang.

McCarthy, M. (1999) *Passing It On: The Transmission of Music in Irish Culture*. Cork: Cork University Press.

McFarlane, A. (2006) 'ICT and the curriculum canon: responding to and exploring "alternative knowledge"'. In Moore, A. (ed.), *Schooling, Society and Curriculum*, pp. 130–42. London and New York: Routledge.

McPherson, G.E. and Gabrielsson, A. (2002) 'From Sound to Sign'. In Parncutt, R. (ed.), *The Science of Psychology of Music Performance*, pp. 99–116. Oxford: Oxford University Press.

Merriam, A. (1964) *The Anthropology of Music*, Evanston, IL: North Western University Press.

Mills, J. (2005) *Music in the School*, Oxford: Oxford University Press.

Monson, I. (1996) *Saying Something: Jazz Improvisation and Interaction*, Chicago, IL: and London, Chicago University Press.

Moore, A. (1999) *Teaching Multicultured Students: Culturism and Anti-culturism in School Classrooms*, London and New York: Falmer Press.

Moore, A. (2000) *Teaching and Learning: Pedagogy, Curriculum and Culture*, London: RoutledgeFalmer.

Moore, A. (ed.) (2006) *Schooling, Society and Curriculum*, Abingdon and New York: Routledge.

Morgan, L., Hargreaves, D. and Joiner, R. (1997) 'How do children make music? Composition in small groups'. *Early Childhood Connections*, Winter, 15–21.

National Advisory Committee on Creative and Cultural Education (NACCCE) (1999) *All Our Futures: Creativity, Culture and Education*, London: Department for Culture, Media and Sport.

Negus, K. (1999). *Music Genres and Corporate Cultures*. London and New York: Routledge.

Nettl, B. (1983) *The Study of Ethnomusicology: Twenty-nine Issues and Concepts*, Urbana and Chicago, IL: University of Illinois Press.

Nettl, B. (1995) *Heartland Excursions: Ethnomusicological Reflections on Schools of Music*, Urbana: University of Illinois Press.

Newsom, D. (1998) 'Rock's quarrel with tradition: popular music's carnival comes to the classroom'. *Popular Music and Society*, **22**, 3, 1–20.

Nielsen, K. (2006) 'Apprenticeship at the Academy of Music'. *International Journal of Education and the Arts*, **7**, 4.

Nketia, J.H.K. (1975) *The Music of Africa*, London: Gollancz

Nwezi, M. (1999) 'Strategies for music education in Africa: towards a meaningful progression from tradition to modern'. *International Journal of Music Education*, **33**, 72–87.

O'Flynn, J. (2006) 'Vernacular music-making and education'. *International Journal of Music Education*, **24**, 2, 140–47.

O'Neill, S. (1997) 'Gender and music'. In Hargreaves, D.J. and North, A.C. (eds), *The social Psychology of Music*, pp. 46–63. Oxford: Oxford University Press.

O'Neill, S. (2002) 'The self-identity of young musicians'. In MacDonald, R., Hargreaves, D. and Miell, D. (eds), *Musical Identities,* Oxford: Oxford University Press.

O'Neill, S. and McPherson, G. (2002) 'Motivation'. In Parncutt, R. and McPherson, G. (eds), *The Science and Psychology of Music Performance: Creative Strategies for Teaching and Learning,* pp. 31–46. Oxford: Oxford University Press.

Odam, G. (1995) *The Sounding Symbol*, London: Nelson Thornes.

Odam, G. (2004) 'Music education in the aquarian age: a transatlantic perspective (or "How do you make horses thirsty?")'. In Rodriguez, C. (ed.), *Bridging the Gap: Popular Music and Education*, pp. 127–40. Reston, VA: National Association for Music Education (USA).

Oldfather, P. (1995) 'Songs "come back to most of them": students' experiences as researchers'. *Theory into Practice*, **34**, 2, 131–7.

Osler, A. (2006) 'New directions in citizenship education: re-conceptualizing the curriculum in the context of globalization'. In Moore, A. (ed.), *Schooling, Society and Curriculum*, pp. 100–114. London and New York: Routledge.

Paynter, J. (1982) *Music in the Secondary School Curriculum*, Cambridge: Cambridge University Press.

Paynter, J. and Aston, P. (1970) *Sound and Silence: Classroom Projects in Creative Music*, Cambridge: Cambridge University Press.

Peters, R.S. (1978) *Ethics and Education*, London: Unwin.

Piaget, J. (1926) *The Language and Thought of the Child*, New York: Harcourt, Brace

Pitts, S. (2000) *A Century of Change in Music Education: Historical Perspectives on Contemporary Practice in British Secondary School Music*, Aldershot: Ashgate Publishing.

Pitts, S. (2005) *Valuing Musical Participation*, London and Burlington, VT: Ashgate Publishing.

Price, D. (2005) *Musical Futures: An Emerging Vision*, London: Paul Hamlyn Foundation; <www.musicalfutures.org>.

Price, D. (2006a) *Personalising Music Learning*, London: Paul Hamlyn Foundation; <www.musicalfutures.org>.

Price, D. (2006b) *Supporting Young Musicians and Coordinating Musical Pathways*, London: Paul Hamlyn Foundation; <www.musicalfutures.org>.

Rainbow, B. with Cox, G. (1989/2006) *Music in Educational Thought and Practice*. Woodbridge: Boydell.

Regelski, T. (2005) 'Music and music education: theory and praxis for "making a difference"'. *Educational Philosophy and Theory*, **37**, 1, 7–28.

Reimer, B. (1989). *A Philosophy of Music Education* (2nd edn), Englewood Cliffs, NJ: Prentice-Hall.

Renshaw, P. (2005) *Simply Connect: Best Musical Practice in Non-formal Learning Contexts*, London: Paul Hamlyn Foundation; <www.musicalfutures.org>.

Renwick, J.M. and McPherson, G.E. (2002) 'Interest and choice: student-selected repertoire and its effect on practising behaviour'. *British Journal of Music Education*, **19**, 2, 173–88.

Rodriguez, C. (ed.) (2004) *Bridging the Gap: Popular Music and Education*, Reston, VA: Music Educators' National Conference, National Association for Music Education.

Ross, M. (1998) 'The aim is song: towards an alternative national curriculum'. In Edwards, G. and Kelly, A.V. (eds), *Experience and Education*, London: Paul Chapman.

Rousseau, J.-J. (1762/1974) *Emile*, London: Dent.

Schafer, M. (1967) *Ear Cleaning: Notes for an Experimental Music Course*, New York: Associated Music Publishers Incorporated.

Scholes, P. (1972) *The Oxford Companion to Music*, Oxford: Oxford University Press.

Sefton-Green, J. (2003) 'Informal learning: substance or style?'. *Teaching Education*, **14**, 1, 37–51.

Seifried, S. (2006) 'Exploring the outcomes of rock and popular music instruction in high school guitar class: a case study'. *International Journal of Music Education*, **24**, 2, 168–77.

Self, G. (1967) *New Sounds in Class*, London: Universal Edition.

Shah, S.M. (2006) 'Popular music in Malaysia: education from the outside'. *International Journal of Music Education*, **24**, 2, 132–9.

Shepherd, J. and Vulliamy, G. (1994) 'The struggle for culture: a sociological case study of the development of a national music curriculum'. *British Journal of the Sociology of Education*, **15**, 1, 27–40.

Shepherd, J., Virden, P., Vulliamy, G. and Wishart, T. (1977) *Whose Music? A Sociology of Musical Languages*, London: Latimer.

Simpson, K. (1976) *Some Great Music Educators: A Collection of Essays*, London: Novello

Slavin, R.E. (1995) *Cooperative Learning: Theory, Research and Practice* (2nd edn), Boston, MA: Allyn and Bacon.

Small, C. (1977) *Music–Society–Education: A Radical Examination of the Prophetic Function of Music in Western, Eastern, and African Cultures With its Impact on Society and its Use in Education*, London: John Calder.

Small, C. (1998) *Musicking: The Meanings of Performing and Listening*, Hanover, NJ: Wesleyan University Press.

Smith, A. (1996) *Accelerated Learning in the Classroom*. Stafford: School Network Educational Press.

Somekh, B. (2006) 'New ways of teaching and learning in the digital age: implications for curriculum studies'. In Moore, A. (ed.), *Schooling, Society and Curriculum*, pp. 119–29. London and New York: Routledge.

Stålhammar, B. (2000) 'The spaces of music and its foundation of values – music teaching and young people's own music experience'. *International Journal of Music Education*, **36**, 35–46.

Stålhammar, B. (2003) 'Music teaching and young people's own musical experiences'. *Music Education Research*, **5**, 1, 51–68.

Stålhammar, B. (2006a) *Musical Identities and Music Education*, Orebro: Universitetsbiblioteket.

Stålhammar, B. (ed.) (2006b) *Music and Human Beings: Music and Identity*, Orebro: Universitetsbiblioteket.

Stolzoff, N. (2000) *Wake the Town and Tell the People: Dancehall Culture in Jamaica*, Durham, NC: Duke University Press.

Swanwick, K. (1968) *Popular Music and the Teacher*, Oxford: Pergamon Press.

Swanwick, K. (1988) *Music, Mind and Education*, London: Routledge.

Swanwick, K. (1992) *Music Education and the National Curriculum, the London File: Papers from the Institute of Education*, London: The Tufnell Press.

Swanwick, K. (1994) *Musical Knowledge: Intuition, Analysis and Music Education*, London: Routledge.

Swanwick, K. and Tillman, J. (1986) 'The sequence of musical development'. *British Journal of Music Education*, **3**, 3.

Tagg, P. (1998) 'The Göteborg connection: lessons in the history and politics of popular music education and research'. *Popular Music*, **17**, 2.

Talbot, M. (ed.) (2000) *The Musical Work: Reality or Invention?*, Liverpool: University of Liverpool.

Tarrant, M., North, A. and Hargreaves, D. (2002) 'Youth identity and music'. In MacDonald, R., Hargreaves, D. and Miell, D., *Musical Identities*, Oxford: Oxford University Press.

Vakeva, L. (2006) 'Teaching popular music in Finland: what's up, what's ahead?'. *International Journal of Music Education*, **24**, 2.

Volk, T. (1998) *Music, Education and Multiculturalism: Foundations and Principles*, New York: Oxford University Press.

Voss, J.F. and Wiley, J. (2000) 'A case study of developing historical understanding via instruction: the importance of integrating text components and constructing arguments'. In Stearns, P.N., Seixas, P. and Wienburg, S. (eds), *Knowing Teaching and Learning History: National and International Perspectives*, pp. 375–89. New York and London: New York University Press.

Vulliamy, G. (1977a) 'Music and the mass culture debate'. In Shepherd, J., Virden, P., Wishart, T. and Vulliamy, G. (eds), *Whose Music: A Sociology of Musical Language*, London: Latimer New Dimensions.

Vulliamy, G. (1977b) 'Music as a case study in the "new sociology of education"'. In Shepherd, J., Virden, P., Wishart, T. and Vulliamy, G. (eds), *Whose Music: A Sociology of Musical Language*, London: Latimer New Dimension.

Vulliamy, G. and Lee, E. (eds) (1976) *Pop Music in School*, Cambridge: Cambridge University Press.

Vulliamy, G. and Lee, E. (eds) (1982) *Pop, Rock and Ethnic Music in School*, Cambridge: Cambridge University Press.

Vygotsky, L. (1978) *Mind in Society*, Cambridge, MA: Harvard University Press.

Watkins, C. (2005) *Classrooms as Learning Communities: What's in it for Schools*, London: Routledge.

Webster, P. (1992) 'Research on creative thinking in music'. In Colwell, R. (ed.), *Handbook of Research on Music Teaching and Learning*, pp. 266–80. New York: Schirmer.

Weimer, M. (2002) *Learner-centred Teaching: Five Key Changes to Practice*, San Francisco, CA: Jossey-Bass.

Welch, G. (2001) 'UK'. In North, A. and Hargreaves, D. (eds), *Musical Development and Learning: The International Perspective*, pp. 202–19. London: Continuum.

Wemyss, K.L. (1999) 'From T. I. [Torres Strait] to Tasmania: Australian indigenous popular music in the curriculum'. *Research Studies in Music Education*, **13** (December), 226–40.

Wemyss, K.L. (2004) 'Reciprocity and exchange: popular music in Australian secondary schools'. In Rodriguez, C. (ed.), *Bridging the Gap: Popular Music and Education*, pp. 141–57. Reston, VA: National Association for Music Education.

Westerlund, H. (2002) *Bridging Experience, Action, and Culture in Music Education*, Helsinki: Sibelius Academy.

Westerlund, H. (2006) 'Garage rock bands: a future model for developing musical expertise?'. *International Journal of Music Education*, **24**, 2, 119–25.

Wiggins, J. (1999/2000) 'The nature of shared musical understanding and its role in empowering independent musical thinking'. *Bulletin – Council for Research in Music Education*, **141**, 65–90.

Wiggins, J. (2001) *Teaching for Musical Understanding*. New York: McGraw-Hill.

Wiggins, J. (2006) 'Compositional process in music'. In Bresler, L. (ed.), *International Handbook of Research in Arts Education*, pp. 451–67. New York: Springer.

Wiggins, J. (forthcoming) 'When the music is theirs: scaffolding young songwriters'. In M. Barrett (ed.), *A Cultural Psychology for Music Education*. Oxford: Oxford University Press.

Wiggins, T. (1996) 'The world of music in education'. *British Journal of Music Education*, **13**, 1, 21–30.

Wiggins, T. (2006) 'Cultivating shadows in the field? Challenges for traditions in institutional contexts'. In Campbell, P.S., Drummond, John, Dunbar-Hall, Peter, Howard, Meith, Schippers, Huib and Wiggins, Trevor (ed.), *Cultural Diversity in Music Education: Directions and Challenges for the 21st Century*, pp. 13–21. Brisbane: Australian Academic Press.

Wishart, T. (1977) 'Musical writing, musical speaking'. In Shepherd, J., Virden, P., Vulliamy, G. and Wishart, T. (eds), *Whose Music? A Sociology of Musical Languages*, pp. 125–53. London: Latimer.

Woodford, P. (2005) *Democracy and Music Education: Liberalism, Ethics, and the Politics of Practice*, Bloomington, IN: Indiana University Press.

Wright, R. (2007) 'Reconsidering inclusion in music education'. In H. Coll and J. Finney (eds), *Ways Into Music*, Matlock: NAME Publications, pp. 40–43.

Yang, M. (2006) '*Für Elise*, Circa 2000: Postmodern readings of Beethoven in popular contexts'. *Popular Music and Society*, **29**, 1, 3–23.

York, N. (2001) *Valuing School Music: A Report on School Music*, pp. 1–7. London: University of Westminster and Rockschool Ltd.

Young, M.F.D. (2006) 'Education, knowledge and the role of the state: the "nationalization" of educational knowledge?'. In Moore, A. (ed.), *Schooling, Society and Curriculum*, pp. 19–32. London and New York: Routledge.

Youth Music (2002) *Creating a Land with Music: The Work, Education and Training of Professional Musicians in the 21st Century*, London: National Foundation for Youth Music.

Zervoudakes, J. and Tanur, J. (1994) 'Gender and musical instruments – winds of change?'. *Journal of Research in Music Education*, **42**, 1, 58–67.

Index